Praise for

HER WORD IS BOND

"If there's one voice missing from the ongoing conversation about representation, equity, and the intersection between queerness, the femme experience, and Black lives in the hip hop scene—it's Psalm One's. A prolific lyricist, poet, philosopher, and emcee, Psalm One is the visionary chemist of our alt hip hop dreams; an artist whose buck is def as good as their knuck, both on and off the page. And we know that Cristalle Bowen has always championed for the rights and protections of those most neglected and harmed by the music industry—Black womxn—but in *Her Word Is Bond*, readers receive an in-depth look at the complex and vibrant brilliance that is the renegade known as Psalm One. Epic from beginning to end—this is a book every warrior for equity and representation in the music industry needs to have on their shelf." *—Faylita Hicks*, author, poet, 2021 Shearing Fellow and Recording Academy Member

"Reading Psalm's music business travails triggered my PTSD. Then I realized how lucky I was to be single through most of mine, because only a true psychopath or someone with the tenacity of a honey badger and patience of Job can handle the rap game and romance at the same Goddamn time." *—J-Zone*, drummer, musician, author, and retired former hip hop artist

D1532132

"*Her Word Is Bond* is a long overdue and necessary memoir about not only fighting other people's expectations, assumptions and projections about who you are while constantly feeling judged, marginalized, tokenized, exploited and underrepresented. Psalm One is brutally honest about the struggles of just trying to function in a male-dominated, black & white binary world when she should've been given the support, space, and freedom to grow and thrive." *—Dart Adams*, journalist, historian, researcher, and author of *Best Damn Hip Hop Writing: The Book of Dart*

"I have the utmost respect and admiration for Psalm One, not just as a rapper and artist but as someone who lives by their word and always stands for something. As an emcee, her lyrics were always very visual and colorful, and her foray into becoming a published author is no exception. Her story is one that needs to be told, and I highly recommend this memoir to all, especially those looking to jump into the world of professional music. I've truly enjoyed the journey thus far and look forward to what's next."
—Andrew Barber, hip hop historian, Recording Academy member, and owner of the iconic FAKESHOREDRIVE platform

HER WORD IS BOND

NAVIGATING HIP HOP AND RELATIONSHIPS IN A CULTURE OF MISOGYNY

CRISTALLE "PSALM ONE" BOWEN

Haymarket Books
Chicago, IL

Published in 2022 by
Haymarket Books
P.O. Box 180165
Chicago, IL 60618
773-583-7884
www.haymarketbooks.org
info@haymarketbooks.org

ISBN: 978-1-64259-461-4

Distributed to the trade in the US through Consortium Book Sales and Distribution (www.cbsd.com) and internationally through Ingram Publisher Services International (www.ingramcontent.com).

This book was published with the generous support of Lannan Foundation and Wallace Action Fund.

Special discounts are available for bulk purchases by organizations and institutions. Please email info@haymarketbooks.org for more information.

Cover photo by Rena Naltsas. Artwork and design by Patrik Oser.

Printed in Canada by union labor.

Library of Congress Cataloging-in-Publication data is available.

10 9 8 7 6 5 4 3 2 1

CONTENTS

PREFACE

This book is part cautionary tale, part celebration, and part medicine. I told my therapist, wholeheartedly and with full conviction, writing this thing would change my life.

I'm not the first emcee (MC) to write a book. In fact, the first book by an emcee I ever read was J-Zone's *Root for the Villain*. Zone's music was ever present when I was in college. My homies and I smoked many a schwag blunt to his album *Pimps Don't Pay Taxes*, and I became a fan for life. I never thought he fell off, but outside of my homies and time at the University of Illinois in the late 1990s and early 2000s, his music wasn't widely heralded. After I began taking rap seriously, he seemingly disappeared from rap altogether. Years later, his book, which now reads like a documented acceptance of his fate, was more inspiring to me than a book by a person who writes about rap life like it's all shits and giggles. Believe me: it's way more shit than giggle.

But you know what *is* funny? The word FEMCEE. Who came up with that shit? It's so fucking stupid. We don't employ this distinction for male emcees because they are the standard. You would think just *being* an emcee is enough to be labeled one. Never mind that this "nod to gender" might even hurt your chances of acceptance, depending on who you are or how you look. Male emcees shouldn't be the standard. Fuck that. Because *MANcee* sounds stupid, too. Jesus, take the wheel and the brake pedal.

Is an emcee blowing your head open with wordplay or nah?

Is an emcee taking me on a ride with their bars or nah?

Either you're an EMCEE or you're not. In fact, referring to human beings as male or female is way too biological. I don't do biology; I'm a chemist. It's all about the breakdown, baby, not the genitals. However, those are ideas for another book. Back to emceeing. Either you're an emcee or a rapper or nada. To be an emcee, you gotta be *more* than good. You gotta *drown* in hip hop. While I will use the term *rap* a lot in this book, being an emcee is far more serious than being a rapper. We're dealing with emcees in these pages.

There's no manual for how to navigate being really fucking good at rap music while dealing with puberty. Add being queer to the mix, and you can stop wondering why I'm writing this book. Also, dudes' silly rap fantasies often feature the chick who is seen and not heard. She's allowed in the boys' club temporarily, with a chaperone, but when she's alone, she's prey. Sadly, they never tell little girls who want to make music that pursuing that dream means experiencing heaping helpings of misogyny, violence, and scrutiny. We like the music because it invites us to play in a world where we'd rather be. It's escapism. It's release. It's joy, pain, and all of that emo shit. This is a manual for the misogyny-resistant artist. This is also a tale for queer kids in hip hop.

Besides being a writer at heart—I vowed to write the "great American novel" at fifteen but started rapping at sixteen—I've lived a life worth jotting down. Hip hop has shaped my bisexual, polyamorous, scientific, native-of-the-South-Side-of-Chicago, Black-ass existence. Manuals are good. Therapy is good.

Emcees with college educations are becoming less rare, but when I was coming up, rappers didn't normally boast having a GED, much less a bachelor's degree. I was coming of age in arguably the golden era of rap, circa 1996. Slick Willie Clinton was president. The Chicago Bulls and, more specifically, Michael—fucking!—Jordan had everyone in Chicago thinking we ALL played in the NBA. (LeBron, who?) We were starting *another* three-peat. (Steph, who?) You couldn't tell Chicagoans shit in the '90s. And if you were into hip hop, not merely rap, chances were you were *really* into it. Like, hardcore into it. Being into hip hop, as opposed to just rap, meant you were seeking out this style of music outside of mainstream radio. You were immersed in the whole culture, not just the music. Most rappers claimed to be super-duper hardcore. If they had anything other than a PhD in the street life, their fans had no idea. Rap/hip hop back then was not exactly synonymous with a good upbringing. At least not the stuff we were listening to.

I remember not quite understanding rap music in the 1980s. To be fair, I was way too young to get it, yet I remember being drawn to the beats and the Blackness of it all. Poor Righteous Teachers, Boogie Down Productions (BDP), and Queen Latifah come to mind immediately when I think of that period. These were educators—scholars, even. But by the '90s, rap had expanded beyond songs for dancing and educating folks. Rap was on some other shit. Some gangsta shit.

In 2021, we seem to be collectively embracing stupidity more than ever when it comes to the modern, successful, mainstream rapper. Lil Uzi Vert put a $24 million pink diamond in his forehead just to make more music about . . . money and bitches. (Sigh.) Rappers are getting shot and going to jail left and right. (RIP, King Von. RIP, Pop Smoke.) It seems like we're losing rappers all the time. Overdosing. Overclouting. Just overdoing it. Capitalism has completely taken over the subject matter. You have to dig deep to find content that's about something other than money, clothes, jewelry, and throat babies. You read that right. There's a song trending *right now* called "Throat Baby," and, as you can guess, it's about swallowing semen. These are the times. Yet with all these distractions from real emcees, the ones focused on different content and heady lyrics can still be found in the Kendricks and the Rapsodys. The J. Coles and the Tierra Whacks. (RIP, Nipsey Hussle.) Some of these emcees are in the mainstream, but for the most part, we're stuck with sex-crazed, money-worshipping, indecipherable druggies with penchants for neon hair.

Before going any further, we have to acknowledge the distinctions between casual rap fans and passionate underground heads because there is a true difference between independent or underground acts and mainstream ones. There is also an elitist view of music that can separate "McDonald's" tunes from "farm-to-table-cuisine" tunes.

When we talk about the monotonous rap heard on the radio versus what fans have to seek out, these separations are implied. If you've been a casual rap fan and you're reading this, good portions of this book will be new to you. Getting into independent/underground rap music opens up a whole-new universe of artists. And when you start getting deeper into the women, and LGBTQAI+ folks, who've made hip hop tunes throughout history, you're opening up that universe even more. And when you start talking about the best emcees, PERIOD, you HAVE to talk about women. But please, don't call us femcees.

When I first started rapping, my only goal was to be able to rap on any beat. I just wanted to sound good flowing on different tempos. That was it. I had no idea some of my peers were gonna one day be considered among the best emcees. I didn't know anyone would care about what any of us did, much less call us great. A very wise rap mentor of mine said, "Most legends exist in their own minds." You ain't a legend just because you did it and love it. What have you given? What have you offered? What have you done? And, who cares?

I wouldn't call myself a legend, personally. I'm a medium deal within an elite rap club. But if I'm being honest, I am a legend in many underground-rap circles. The shoe fits. Fine. It fits. I've walked in these hip hop shoes for a long-ass time. I've given my adulthood to this shit— and I have a degree in fucking CHEMISTRY. If legendary things didn't happen, and weren't happening, I don't think I'd have stayed in this life this long. This music is running through my veins. You know what they say about eating, drinking, and breathing this shit? Yeah, I do that.

My mother is a writer. My father was a writer. (RIP, Alvin "Corky" Bowen, Jr.) The majority of my family has lived in Chicago for decades. My mother's parents migrated to Chicago from Mississippi in the 1950s. I spent most of my childhood living in Englewood, which, by the time my maternal grandparents were older, seemed like a war zone torn apart by crack cocaine and street gangs. But when they first moved there, they were one of the first Black families on the block. It's a respectable home with hardworking spirits in there. My grandmother refuses to leave. I don't blame her.

I come from a long line of seekers of knowledge, including writers, comedians, and singers. Hanging out with my family is always educational AND entertaining. I constantly learn stuff, and I perpetually laugh my ass off. As an only child, I was doted upon—a latchkey kid with all the toys and no one to play with. My father's side of the family boasted tons of cousins to hang with, but growing up it was mostly me and my mom, with my mom either working or studying to give us a better go of it. She committed herself to education—hers and mine. I still beam with pride when I reflect on those late nights with her studying for a degree in journalism while I was studying in high school. We'd spread our books and work on her bed and just *get to it*. My mom literally slept with the *AP Stylebook*, and I literally slept with a chemistry book. I didn't have a choice about whether or not I went to college. Education was the ONLY priority for me, according to my mom. She knew early on my intellect and interests would take me far, so she insisted, no, DEMANDED, the best education possible. I wasn't gonna be a statistic on her watch.

Yet sometimes I wish I hadn't wasted all those silly years committing to college and started taking music seriously way earlier. Now THAT would have been the difference between fame and fringe. Yeah, right. Early fame was certainly not in the cards for me. That alignment might have killed me. I love chemicals. I love humans. It wasn't until I started touring consistently that I discovered I was good at alcohol and drugs. Having too much too soon could have proven fatal. I'm thankful I'm here, sober, and reflective. Perspective is a bitch, and we'll discuss my brushes with drugs throughout this book. It's part of the medicine.

I thank God daily for my life and outlook. I overthink everything. I overanalyze, often to a fault. However, if being an emcee has taught me anything about life, it's you either connect or you don't. You're either creating a character or you're searching for self, but either way art is imitating life. You're speaking shit into existence, you're speaking prophecy, you're pouring energy out, and you're inviting energy in. I had to get a degree in chemistry before becoming a professional emcee. And I had to bust my existential-thinking ass all the way open being a professional emcee before becoming an author. *In that order.*

My life surrounding the music has taken me higher, and lower, than I've ever been. In *Her Word Is Bond*, I'm focusing on my career especially, but being in love while pursuing a rap career can bring out the ugly side in anyone. Women, most often, are on the receiving end of so much hip hop–based trauma. Domestic issues. Professional damage. Naïveté. Many women quit rap for these reasons, and you'd never know how much abuse they'd endured unless they split themselves open and told you. Lots of these stories never see the light of day.

But how does one do all this life and music and art and love and hate AND stay sane? What's the secret to surviving this game as a woman emcee? I guess we'll all have to keep reading to find out.

HOUSE RULES,

OR THINGS TO CONSIDER WHILE READING

My book, my house, my rules.

Please keep in mind: Some of the identities in this book have been protected, because even though we might have been through some wild shit together, I want to honor their anonymity. Some names have not been changed. Some names have been omitted for not only the person's protection, but mine. When you speak up for survivors, some abusers get mad and do what they do best. Safety first.

This isn't a book meant to slander anyone or ruin anyone's life, even if some of the folks mentioned in this book tried to ruin mine. Let's just call it even.

Some of the book chapters have interludes. They are meant to add extra context to the timeline of my story via some of the music I was obsessed with during those moments. Also, a few of the chapter breaks help to compartmentalize the memories in my brain. They are part of the roadmap.

Everything in this book happened to me. But because I've never pressed charges or gotten the law involved, they will be considered *allegations*. That's fine with me.

My story is one that might help an up-and-coming artist or a person dealing with the fear of failure. The fear of scrutiny crippled me for years—coming out of it took decades.

I am sober. Sobriety has been one of the biggest life changes I've made. If you're struggling with addiction, please tell someone. In music, it's almost comical to be sober. Believe me, you cannot work in your truth when you're fucked up all the time. But you can make powerful changes. If I can do it, you *certainly* can do it.

I am bisexual. Being a queer artist in hip hop, while getting easier, is difficult still. Homophobia, transphobia, and the like have made it almost impossible for some queer artists to create in a healthy way. Some folks wanna be near you because it makes them seem more progressive. Some folks will want to fuck you on the low but never stand up for you in public. Some folks will just want to exploit you. But until *you* know someone stands explicitly for gay and trans rights, *you don't know*. Find out where they stand before it bites you in the ass. (No pun intended.) Black trans rights are HUMAN rights. Don't get it twisted.

Fuck the police.

I believe in God, and God is great.

CHAPTER 1

TODAY WAS A GOOD YEAR

n 1993, I was attending William H. Ray Magnet School in Hyde Park in Chicago. Hyde Park is known now as the neighborhood near where the Obamas lived before they moved to the White House, but back in the '90s it was still a very nice, historic neighborhood, a place where you could see many affluent people of color. Home to the University of Chicago, it was cheap eats and WHPK, the college radio station. I was in the eighth grade and not looking forward to high school at all. A nerd by hood standards, I wanted nothing to do with college prep. I just wanted to fast-forward to college. Only a few of my family members had gone away to college, and soon I would be among them. At that point in my life, I was big on academic praise, and high school seemed so . . . mean. All my older cousins had told me all these horror stories about ninth grade through twelfth grade. I wanted to skip over all that. No dice.

I'd passed the entrance test to get into Whitney M. Young Magnet High School (alma mater of many influential Chicagoans, including Michelle Obama), so that's where I was going. My mother would have nothing less. One thing about Elaine Hegwood Bowen: She was gonna see to it that I went to a "good" school. I had no say in the matter. A lot of my friends from Ray were going to go to Kenwood High School, a few blocks away, but not me. That kinda made me nervous. I had made some good friends by eighth grade, even though I'd only attended Ray for two years. I got along with all the slick-talking nerds who finished their homework early and disrupted class. Some of the friends I made at Ray are still my friends today. I wanted to stay at that school forever. Ray was small; Young was big. I felt very small.

And teen angst was life at this point because, well, teens are normally angsty. I was a chubby kid, an only child, and I was a "smart" kid from the hood. I never felt *cool*, per se, but I always felt creative. Music already had its hold on me, and I was dreading going to Whitney Young. I wasn't sure I was up to it. I blame it on *House Party 2*, released in 1991, starring iconic hip hop duo Kid 'n Play (Christopher Reid and Christopher Martin), Queen Latifah, a budding Martin Lawrence, and many more great Black actors. That movie made me wanna live in dorms, pick out silk numbers for pajama jammy jams, not study for the ACT, and dodge bullies in the cafeteria.

The year 1993 is a great starting point because hip-hop-ya-don't-stop aficionados love to stamp it as one of the best years in the genre. That stance is hard to argue. Some very big, very classic hip hop albums were released in 1993. That year also boasted huge moments for pop culture, and hip hop was right there, grabbing my attention and spinning in my Sony Discman—complete with huge, obnoxious Sony headphones to let everyone know I was *deeply* into music.

In '93 I was thirteen years old and hip hop was around twenty. Even though I was preparing to graduate from Ray and head to Whitney Young in the fall, my home life was pretty boring. I wasn't really allowed to just hang out on the block for fear of violence or negative influence. Art really helped shaped most of my youth; reality was spoon-fed to me. (Again, I was severely overprotected.) My friends were at school; they didn't live in my neighborhood. TV, people watching, and music got me through a good amount of loneliness. So let's talk about some of the genre- and puberty-defining music that shaped this time in my life.

Ice Cube, "It Was a Good Day"

The single and accompanying music video made the West Coast look dangerous yet very cool. F. Gary Gray directed the video and would go on to direct some of my favorite movies. Leaving a decent neighborhood and moving back to Englewood in 1986 had me really disliking the ghetto, as it were. My mom and I had relocated to the house where she grew up, in Englewood, a neighborhood that would soon become arguably the worst in Chicago, after my grandfather's death that same year. Relocating was good because I was closer to my extended family. Living on the North Side of Chicago had made commutes to see my people long and arduous. At least in Englewood I was closer to my relatives. But relocating was also bad because, well, danger. By '93, crack and gangs were epidemics and I hated them. But Cube and Gray reminded me of how cool and plentiful the ghetto really was. When you don't have to use your AK, it is indeed a good day.

Fun fact: Two of my best friends were allowed to recite Ice Cube's lyrics in poetry class. Our teacher let them say the curse words and everything. That was probably the coolest thing to ever happen during my time at Ray. That's the spirit of what I eventually brought to my own hip hop–based after-school program.

Tour poster for a Digable Planets show with support from hip hop band Abstract Giants and Psalm One.

Digable Planets, *Reachin' (A New Refutation of Time and Space)*

I know this album word for word. Digable Planets' debut single, "Rebirth of Slick (Cool Like Dat)," was a smash— and so jazzy my mom bumped the album on her own. She disliked most hip hop. To be fair, most parents at the time were utterly shocked by this pounding, vulgar music. My mom liked some stuff, like Heavy D, Run-DMC, and Kool Moe Dee, but really didn't allow rap in the house. I had to sneak to listen to it. But Digable Planets? She let their music ride, and we often discussed their album's merits. Discussing hip hop with my mom is still so much fun.

I played that album constantly. It was a sonically interesting record for kids like me who didn't fully get or subscribe to gangsta or pop rap. Digable Planets was different; it showed in the samples the group rapped over. Digable Planets was groundbreaking and—wait for it—there was a woman in the group.

Ladybug is very important to the legacy of Digable Planets. She has the trippiest wordplay and the softest, yet most commanding voice. Often, she sounded better than her male counterparts, and the way she rapped moved my young soul. Having that one woman in the crew was important for little girls to see. Hearing her higher-pitched voice cut through the bass and the machismo of hip hop let me know it could be done. She was different. She stood out. Even though I know now that having one woman in a sea of men is patriarchy at play, back then, when I was a future lyrical assassin, I couldn't care less. I didn't see the nuance there. I didn't understand how being the lone woman in a crew could spark a deeper conversation about exclusion. I just knew it was fucking awesome seeing Ladybug shine. The truth is, many women in hip hop go uncelebrated. That's why, even today, I celebrate the fuck out of Ladybug Mecca.

Fun fact: I opened for Digable Planets in Chicago in November 2009. They were playing without Ladybug, which was a real bummer, but they still put on a great show. I met Doodlebug and Butterfly that night; I had the pleasure of chatting it up with Ladybug on a random visit to Oakland, California, a few years later. It's crazy to think about being so influenced by their music and having no idea I'd meet them later in life.

Naughty by Nature, *19 Naughty III*

At this point, Naughty was hot in the streets. After "O.P.P." took off (I wasn't allowed to sing it in the house), they followed up with an album boasting one of the biggest hip hop anthems of all time, "Hip Hop Hooray." Play that one at a party right now, and somebody will start doing the wave during the chorus. This is a song we couldn't escape in '93, and nobody wanted to. Yelling "hip hop hooray" was a genius play on the old time "hip, hip, hooray" chant, which many scholars say has anti-Semitic roots—yikes—and it cemented Naughty's anthemic capabilities.

19 Naughty III went platinum and, quiet as it's kept, Treach is one of hip hop's greatest lyricists. But Naughty by Nature soon went pop, and my budding hip hop elitism didn't allow me to stick around for the ascension. I know better now than to chuck an artist *just* for going pop. But back then nothing was cornier than going mainstream.

Fun fact: Track eleven on *19 Naughty III* is a song called "Hot Potato," and it features Freddie Foxxx. In 2012, Foxxx played my boyfriend in the music video for my song "Open Relationship." If y'all know anything about Freddie Foxxx (aka Bumpy Knuckles), y'all know he doesn't fuck around. He's one of the most feared heads in hip hop. So, you know how hilarious it is to see him in a video playing my boo. I couldn't help but hum "Hot Potato" to myself at times during the video shoot.

A Tribe Called Quest, *Midnight Marauders*

I also know this album word for word. *Midnight Marauders* is my favorite Tribe album. I'll argue with anyone who questions whether it's their best effort. I still remember going to one of my first shindigs with my old friends from Ray when the music video for "Award Tour" was released. Standing around with awkward kids trying to decipher this classic hip hop and knowing it was important sticks in my mind. We knew this was some cool shit, we just didn't know why. This was still all very new to us. *Marauders* is Tribe's third album, but it was the one that hit me the hardest. The samples, the rhymes, the concept. The interludes? Flawless.

Fun fact: In 2006, I saw Tribe perform *Marauders* and other classic material at Bumbershoot, a Seattle-based music festival. I was touring with a group on the festival's bill and was given all access. The festival also boasted a Kanye West performance, but in 2006 I was more interested in seeing Tribe. Gaining access to this performance and being on the wing of the stage while they performed "Electric Relaxation" to a crowd of one hundred thousand is bucket list stuff. I almost cried. I probably did cry. (RIP, PHIFE DAWG.)

Souls of Mischief, *'93 'til Infinity*

A-Plus and Psalm One at South by Southwest (SXSW), Austin, Texas, March 2014.

The title track, an era-defining classic that still slaps, is one of the biggest rap songs in history. Souls of Mischief is one of the most famous rap groups ever, and this album was prophetic. Released during the onslaught of G(angsta)-funk, the album takes a sharp turn from what we were used to hearing on the radio, especially from a West Coast group. Souls and the entire Hieroglyphics Crew were putting Oakland, and ultimately independent hip hop, on the map in a big way. Hiero gave us a long-standing, successful indie blueprint, and they have one of the most recognizable logos of all time. "'93 'til Infinity" was inescapable, and Hiero was right about building a legacy and having longevity. This song specifically has proven time and again its significance in hip hop.

Fun fact: I was offered my first record deal by Casual of Hieroglyphics and was featured on his *Smash Rockwell* album.[1] That feature was my introduction to the independent–hip hop game and was my first album placement. I've toured with Del the Funky Homosapien and have songs[2] with him, too. A-Plus of Souls of Mischief coproduced my 2013 project, *Free Hugs*.

Nirvana, *In Utero*

Ok, so this ain't hip hop, but in 1993 Nirvana was one of the biggest acts in music—period. I can't lie. I *pretended* to love them at first. I was at Ray and my white friends were into them, so by default I was into them. The music video for "Smells like Teen Spirit" changed pop culture for certain. *Nevermind* was my JAM, and the song "Lithium" got played repeatedly for days on end. I thought I was the weirdest kid in the hood for loving that song. Nirvana's follow-up, *MTV Unplugged in New York*, was also my jam. *In Utero* wasn't my favorite album, but I let the tape rock because of peer pressure. "Heart-Shaped Box" was pretty dope, though. I should revisit that album with adult ears. (RIP, Kurt Cobain.)

Fun fact: Super engineer Steve Albini worked with Nirvana on *In Utero,* and I was privileged to work with him on a mixtape I released in 2010, *Woman at Work Volume 2*. I was a complete fan girl and wouldn't stop asking Albini questions about the Nirvana sessions during my own marathon session. Even though I'm sure

Albini gets really tired of people asking him questions about Nirvana, he was really nice to me and answered most of them.

Snoop Doggy Dogg, *Doggystyle*

DOGGYSTYLE IS THE MOST IMPORTANT DEBUT ALBUM BY A RAP ARTIST. You can argue with your creepy cousin about it. It peaked at number one on the *Billboard* charts in December '93 and sold just shy of one million copies in its first week. This is when people had to *leave their homes* to buy albums—and I was one of those people. Snoop's cameos on Dr. Dre tracks had me eagerly anticipating this album. Since I wasn't allowed to listen to "vulgar" hip hop in the house, *Doggystyle* was relegated to my headphones. The way "Lodi Dodi" was mixed still gives me chills. I can remember being on the school bus, my Sonys pressed up against my ears, eyes closed, trying to understand why this album was such an earworm. I wanted to hear it every minute of every second of every day. I've been a full-on Snoop Dogg STAN since the beginning.

Snoop remains on my personal top-ten list of rappers. He has such a distinct voice and a penchant for business that's almost unmatched. He's said some questionable things about women in recent years, and honestly most of his discography is a calling-women-bitches fest. But fuck all that for now. When this album dropped, I changed. I was fully on board, but still wasn't allowed to buy a Pittsburg Penguins jersey, like the one Snoop wore in the "Gin and Juice" video.

Fun fact: In 2008, I recorded a few songs at Hyde Street Studios in San Francisco. The literal *only* reason I wanted to record there was because Snoop allegedly recorded in one of the rooms. The session was very expensive. The song was never released.

Insane Clown Posse, *Beverly Kills 50187*

Say what you want about Insane Clown Posse (ICP), but you can't say they aren't one of the most successful rap groups of all time. I didn't own their album in 1993. To be honest, I wasn't aware of ICP until Eminem dissed them years later. I wasn't a Juggalo growing up. But in 2017, I was lucky enough to tour with ICP via RA the Rugged Man. You read that right. I was RA's touring DJ, and we were direct support for ICP's The Great Milenko Tour, celebrating twenty-plus years in the industry. They make millions every year while remaining the butt of many hip hop jokes. The clowns are still laughing all the way to the bank, and I gained a lot of knowledge being on the road with them for five weeks.

Fun fact: Juggalos are one of the only remaining American subcultures that doesn't specialize in race war. They marched on Washington, DC, for Chrissake. I also went to a Jacksonville, Florida, strip club with ICP, but that's a story for another book. Oh yeah, and I sprayed Faygo on fans during ICP shows. That really happens. That was a fun tour.

Insane Clown Posse and Psalm One at Basement Transmissions,
Erie, Pennsylvania, October 2017.

Wu-Tang Clan, *Enter the Wu-Tang (36 Chambers)*
The Wu made such an intense splash in hip hop, we didn't know what
to make of them. We just knew they were hot. By the time *Forever*, their
second album, dropped, I was borrowing bubble coats and ski goggles
from my more fashionable friends to rock in the halls at school. When
those killer bees swarmed, we were ready, son. I do maintain that this
double album could have been condensed into one amazing effort, but
I understand what they were doing. They were making a full-on domi-
nant statement, and I was here for it. All hip hop heads were.

Fun fact: I opened for Wu-Tang a few times in my career, but
the most important one was when I was direct support for them at
the old Congress Theater in Chicago, circa 2011. It remains one of
the more violent hometown crowds I've ever performed for (the
other was the crowd at a 50 Cent show—I opened for him before
his debut album dropped), but one of the most rewarding shows I
endured. I left everything on the stage. Because hip hop groups with
cult followings are NOT there to see the openers, I had to bring it. A
young Chance the Rapper, before he was a super-famous artist, was
in attendance, and every now and then we bump into each other and
bring up that performance. What a fucking night.

Honorable-mention fun fact: I opened for Ghostface Killah
later down the line and was too afraid to ask him for a picture when
I saw him backstage. Tragic.

I could write a whole book on hip hop in 1993. However, I'll
stop. What's more interesting to me, while reflecting on the above
list, is how few women are represented. I'm sure there were *plenty*
more unsung woman heroes making hip hop a phenomenon in 1993,
but they aren't highlighted. I sure as hell wasn't aware of too many.
But I'm positive these women exist. I'm also quite sure some readers
will find glaring omissions, but keep in mind these were only SOME
of the albums and singles defining MY '93, a few years before I ever
picked up a microphone and more than a decade before I became a
professional rapper.

The summer of '93 was an epic time for hip hop and for me: I was nervously preparing for my high school career. I had no idea what to expect, but I knew music was gonna be there for me. Whenever I felt invisible, which was often since I was an only child, I simply had to slip on those big-ass Sony headphones. When those things were on my dome, nothing mattered much.

Whitney Young was intimidating. It was the most competitive public high school in Chicago, and I'd tested in with flying colors. My mother couldn't have been happier. This was confirmation of my young Black intelligence. My ambition. My comfortable future.

But I wasn't popular as a freshman. My first year of high school was brutal. I had exactly one friend from Ray with me at Whitney Young, Luis, and we hung out constantly. During lunch, we'd go off campus and walk down Jackson Boulevard, singing Bone Thugs-N-Harmony songs for fun. Whitney Young was massive—three big buildings connected by bridges—and it was easy to get lost. The location of the school was an intersection of the hood and the burbs. It was right in the middle of a few housing projects and million-dollar homes. Coming off I-290 and driving down Ashland to Jackson was like night and day. From hood to hope.

I've experienced this kinda duality my whole life—one foot in the ghetto and one foot in that deluxe apartment in the sky. Since Luis was also coming from the allegedly dangerous South Side of Chicago, we stuck together naturally. Navigating that red brick and black metal, those huge hallways, and those intimidating upperclassmen was a course in itself.

Being impressionable and around so much opportunity and privilege was daunting, but I was up for the challenge. I wanted my education to take me away from the hood, permanently. Freshman-year classes weren't too difficult yet, but coming from a small magnet school to this big-ass high school was a lot for my nerves. I was pretty shy and quiet freshman year. However, that wouldn't last.

By sophomore year, I had fully remixed my wardrobe: khakis and Reeboks and Ralph Lauren polo shirts, which was the uniform of the kids who were into hip hop. My locker mate was a dreamy, break-dancing senior nicknamed Relay, and I was IN LOVE with him. I had stalker-like tendencies when it came to Relay, and he was *really* into hip hop. I wanted to relate to him, so I made sure to keep up with the music he liked (enter Mobb Deep's *Juvenile Hell*). To be honest, I don't even think I'd be rapping if he hadn't encouraged me to after seeing my poetry book. Besides hanging with Luis and listening to music, writing bad poetry was my thing. I wanted so bad for Relay to like me that I dove head first into "being" hip hop. Boys, right?

Relay was older and more popular, and he had the respect of everyone in school. It was through my love of Relay that I met my first rap crew, which included the brilliant Open Mike Eagle. We weren't tight yet, but because all the hip hop kids hung around each other, it was only a matter of time until we connected. I believe we had one class together, but I was still too shy to introduce myself to other kids. Who knew we'd all go on to do super cool things?

End-of-year cipher, PDX crew (Mike and Psalm One in front), Whitney Young High School, 1998.

PDX, my first crew, included kids who would go on to become engineers, photographers, and scholars. Open Mike has performed his critically acclaimed music around the globe, and he even had a TV show on Comedy Central. I'm so proud of him. He's still on TV quite a bit and is doing great things in the arena of podcasting.

To brag a bit: I was the first one in this crew to rap. All the guys were originally avid break-dancers, but it wasn't long before the whole crew was rapping. Mike, Rift, Sonar, Misfit, Antimatter Bonecrusher, and a few other new hip hop converts were becoming pure heads. But let the record show: I was the first one in PDX to consistently rap my lyrics in ciphers. They couldn't let a girl get all the attention, so they all quickly followed suit, but I digress.

In addition to beginning to pursue hip hop, by sophomore year, I took my first chemistry class, an honors version that cemented my love for science. Something happened to me when I began studying chem. It was a language I felt compelled to learn. The term *breaking it down* was also synonymous with the breaks in disco records, which were adapted for hip hop breaks. The same certainly applies to this field of study. Chemistry is the explanation of what occurs when you "break down" matter. The combination of science and hip hop helps define me, and to this day, I'm still breaking shit all the way down.

Hip hop, like chemistry, is a language. But hip hop is also culture. It's a lifestyle. And it's also very unforgiving to women and queer folks. To have love for hip hop as a woman toughens you. I wasn't too tough yet, but high school was certainly helping with that. Being the lonely, overprotected girl was a reputation that was slowly changing. What a crazy year to evolve.

Thanks, 1993. You're the GOAT.

CHAPTER 2

THERE'S NO CRYING IN THE STUDIO

Sixty-Second Bishop is the song I quote/
Weaker people never get the prawns I smoke/
Cooked shrimp and corruption is the cross we bear/
Awe yeah, if you pilot, put your wings in the air.
—"Kids Right Now"

As an only child growing up in the increasingly dangerous terrain of Englewood in Chicago, I was smothered with protection. I can recall whole summers when I wasn't allowed to leave the front porch for my mom's fear of me getting into trouble. What the fuck this trouble was largely escaped me, but it made me crave the freedom that most of my friends seemed to have.

Englewood—about a twelve-minute drive from Hyde Park, on the city's South Side—has never fully recovered from the crack-cocaine epidemic, race riots, or white flight. In the 1950s, whole swaths of the South Side were burned down by white people who inhabited the area, sparking all sorts of crime. By the 1960s, the white folks started moving out in droves. By the '70s, more crime. By the Reagan era, it was a war zone. In the '90s, gangs. But for me, this was where my family stayed. This was my home.

I lived in a house right near Sixty-Third and Ashland, a major intersection in the area. I can recall nothing but fast-food restaurants, liquor stores, storefront churches, and shitty apartment buildings as far as the eye could see. And crack houses. We were very close to the train station and on a main bus route, so that made the hood a *little* safer for me. Still, my mom worried herself sick about my safety in the neighborhood. Easy to get shot. Easy to get grabbed. And worse: it was easy to be impressed by the streets.

I hated being so lonely. I rarely got to see any of my school friends because my mom didn't dare let me go to my neighborhood schools. Because she was so overprotective, I didn't have any friends in my neighborhood. No siblings to watch my back. I was only allowed to play with my cousins when I went to my father's mother's house, near Sixty-Third and Halsted. It's not surprising that my imagination was a pillar of my latchkey childhood.

By the time hip hop as lifestyle consumed me, I had my driver's license. My first car was a 1987 Ford Mustang, gifted to me by my aunt, who had recently purchased a Mercedes-Benz. That was one helluva hand-me-down, and the newly acquired freedom it brought me had me seeking out the latest Redman cassette to blast in my first vehicular tape deck. *Muddy Waters* was his 1996 opus—and the soundtrack to the world I explored in my first whip.

I wasn't cool, per se, but I was far from unpopular. My chubbiness knocked my clout score down a bit, but I could rap and didn't pose a threat to the popular girls. Those girls would've literally clawed each other's eyes out to be seen as the hottest. I'm happy to announce we called them plastics way before the great American classic film *Mean Girls* made that term popular. Many of them were just so fake, so it was an easy moniker to place on them. Little did I know, high school would reflect the rest of life.

My first actual crew was PDX, also known as Paradox or PHactory Defects. In the '90s, every hip hop entity needed to have multiple names with multiple meanings. I remember my best friend,

Colin, looking at me in disgust when he found out I hadn't realized the Notorious BIG was also Frank White, one of Biggie's many pseudonyms. Pseudonyms? We all had 'em. Hell, I've got at least three.

The main members of PDX were: Rift Napalm, Antimatter Bonecrusher, Sonar, Open Mike, Kizzie Tangents (ME), and Misfit, who would become my first real boyfriend. All these super interesting guys . . . and me. This would prove to be a running theme in my life, being the token woman. The guys were mostly break-dancers, but soon we were a budding rap crew. (Enter the proverbial banging on lunch tables during freestyles and huge rap ciphers where we would get half our class to surround us while we performed.)

Those lunchroom and behind-the-arts-building ciphers were the stuff of lore and glory. At Whitney Young, we had four lunchroom areas, each with a designated color. We were all about red- and blue-house ciphers. That's where, when the bell rang to signal a class change, hundreds of kids, maybe even a cool thousand, would be shuffling through the school to their next class. And we would be there. Freestyling. Spitting writtens. Battling. Nobody was safe. Damn near every day there could be a huge group of kids circled around one of us, trying to hear these rappers. Enter a taste of high-school fame. Enter the intense rap battle. Enter us no longer being on the fringes of what was cool. Our nonrapping peers were trying to figure out what the fuck these weird-ass kids were doing and why so many *other* kids were interested. We were becoming a threat to what had been traditionally popular. Kids who could actually rap were all the rage. Still are. And I was right there. The pulsing nucleus of rhyme, in female form, oozing insecurity, but attracting attention.

By around the time I turned fifteen, I'd started kissing girls. One girl, actually. Let's call her Stevie. Stevie was older than me. I was barely a sophomore, and she was a senior at a different high school. She was also a little older for her grade, making her a few months shy of nineteen. Stevie was convinced my mom would have her locked up for statutory rape if moms ever found out we were dating. I can't say what my mom would have done if she found out her fifteen-year-old daughter was seeing a nineteen-year-old, a legal adult, who was about to graduate high school her damn self. Yeah, my mom probably would have advocated for Stevie to be placed swiftly UNDER the jail.

I had been battling some real homosexual feelings since I was a little girl. I remember having a crush on a dance teacher when I was around six years old. I remember dry humping with a few family friends when I was around eleven, for research purposes. I remember understanding Denise was the hottest Huxtable, but constantly hearing about Theo. You gotta understand: Growing up in a semistrict, very respectable Baptist household meant being *any* kinda gay was punishable. And I didn't like punishment; I liked praise. So, I kept my curiosities and my sexuality a secret for decades.

Mom and a young Psalm One during the summer Psalm lived in New York City, circa 1997.

By my final year of high school, most of my friends knew I was bisexual. I'd dated and broken up with Stevie, a devastating event brought on by mom finding some letters addressed to Stevie. (Though, thankfully, none of the letters mentioned how old Stevie was.) I promptly denied any romantic involvement with her even though I'd already come out to my closest cousins. I couldn't fathom completing high school without a proper boyfriend, so I lost fifty pounds between junior and senior year, after staying with my aunt and uncle that summer. They had a treadmill I took full advantage of. After that, I finally felt confident enough to talk to boys. Thinking back, this was actually insane, because I was rapping and battling guys for a couple years before feeling like I could flirt, albeit badly. I'd just never considered myself the kind of girl guys would be interested in. I had such low self-esteem.

Misfit was the young man I felt safest with. He was cute, funny, smart, and a former fat kid. He felt the pain of being shunned by popular kids just because of a little extra chubbiness. I think it was this chip on our potato chip–loving shoulders, plus our love of hip hop, that made us work. Rumors were also flying around school that I liked girls, so courting Misfit helped me avoid being labeled the gay kid. I was scared shitless of the prospect of being branded gay, when in fact I am bisexual. No shade to homosexuals, though.

In the '90s, there was no nuance in talks of sexuality or gender identity at my high school. Even the slightest whisper that you weren't heterosexual could lead to violence. Hip hop was the same. The f-word—the six-letter one, not the four-letter one—was thrown around so flippantly most folks wouldn't dare embrace queerness. If you were a lesbian, it was sexy to guys *if* you were attractive to them. If you were an "ugly" gay girl or a gay guy, you were a target. And gender identity beyond boy/girl, man/woman was unthinkable. There was no education or compassion for people living between the spectrum ends of man and woman. You were either a straight guy or girl (aka "normal"), or you were prey. I wanted no parts of it, so even though I truly loved Misfit, I had a very real internal struggle about who I was, and what I was presenting, when we dated. We had a lot of fun and laughs together. We went to prom together. But I also cheated on him by smooching a girl here and there. In college, I cheated on him with a mutual guy friend. He found out and almost battled me. I was a *very* shitty girlfriend. We are, however, currently friends, and I'm so grateful for him. It's water under the bridge, but I still actively hope he forgives me. I love him so very much to this day. If you're reading this, Misfit, I know I told you but I'm really sorry. Thank you for loving me. Thank you for forgiving me.

Misfit and I also gave each other the gift of nonvirginity. We still joke about it. We were so hip hop with it, too. Just imagine battling your high school boyfriend a week after losing your virginity to him. Rap love is real.

At this point in my life, I was still sheltered in comparison to most of my friends, but my mom had loosened my leash a bit. I was allowed to stay out late, sleep over certain friends' houses, and date. I wasn't too wild. No arrests. Only one in-school suspension. I snuck and drank Zima when my friends could get their hands on booze. I'd smoked a little weed and got caught, so I was real careful with my marijuana intake. (My mom is still very much antipot, but I know weed is medicine.) Other than a few minor offenses, I didn't give my mother too much trouble. I was constantly looking ahead to college. I knew she really trusted me, and I couldn't wait to experience what Kid 'n Play experienced in their fictional, Hollywood-ized, post-high-school fantasy. Dorms and pajamas, baby.

By the time I graduated, in 1998, I was a hip hop aficionado. I came of age in the golden era. And that year, hip hop gave us Black Star's *Mos Def & Talib Kweli Are Black Star*; Lauryn Hill's iconic debut, *The Miseducation of Lauryn Hill*; Tribe's *The Love Movement*; Big Pun's first joint, *Capital Punishment*; an intro to DMX, who dropped two albums that year, something that was unheard of; the emergence of Canibus; and Hieroglyphics' classic album *3rd Eye*

Vision, just to name a few. I got great grades and hip hop was the soundtrack to my studies. All I wanted to do was rap, but I knew I had to do my homework first. Luckily, I was on pace for a handful of academic scholarships. I had time to dream.

I'd performed in one talent show with PDX and had one particularly intense school-wide cipher where we were the focal point. I'd also gone to a "studio" for the first time with the guys. The producer/engineer was a friend of a friend who had a four track and a mic, and was looping samples to make songs with whatever rappers he could find. For the production-gear ignorant, a four track is an old-school recorder based on the cassette tape and was used for multitrack recordings. It was the standard for years. Now the standard is digital, with software like Ableton and Pro Tools. The four track THEN was what Pro Tools is NOW.

One of our first recording sessions as a crew was a circus. We had no idea what we were doing, but we were doing something NOBODY in our social circle had done. We were getting our rhymes recorded. Still, it was Barnum and Bailey.

We were running late because we'd never bothered to think just how long it would take for five newbies to lay down vocals in a time when, if you messed up, you had to do the WHOLE THING OVER. OMG, I shudder just thinking about it. There was no copy and paste, no drag and drop. It was tape. None of us were pros, but some of us were more comfortable, naturally, on the mic. I remember having to be home by nine that night, and we'd driven about thirty miles outside of the city, to Indiana, to record these tracks. A whole other fucking state! I hadn't informed my mom of any such thing. She didn't even know I rapped. She didn't know I was the only girl in a crew with a bunch of other guys and that we occasionally smoked weed and left the city to record songs with lots of curse words in them. We didn't even get to the studio until well after five. I was scared as fuck.

Curfew be damned. It was around nine, my curfew time, when we finally left the studio, and I was driving. I was so mad and fearful that I'd get in trouble for coming home late, I started bawling my eyes out. Speeding down I-94 to get my crew home and then myself home without encountering my mother's wrath was the mission. I was very much wearing the façade of a good kid by being a good student. Indiana studio sessions with my all-male crew did not fit the description, and I was desperate to keep my good standing with Elaine.

Thankfully the mission was completed without incident. My mom was tired from work and not too concerned with my tardiness, so all that crying and yelling had been unnecessary. At least for now, my horrible hip hop secret was safe. We got our first music recorded, nobody got in trouble, and we were now *immortalized* on cassette tape. But the next day, my crew clowned the fuck outta me for crying. I told them I was just passionate about my shit—and my freedom.

Hip hop–obsessed teenagers from all over the city were starting to hear about these kids from Whitney Young who really stretched metaphor and could freestyle all day. And with recordings, word spread fast. We were quickly recognized as the best rappers in the school. Little did we know, we were even becoming known outside of our respective neighborhoods.

CHAPTER 3

LIFE IN CHAMPAIGN COUNTY

The stretch of time between graduating high school and entering college is probably monumental for everyone. The class of '98 was one of the most successful in Whitney Young's history. We won the academic decathlon that year, which was kind of normal, but our boys basketball team also won the Illinois High School Association (IHSA) state championship for the first time. (Young has produced a few pro basketball players, like Quentin Richardson, who was in my graduating class.) Oh, and the mothafuckin' Chicago Bulls won the NBA championship that year, too. It was a three-peat, and I was ecstatic. We all were.

I had *just* under a 4.0 GPA when I finished there, which put me among the top one hundred students. I don't know why it was so fucking important for me to be smart among smart kids, but my fear of scrutiny probably had everything to do with it. I was also very active in church and quite sneaky with anything that had to do with hanging out with friends. I wasn't even doing a lot of "bad" stuff so much as I had a fear my family wouldn't accept anything about me that didn't have to do with church or school. But I was finishing high school. It was a feat in my community. I graduated with honors and was heading to the University of Illinois to study chemistry. This was monumental stuff.

I had also finally lost my hetero virginity and started finding my young voice as a rapper. All that ciphering and cutting a few tracks in Indiana were paying off. Even with low self-esteem, I was expressing myself in important ways, and it was helping me cope. I was an adult—maybe? Ain't it funny how when you're eighteen years old, you're all like, "I'm an adult!" when you don't know shit? And in society we all recognize it. I swore I was grown but I sure as hell wasn't. I was ready to head to college, but I was definitely scared of being unpopular again. I was scared to have no friends. But I still had one last summer in Chicago.

I still had a crappy, little car. My aunt had bought me a used one after the Mustang blew up, a casualty of letting my then drug-addicted uncle borrow it. (When he returned it, it was in need of major repairs, but I hadn't known.) I had a temp job doing mailings for The Chicago School of Professional Psychology, thanks to my mom, who was working there full time. The school was located near the Printers Row area in downtown Chicago. I was driving from Englewood every day and parking down there. I felt adult as hell, with my own parking spot, an hour lunch, and a little money in my pocket. My checks went to gasoline, food, and reggie weed. (*Reggie weed*, for the slang ignorant, was the term we used for regular, or terrible, marijuana. It's wild thinking I can just go to a dispensary now in Chicago and buy the best; legal weed back then was a pipe dream. As a young adult, reggie was all we had access to.) Every now and then I would buy music and shoes. Those were the necessities.

I mainly hung out with my crew members and a few friends I still have to this day. My circle was pretty small. We were all at the top of our classes and headed to college. I think I gravitated to overachieving kids who smoked weed and listened to hip hop because despite the stigma of drugs and rap music, we were still doing well in school. It was like a cloak. I also had a few friends on the South Side whose parents let us come over all the time.

We definitely smoked enough reggie in their basements while freestyling for hours and debating whether Eminem was white. Nobody seemed to know. Even the rap "scholars" couldn't say with any certainty. We automatically thought anyone who was insanely good at rap had to be Black or Latino. We were at the tail end of this particular golden age of hip hop. We were living in a very popular time. It seemed like every other day something incredible was released. But there was no user-friendly internet. You were either aware of the dope rappers or you weren't. Thank God my friends were all hip hop junkies. Without them I wouldn't have been as aware of all the great music happening in that era.

Back then, we'd often get music without ever seeing pictures of the artist. We hadn't SEEN Eminem yet. We'd only heard some of his music. We didn't always have access to rap magazines either, so we were stumped about this particular soon-to-be legend. *Infinite* was Eminem's underground debut album, released in late 1996. In the summer of 1998, he'd release the *Slim Shady EP*, a precursor to his major-label debut on Dr. Dre's Aftermath imprint. The debates about him, held in smoky basements as I swigged my Zima, went something like this:

"He's Black. Listen to that flow."

"He doesn't say nigga, and he talks about trailer parks."

"I think I heard him say nigga before, and brown people live in trailer parks, too!"

"I don't know, man. I never heard a white dude spit like that. He gotta be Black."

"Yo, he's talking about raping and hating his mother. He's white."

"Whatever he is, he's dope!"

I hadn't really heard anyone rap like Eminem before. His higher-pitched, almost-violent flow and his wordplay were groundbreaking to me. Rap nerds can trace Em's flow back to Kool G Rap's style, but back then I ain't know that. Em had multisyllabic rhymes, crazy metaphors, and shocking lyrics. Listening to him was like watching a movie. My crew and I were instant fans, and we all but studied his music like it was an actual course.

You couldn't tell us shit as a crew. Me, Antimatter, Open Mike, Sonar, Rift, and Misfit were very good at rapping and getting better all the time. Kids were *requesting* we come to ciphers and rap. We were all still years away from our first real shows, but in the back of school buildings, we were headliners. We were too young for "da club," but we had these public meetups and the occasional hip hop party at all-ages spaces. Those were rare, though. PDX had a tape of a few songs out, and it was getting dubbed constantly. (A dub on tape is the equivalent of burning a CD.) We found out kids were copying our tape onto blank tapes and sharing the music with their friends. You had to *physically* give someone else music if you wanted to share it during those days.

It's funny to think about how now, in the streaming era, where every download counts and you get percentages of pennies on it, we were giving out tapes to friends and spending hours making duplicates to circulate. We weren't too familiar with other crews or bands during this time, except for Nacrobats, who I'll talk about later. We sold a few tapes here and there, but we really just wanted people to know we were making music. As much as I bust my ass for these streams and stand at merch booths slanging T-shirts and vinyl now, some things never change. You gotta spend money to even GIVE away an album. We were doing that early.

Being the only woman voice on that first tape was important and would become a consistent, running theme throughout my life until now. I was always so used to being the only girl interested in the shit I was into. Back at Ray Elementary, for a short stint, I was the only girl on the boys basketball team. There was no girls team. It caused an uproar at PTA meetings. A lot of daddies hated that their sons had to play with me. I was a decent player for a little while, too. I've been playing basketball my whole life, and I always had a decent shot. In practice I dominated. However soon after, in one of our first official games, I made a crazy mistake: I ran the wrong way and actually scored on the opposite team's basket. The daddies had a field day with that. Afterwards, I was called Wrong-Way Cristalle for weeks, and I finally quit the team out of embarrassment and fatigue from all the daddies who wanted me gone anyway. As a kid, looking over to the audience to see dudes, red in the face, screaming about how I "didn't belong there" took its toll. Now, it makes me laugh. But then, I couldn't handle it. And when I quit, nobody made a fuss.

Back at Whitney Young, I had been on the Lady Dolphins basketball squad, and it was the first time I ever played with other girls. I actually ended up quitting that team after two seasons to concentrate on my studies, a decision my mom made for me in order to get a jump on academic scholarships. In my high school chemistry classes, I was usually one of a handful of ladies. So yeah, even though spitting raps on that first crew tape made me an obvious standout, it was something I was used to.

But don't get it twisted: PDX had no weak links. Rapping with those guys was no walk in the park. It was easy, very easy in fact, to get overshadowed. Open Mike, Misfit, and Antimatter were all genius freestylers. Quiet as it's kept, I was usually intimidated rhyming with them. I held my own, but it was something I worked very hard at. I sharpened my skills with them. Being in a crew with those dudes made me a better rapper and, eventually, a better artist. I was gonna miss them in college.

Top: Closeup of Psalm One (middle) on the Whitney Young girls sophomore team, circa 1996. Bottom: Team picture, circa 1996.

I had exactly one crew member I'd graduated high school with who was enrolled at the University of Illinois (U of I) along with me. U of I was a two-hour drive from Chicago, south on I-57, near central Illinois, in Champaign. Though it's definitely not Kansas, it's light years from home. It's a tiny town with a flagship campus and a smattering of Black people. U of I wasn't my first choice, but they gave me the most scholarships and financial aid. A BLACK FEMALE CHEMISTRY major? And it was my state school? I couldn't get more bang for my buck if I wanted. (Education in America is quite the scam, but by the time this book is published I will have paid off my student loans. Take THAT, Sallie Mae.)

East-central Illinois was another world entirely. Chicago is a huge industrial city. It's a metropolis, and I'm convinced Gotham City is modeled after it. (I love you, NYC, but Chicago *is* Gotham.) I love my city. No matter where I'm at in the world, I love being from and having grown up in such a culturally rich place. The diversity, the food, the people, and the music are all world class. I was exposed to a lot of it as a kid, so I was spoiled. My experiences, even living in Englewood, were so important and dynamic because I'd always gone to "good" schools. I've always had family that insisted on experiencing the "finer" things, even when they had to scrimp and save for those things. That juxtaposition is one of the coolest things about me. Being from Chicago is another one.

However, once you leave Chicagoland? The rest of Illinois is country as fuck. Champaign-Urbana was another world. Little to no diversity at all, and when you saw Black people outside of campus they were usually living in complete poverty. That college town was also the first time I ever saw a trailer park. So, THIS was the shit Eminem was talking about? (Oh yeah, by that time we'd all figured out Eminem is a white man. Imagine that.)

I had a whopping one crew member, Antimatter Bonecrusher, and one middle-school friend, Colin, with me my freshman year in college. Every other friend I would have to earn. That low self-esteem was still quite active, despite hip hop giving me some confidence. My friends and I carried hip hop everywhere we went, so pretty soon my reputation started to precede me.

In the late '90s, if you were into hip hop, a person could tell just by looking at you. Those big-ass headphones and the baggiest jeans you could find were dead giveaways. Beanies and backpacks, even when you weren't going to class, were others. I literally carried a backpack way past college, and it wasn't because I had so much shit to carry. It was hip hop. Fashion has been so inspired by hip hop culture, you can see someone today rocking a Run-DMC T-shirt who has never heard their music. What a bittersweet, cool-ass shame. Hip hop is so global now you can *look* like it without being interested in it at all. But down at Chambana back then, when I was a spring chicken, hip hop heads could smell it on me.

The quad on most college campuses is a centrally located meeting zone where you can figure out who your friends are. U of I was no exception. We didn't know of anything else to do, but we knew where the other students congregated. Antimatter Bonecrusher would wear some outlandish shit. Huge fuzzy Kangol hats with oversized hockey jerseys that adorned his long, lanky body and sloppy, never-tied Timbs. He particularly loved neon-colored pants, with tons of jewelry, accessories, and rap flare. He swore he was André 3000 way back then. Walking up to ciphers with Antimatter was in and of itself an event.

There was a small, but tightly knit, hip hop community at my alma mater. When we walked into a quad freestyle cipher our freshman year, we didn't know we were being recruited. Anyone who even thought about rapping, break-dancing, graffiti, or DJing would be at the quad during a cipher. My first college cipher wasn't much different from the lunchroom ciphers in high school, where we'd sprinkle in a little break-dancing. I would NEVER call myself a B-girl, but I had a little uprock move. It's pretty basic: foot shuffles, spins, and turns. And I can do it still.

I quickly gained respect on the quad because I was rapping, period. During that time, you just didn't see women doing it. But when I added in my little uprock after spitting some raps, I killed the game. Niggas thought I was hip hop in the flesh.

Above making with gangsta for makin' hits sake/
And those thinkin' I ain't quite found my niche, wait!/
Escape, shaft and avoid the Blair Witch fate/
Droppin' cuts while holdin' the hottest switchblade/
A mixed fate, sky open to all options/
My small squadron consists of flawed marksman . . .
—"Life After Champaign County" (album version)

My rep as this girl from Chicago who rapped and was break-dancing on the quad spread like wildfire across campus. Antimatter could cipher for hours and had the sickest Eminem- and horror core–inspired bars. While there were other kids on campus who rapped, very skilled rappers were few and far between. The emcees were rare but audiences were plentiful. Our fellow students would just stand in awe after we rapped. Some would even come up to us randomly and identify us as "those rappers." Niggas thought Antimatter was the rap boogeyman and thought I was a unicorn. I wasn't sure if this equaled popularity, but I did think that maybe that Kid 'n Play fantasy wasn't so far-fetched.

I was definitely seeking out like-minded rap fans in college to debate shit like The Roots' best song and if Lauryn Hill was the best Fugee (spoiler alert: she was), but the music-as-serious-hobby bug had bitten me. I wasn't even thinking about music as a profession, but I was certainly rapping more than ever.

Enter Peppa's, an open mic for students of color at a space racially dubbed The Black House, which was a small building on the opposite side of campus from my dorm. How fucking racist is that name? They even sold fried chicken in the back after open mics, which usually happened every weekend. The university didn't call it that. They named the building the Black Student Union. But everyone else, including white folks, called it The Black House.

Now that I think about it, Peppa's was like the Black Twitter of Chambana. You basically had to go there to get any semblance of Black culture on campus. If you went to Peppa's, you got the tea, or the spicy news and gossip of the week. But boy, it was also crawling with hip hop. Peppa's was a place to bring your bars, if you had 'em. A place to express ranges of color, air out the person who ghosted you, or just try out your poetry. Our quad rap ciphers moved indoors, then back outdoors, after Peppa's sets. While mostly poets came to flex their skills during the weekly gathering, the real action happened afterwards. Students who dared rap in front of damn near every creative person of color on campus took on an arduous task. That shit felt like the Apollo. Like, you could seriously get booed off stage, Sandman style, and hear about it until another rapper got booed. And there wasn't even a stage. That's the funniest part. Most of the entertainment was offstage, right outside the hallowed halls of The Black House.

The Black House allowed me the opportunity to meet and eventually collaborate with other artists. I sharpened my artistic knives quickly just being around the property. I performed twice at Peppa's, and both times were nerve-racking. Fortunately, I was well received, but I remember having that feeling in the pit of my stomach before performing at those first college functions. What if everyone thought I was wack? What if they . . . booed ME? I'd be scarred for life. Luckily that didn't happen, there would be plenty of future events to scar me. Even as I write this, I'm laughing nervously at those memories.

By performing at Peppa's, we put all rappers in the area on notice that these freshmen from Chicago were really good. I ultimately got recruited into a rap super crew called Bionic 6ix. Our objective was to lyrically demolish any rapper within a one hundred–mile radius. It was all violently hip hop. So beautiful. As a crew we performed at the University-wide talent show called Cotton Club. We had praise in the bag from sheer numbers. A lot of students already knew us from ciphers and Peppa's, and there were just six of us, plus a DJ. We WERE hip hop, man.

During our first Cotton Club, I had a legendary moment where our DJ stopped the track and I spit a capella in front of thousands of students. I got some big, raucous applause for my verse, which I don't fully remember. (I *do* remember rapping a line mentioning something about getting head from a little person while standing up. Those '90s punchlines were ruthless, and our crew had no shortage of them.) We crushed that show and went on to crush everything hip hop related on that campus.

I was barely able to juggle rapping on the side while studying for a major that was becoming increasingly difficult. Chemistry was easy in high school, and freshman-year chem 101 was a breeze. But by sophomore year, the shit was getting hard. I'd never really had trouble in school before. This was new territory. School had always been kinda easy for me. I'd sorta study, but I'd pass. Getting As with a sprinkling of Bs was custom. But things for me were changing quickly. U of I was a great school for a chem major, which meant my ass had to study more than I'd ever studied before.

I don't know if working on music hindered or helped my chemistry studies. It probably helped. I have always been proud of my ability to switch from left- to right-brained activities. Music helped me unwind from chemistry, and chemistry helped me attack the music methodically. I don't really think I could have one without the other; residual lessons from a life with both have served me well. Maybe I'm too smart. Maybe I'm so crazy. All I know is, by my junior year I was working on my first EP, *Whippersnapper*. I was also handed my first academic F. Devastation was an understatement. I had to pull my GPA up or risk not graduating in my preferred major.

But I also had these rap songs I was recording.

My first engineer, Manny, was a brilliant dude. He was an electrical engineering major who loved Warren G, Nate Dogg, and video-game soundtracks. He'd heard me at Cotton Club and approached me after a calculus study group we'd both attended. He told me I simply *needed* to come to his apartment and record because he loved my voice and he just wanted to hear it on his tracks.

I remember flashing back to that disastrous first recording session in high school. I think I still had lingering PTSD from all the bad takes, the rushing, the arguing between us crew members and, of course, the crying. That first session just wasn't fun, so I wasn't exactly itching to do it again. However, now I was away at school. That meant there was no curfew and no mom demanding to know why I was gonna be locked in a room with guys for hours. College was the perfect place for me to start my recording career. Elaine Bowen didn't have to know.

One night, a few of us had gone to a friend's dorm to chill and record after Peppa's, and it was fun. We recorded some low-maintenance raps on his four track, which was still the preferred method of the day. But Manny presented an opportunity to have a recording engineer all to myself. He knew how to sample and worked quickly. I didn't realize it at the time, but Manny was helping to lay the foundation for my professional rap career. I was starting to imagine whole CDs—yes, CDs—with my songs on them, and the songs we recorded were starting to accumulate.

Hanging out with hip hop heads in college meant being exposed to a whole-new world of emcees. One artist in particular stood out: Jean Grae, who back then was known as What? What?. OMG, what an influence. I'd first heard of her during her breakout performance on Natural Resource's song "Negro Baseball League," but after the group split up, I caught her on a few Mr. Lif songs. I was in love and hadn't heard an emcee like this before. I would scour local hip hop catalogues, devouring anything with her name on it. Her wordplay, voice, and attitude on the microphone were—and still are—untouchable. She is a literal pioneer in the world of women's rap. She made a name for herself at a time when there weren't a lot of women who were getting recognized in the underground. Sure, we had the big names, like Lil' Kim and Eve, but Jean was more accessible to my underground sensibilities. Much respect to Jean Grae for influencing a baby rapper like me at a time when I didn't have that many influences. She really is one of the greatest emcees of all time.

Jean Grae and Psalm One in the greenroom of The Shrine on my birthday, Chicago, July 2, 2013. Look at me. I was fucking ecstatic.

By the last half of my college career, I was prepping an EP and my eventual first LP. As a chem major with a minor in creative writing, I was tearing my hair out. I was also in a pretty serious long-distance relationship with a girl who was attending Syracuse University. My sexuality was still something I wasn't completely out about, but I'd met Alex through a mutual friend during a summer visit to my family in New York, and we'd hit it off. We decided to go for it. Ah, young love. I'm pretty impressed that I juggled all that. My social life was music, synthesis, and phone sex. Thinking back, I guess it wasn't all that bad.

Partying hard in college was rare for me. I was barely into smoking weed. We couldn't find very good herb, and when we did, I couldn't afford it. Anything that was considered good weed in the area was getting properly taxed. However, I once drank enough during my freshman year to have to get my stomach pumped after guzzling six E&J shots with a friend in a half hour on a dare, so I went from one hundred to zero real quick with the booze. Ecstasy was also a thing at the turn of the century, but it wasn't huge on my campus. I'd tried it a couple of times my senior year. Nothing too crazy. I was sober the vast majority of my time there.

After finding a place to record and befriending the local hip hop buyer at the local record shop, I didn't have much time for anything besides rap and studying. And I was doing more of the latter than ever. Remember the first—and last—F that I got? Well, I busted my ASS to bring my GPA up from that. I was gonna graduate with a degree in chemistry if it killed me. The next course I took after I'd failed organic chemistry was physical chemistry, and I got an A-minus in that, to the amazement of my guidance counselor. My GPA went right back up, but I had to do a few extra classes to get the degree. I always felt like those white people in charge were so horny for me to drop the ball on my coursework. I wasn't having it, though. Maybe it was racism. Maybe it was arrogance, but I set out to show those motherfuckers what my big Black-ass brain was made of. Thank God for study groups and teaching assistants of color.

At that point, I only went out to go to Manny's to record or to the occasional restaurant. Parties weren't a thing for me. By the turn of the century, I was letting a select group of friends hear *Whippersnapper*, which had become a collage of thoughts and old samples I'd always wanted to rap over. I had members of my crew, Bionic 6ix, on it, but I did the lion's share of the rapping. If you can find an old copy, I applaud you. It's RARE, rare. My goal was to sell fifty copies of *Whippersnapper* in one week. And yes, Manny and I were burning the CDs that we were selling.

It came down to the eleventh hour and me hand delivering the last one to a chemistry study buddy, but I did it. At eight dollars a pop, I was rolling in dough. I could sell five MILLION copies in a week NOW, and that feeling *might* come close to the feeling I had reaching that first sales goal. That, and getting a picture of me holding a mic in the school newspaper once, let me know I was a full-fledged rapper and nobody could tell me shit. Hell, I even had a hater or two. So, after word of my first EP spread and people appeared to dig it, I wanted to do more music. My grades were back up and my confidence in recording my raps was high.

Then Manny said his parents would give him $2,000 to do a whole album with me. What the fuck was happening? An album? Like, a whole album? Come to find out, Manny's parents were so happy he had somebody to do "wholesome" activities with, they were game to fund my first full-length project. Wholesome, HA! The occasional reggie weed and dick references weren't *exactly* wholesome, but at least their son wasn't getting into trouble at school. I think that's all they really cared about. We were rap nerds. Most of us cursed like sailors and smoked weed (Manny actually didn't drink or smoke—his vice was Faygo root beer), but we weren't getting into any trouble. Niggas wanted to graduate, and nobody wanted to go to jail in central Illinois. Fuck that.

Manny's parents didn't know they were my first record-label heads, but Manny did. We got a manufacturer to press up one thousand copies of my first album, *Bio:Chemistry*, for two grand. Holy shit. Now we were REALLY in the record business. We split everything down the middle. I guess you could call that my first record deal, and it was more than fair. Manny, if you're reading this, thank you. You really put me on.

I can still remember sitting on the quad, the Illinois sun glistening down as I unboxed my first CD shipment. My house is filled with unsold product now, but that very first box of one thousand CDs felt like every piece of music in the world. Manny and I just sat there for hours, squealing inside and out: We had CDs with our music on it. We even sold a few right there on the quad. We may have even shed a thug tear or five. We were so fucking excited, and my crew homies thought I was the greatest thing since shell toes. A fucking ALBUM. What a marvelous thing.

In the summer of '02, I graduated college with a degree in chemistry and a minor in creative writing. That was the perfect marriage of coursework for me. Science and art still fascinate me and I was always good at both academically; I really feel having both kept me sane at school. Whenever I was frustrated with one, I could always go to the other. For my minor's final I gave the writing professor a shrink-wrapped CD. I hadn't shown up all year and yet had the nerve to waltz in during finals with this music on CD. What bravado. He was impressed. I got an A. I had to take summer school to make sure I locked in the chemistry major, so I didn't get to walk with my class. That was the one thing I'm sorry my mom didn't see me do, walk across that U of I stage with my cap and gown. But I didn't care about all that. I said I wanted a degree in chemistry and I got one. My mom has my degree on a bookshelf at her home in Chicago. So we're good. But I did that. I majored in chemistry and got that fucking degree. Even if it was by the skin of my teeth.

At the time, pressing up my first CD with shrink-wrap and a barcode was more valuable to me than that piece of paper saying I'd passed my classes. I was a RAPPER with a chemistry degree. Something was very cool about that concept, and my nose was wide open to the possibility of taking music even further. Now it was time to go home and see if Chicago would be as friendly to my art as the University of Illinois had been.

CHAPTER 4

I'M A RAPPER, MOM, NOT A WHORE!

He say I love having sex, but I'd rather get some head/
See, I love making threats, but I'd rather make some bread/
And I need it, I plant so many seeds, we got trees/
Yo' feet look tired, you should try it on yo' knees/
I can show you thangs even science can't explain/
Pleasure with the pain and a measure for your strange/
Door open keys and pianos pull the strangs [strings]/
Uh, uh and I will never change . . .
—"Grabbin' Necks"

Since I grew up pretty sheltered and was definitely secretive about mostly everything—including sex, drugs, and rock 'n' roll—college was fertile ground for me to hide even more things from my mom. I've only begun to scratch the surface of why I did this for so long. For the most part, good grades while growing up in my household meant I wasn't a bad kid. So, guess what I did for decades? I got good fucking grades.

My story mirrors that of many kids who grew up in single-Black-mother households. Elaine Bowen worked very hard to make sure I was clothed, fed, and well educated. My mother had "regular" jobs throughout my childhood, but I'd always seen her switch it up. It may have been financial need, it may have been genetic, but she always had an eye out for something better. Another job, another class, another getaway. My mommy is nowhere near a celebrity or a rock star, but as a working journalist, she gets credentials and perks like no one.

I was a spoiled only child, even more so as the only kid on my mother's side of the family. I was one of two children who came around; my other cousin, Jennifer, showed up for some holidays. I saw the extended family on my mother's side even less frequently. I'm not sure if the most pressure was coming from mom, my very invested aunts, or myself, but I felt a lot of it. I was showered with gifts early—a kind of wink-wink, unwritten, unspoken understanding that I was gonna be a kid they could be enormously proud of.

Nope. Cristalle wasn't gonna be one of those hoodlums running around, playing the street corner, and eventually being a drain on society. I was gonna be equipped with all the education, tools, and code switching needed to "make it." I was given a lot of positive reinforcement. I got money to be good. I traveled as young as five years old. I was gonna be impressive by any means necessary.

Early on, around second grade, after I was told I'd get five dollars for each A I received on my report card, I drank the Kool-Aid. I'd like to note that in middle school, you got grades on *everything*—from reading comprehension to gym to listening, penmanship, *and* writing. A bitch got so many high marks my family quickly stopped that policy. I was on the honor roll throughout my college career. To top it off, I was essentially getting paid to go to church every Sunday. I was a youth leader. I taught children's Sunday school and played drums in the church band and choir. During the last few years of high school, it felt more and more performative doing all that. I wanted to spend my weekends hanging out with the crew, smoking the occasional blunt, and listening to whatever new hip hop was coming out. School wasn't really an issue. Joining a gang was never my speed. I wasn't gonna get pregnant liking girls. But it was being this "good," "wholesome," "straight" kid that was becoming more of a performance for me. I was good at it, though. And let's face it: Playing the drums for Jesus is pretty badass. College was a break from all that.

Coming back home to Chicago with a degree in chemistry meant I was fucking smart. Imagine the pride on a mother's face, being able to tell her friends and coworkers that. My chemistry degree was something she could brag about all day. I believe many of us whose parents struggled against poverty, drugs, violence, and teenage pregnancy understand they just wanna see their babies make it out of that. It was my successfully dodging of those statistics that made her gush. I thought a degree in chemistry would not only make my mom so proud she'd overlook me being queer, but it would also shower me in American legal tender, and I'd be able to foot whatever bills came up. What they don't tell you about college is, when you get home, you're literally just another unemployed person. What a fucking scam.

I didn't have any jobs or internships lined up. I'd opted out of working for big pharma because I knew I wouldn't be able to live with myself. But I had a new girlfriend by graduation, and her folks were way richer than my family. They also *knew* I was dating their daughter. I hadn't even really come out to my mom. Not, like, fully. And the thought of being home, in Englewood, with the double secret of bisexuality and rap records proved too much for me to bear.

So, I snuck around. A whole lot.

I wasn't completely out of the closet in college. My closest friends knew. Manny knew. My crew was privy. But I wasn't broadcasting it. My sexuality wasn't something I felt everyone needed to know, so everyone didn't know. I was more interested in being known for rapping and science. That didn't stop me from hooking up with some pretty dynamic women. Queer kids tend to find each other.

My girlfriend at the time of graduation, Meg, was brilliant, sophisticated, and from far more wealth than I was used to. I mean, I had some rich friends growing up, but I didn't get to LIVE with them. By the end of 2002, I was spending the majority of my time in

Warrenville, Illinois, with Meg's family and spending as little time as possible at home in Englewood. The old neighborhood felt even more different than when I'd left. I was told that college would get me out of the hood, and that's the dream we hold onto. But that doesn't just magically happen. A degree doesn't come in the mail and, poof, now you have the resources to defeat poverty. Four years away from home meant, in a lot of ways, four more years of deterioration and the kind of hopeless bullshit that eats away at the fabric of a community. At least at school shit didn't look like a war zone.

Graduating and coming home kinda sucked, not only because I was chock-full of secrets, but because my room had been given away to my uncle, who was again struggling with drugs and had to come back home to get back on his feet. I'd lived with my grandmother and mother, but being away at school meant my empty room was offered. Addiction is a disease and I don't resent my uncle anymore for needing help. At present, he's been clean for years, and I'm proud of him for that. Even though taking in a family member is usually the right thing to do, it fucking sucked for me. It made it way too crowded in my childhood home.

I didn't have my own bedroom anymore and after spending the last two years in my own campus apartment, I couldn't handle it. In Warrenville, I had freedom, privacy, and access to a wealthy white world I hadn't experienced before. Meg was a cool-ass Jewish girl from the suburbs. This was some new territory.

I was looking for a chemistry gig but it would take around nine months of job searching before securing my first job in Chicago. How did I make any money before getting my first job as a chemist, you ask?

I sold mothafuckin' MUSIC, fool.

That box of CDs was slowly selling, and I'd even booked a few very low-paying gigs with some local rappers who were making waves. I didn't have a lot of monthly bills, so I was getting by. However, it was getting more and more difficult to keep this rap shit a secret from my mom. It was time to come clean.

One night, I had a show in the city at the now-shuttered Blue Note on Milwaukee Avenue, and I needed gas money to get there. I wouldn't be going back to Warrenville that night, a minimum forty-five-minute drive out of the city, because the show would end too late. The gig paid something like fifty dollars, and I would sell CDs, so I didn't ask my mom for too much money. I'd planned on coming home, paying back the five-dollar loan, and telling her about my budding rap career—after growing some balls.

The show actually went amazing. I made the fifty-dollar show fee and sold around twenty-five CDs. I came home with $300, gleefully ready to pay my mom her five dollars back. She was a worrier, so she'd waited up for me to come home. I lied and told her I was hanging with the homies all night.

"Hey, baby, how was your friend's house?"

"Oh fine, Mom. I have your five dollars from the gas money you gave me earlier."

As I proceeded to take this substantial stack of tens and twenties out of my pocket, my mother's face flashed with rage. All she could see was me leaving with five dollars and returning with a fistful of money. She actually lunged at me with more angered passion than I'd seen in a long time. Maybe ever.

"Where'd you get that money? What have you been doing all night? Drugs? Prostituting? Are you out there selling your body for money?"

I never liked being hit or punished, so it was now or never.

"I'm a rapper, Mom, not a whore!"

I wanna take this time to say I support and respect all my sex workers out there. That life isn't easy at all. But my mom wasn't having it. She would have killed me. Hell, she was about to kill me that night.

I laugh thinking about this now, because a lot of rappers are whores, with music executives pimping the shit out of us, but I digress. My mom recoiled in pure confusion. While she was relieved that I wasn't out on the streets selling pussy or crack all night, she still didn't understand this . . . rap thing? Rapper? Rapper! Rapper? This was even more confusing for her.

"Don't lie to me! You mean to tell me you made all this money rapping?"

"YES, MOM. I CAN PROVE IT."

At this point there were precisely two articles floating around the internet about Psalm One, the rapper. All the other mentions were about the Bible. (Search-engine optimization, man. Whodathunkit?) The web still wasn't exactly user friendly yet, but it was chock-full of message boards. One board was from Manny, where he talked about our first album together. There was also one review of *Bio:Chemistry* on the now-defunct website hiphopinfinity.com. I had a newspaper clipping of me rapping in college and showed her. It was real.

She was incredulous and asked for further explanation.

"So, you left here earlier tonight, and you performed onstage? Then you sold CDs?"

I pulled out a shrink-wrapped, barcoded *Bio:Chemistry* CD.

"Yeah, and I'm pretty good, too. I'm a rapper, mom. I graduated college and did what I was 'supposed' to do. But I'm a rapper."

As the sky cracked open, she sat with the newspaper clipping all night and asked me questions about how I was able to put music together while getting my degree. She was eerily quiet and looked more worried than ever as I told her. I think she was still processing everything yet thankful I wasn't doing anything illegal for money. I was doing art. It just wasn't something she'd imagined.

The secret rap weight was lifted off my shoulders. I didn't have to sneak around with hip hop so much anymore. But I *did* have to find a job. Making $300 every now and again wasn't exactly gonna cut it as gainful employment.

The Nacrobats crew embraced me when I returned home. Their leader, Pugslee Atomz, escorted me around Chicago, and I'd quickly learned all the consignment shops willing to buy my CDs, but that money was gonna run out soon. Mom-and-pop shops were so important to indie artists at the time. In Chicago, we had Dr. Wax, Hyde Park Records, Reckless Records, and so many more I'm forgetting. Being able to walk in, sell your CDs in bulk at a discount, then come back a few weeks later and get some money was very clutch. I had a barcode on my CD, too, so that meant I could get it in even more stores than I would have with the standard CD-R (recordable CDs) sales of the day. I was ahead of the game with that barcode shit. Manny's parents had me looking super legit and official early on. I even threw a few copies online to sell. This was before streaming, but post Napster. It was relatively easy to make music, get it pressed up, split up the sales, and just keep it moving. Manny wasn't even looking for a profit. His parents weren't looking for profit. This was an experiment gone *right*. This was the golden age of selling CDs hand to hand, or "out the trunk." Slow sales were better than no sales. I was slowly getting the hang of it.

Full-time rap was still a dream, and even though people were discovering me and I was doing a few gigs, I didn't wanna be a broke ass out there. I'd graduated with a degree in chemistry, and damnit I was gonna get a job as a fucking chemist. My friend ThaiOne of Nacrobats gave me some life game and told me that if I was truly cut out to be a rapper, I could take some time off to make sure I was financially ok. So, I took a hiatus from rapping and making new music for about eight months while I searched and interviewed for jobs in my field. I hated the prospect of doing that, but I knew it was the right thing to do. I couldn't be stubborn and broke just because I was good at rapping and had a CD on the shelves. I wasn't rich. I really didn't like it, and I didn't want to do it, but I did. Sigh. Responsibility. I was told if it was truly meant to be, rap would always be there, ready and waiting. Old-school slang for the recording studio is *the lab*. I literally had to go to the lab, a job in my field, to get to the lab, my dream job of rapping.

GOD AIN'T TOO FOND OF PRETTY, EITHER

I got a habit, I didn't think it was bad/
It's like a crack fix, I gotta get me a bag/
I can't be that chick, he gets me off my slab/
Damn, whatcha doin' to me?/
...And when the love comes down/
You can't help it, you need it/
You can't believe this shit/
How'd you get this sick?
—"F*ck Up Your Life"

'd tried cocaine a few times in the past—six times to be exact. The first time was at a childhood friend's house right after college. I was hanging out with her and sharing my new favorite Stevie Wonder songs. I'm such a (musical) slut for Stevie, and I've been this way my whole life. No Stevie Wonder slander, EVER.

I'd contacted her because I wanted some weed. She pointed me in the right direction, but she'd also picked up a side gig of selling fifty bags of coke for her new doctor boyfriend. Yeah, you read that right. She told me it was all the rage. I was curious.

I'd heard a few stories about a few acquaintances doing coke, but it was still very taboo among my peer group. A lot of my friends were solely into weed and were raging alcoholics, nothing too crazy. My childhood friend, who we'll call Suzy, produced a tray of powder, which was cut up into four identical lines. I was already comfortable, I was in a safe space, and Stevie was telling me I was having a thrill. What could possibly go wrong?

This is that damn peer pressure shit they always tell you about. I'd never considered myself susceptible to this shit. After all, I was a college grad on my way to becoming a chemist. I lived in a nice crib with a nice woman in a nice suburb. I wasn't some lowly tweaker. I just wanted to experience something different. Something different than weed and beer.

I stared at those four lines for what seemed like forever. I was thinking about all the things leading up to this moment. Was weed really a gateway drug? Were the two times I'd enjoyed ecstasy in college a precursor to me becoming a cokehead? Would I even feel it? The latter is important, because I eventually gave in and sniffed two lines after Suzy hit me with the greatest peer-pressure jargon I'd ever encountered: "Bitch, this ain't no after-school special! Don't waste my shit. You gonna do it or not?"

Suzy was one of the smartest people I'd ever met. I still feel this way about her. She's brilliant. I'd never seen her tweak or act crazy on the stuff. Her consumption of drugs and alcohol didn't seem to be an issue. She got high marks throughout college and always held a good and demanding job. Hanging out with her and her doctor boyfriend felt sophisticated and grownup.

I didn't do any more than those two lines. But I didn't go back to the suburbs that night either. After I blew those lines, nothing happened, but I still stayed up all night at my mom's house, thinking about what I'd tried. My uncle struggled with cocaine addiction his adult life and was currently sleeping in my childhood room. When you grow up watching an addict do their thing, it's a mind fuck to come home on the same drug they claimed wrecked their life. I don't think it was the amphetamines that kept me up that particular night, though. It was the guilt. But I'd be able to handle it, right? I vowed to never end up like the addicts I grew up watching. This would prove to be harder than I anticipated. I was never too much into any narcotics or even alcohol when I was in college. Drunken frat boys and that stomach-pumping incident my freshman year had turned me off. Weed was expensive in school. I was mostly sober. Up until now. And Suzy was the plug.

When I "woke" up, I went straight back to the burbs. I told my girl, Meg, about hanging out with Suzy. I also noted that she'd given me a little bit of cocaine for the road. What a nice . . . gesture? So, I had some more. I was determined to find out what all the fuss was about. So, every couple of days or so, I'd try a little more. I'd done it four more times and I still hadn't really felt the effects—until one morning before going out for pancakes.

I'd asked Meg to blow a few lines with me before heading out, and she reluctantly agreed. She was a suburban kid. The first time she'd done coke was in junior high, and she'd already kicked a lightweight addiction before graduating college. This was something I didn't really understand or appreciate while coaxing her into indulging with me. Now I know: It was a really fucked-up thing to coerce a former addict to do drugs. But that morning, she agreed.

I placed four medium-sized lines on a clean surface, and we each took turns doing two each. I don't know what it was about the day, the time, my body chemistry, or what have you, but when I tell you that shit WORKED, the shit worked. I was aware of the faint sting of chemicals charging through my nose and into my almost-virgin blood. I could feel the sinful drip hit the back of my throat, smelling like a clean high-school bathroom on a Saturday morning. That smell. That taste. The arrival of the shit into my bloodstream and the fun attack on my central nervous system. I was talkative as FUCK on the way to breakfast.

By the time we got to the pancake spot, I was on some aggressive diatribe about rappers and why they suck or why certain rappers won't work with me, blah blah blah. I was waxing frustrated about everyone in the whole world when the server came by to take my food order.

"Food? FOOOOOOOODDDDDD? Fuck. I can't eat. I just want orange juice and a fruit cup."

Megan was annoyed. "You know what, Cris? You're angry."

"What?"

"You're angry. And obnoxious. Is this what coke does to you?"

"WHAT?"

My girlfriend became a fucking psychiatrist right at the breakfast table. She hadn't done too much for her system, so she was chowing down on some French toast and laughing at me. While this new destructive-but-wonderful chemical euphoria traveled through my blood, I could even hear things differently. All my senses were different. I was so willing to listen to her, and after finally understanding what the fuss was about, I decided that any drugs I did would add to my enlightenment. Besides, Meg had done coke and quit before it ruined her future. Surely I was in good company.

So naturally, we began doing it more. Within several days that little fifty bag was dwindling. Consequently, Suzy introduced us to doctor boyfriend. Now is a good time to say that, in hindsight, going to coke parties with a coke dealer/SURGEON who often would leave us at his apartment while he went to the hospital to HELP PEOPLE wasn't the best idea. He had a dangerous ego and was pretty sloppy with his operation. But we were young and indulgent and finally popular, and I was curious about this shit.

I kept this extracurricular drug use a BIG secret. Only Suzy and Meg knew about it. My white friends, LOL. The Chicago scene was all weed at this point. I'd been going to my fair share of underground shows and ciphers, and I saw neither hide nor hair of cocaine. I mean, it was probably around, but I never encountered it. At this point, everybody was trying to figure out how to press up CDs and stand outside of shows selling them. Shit wasn't glamorous at all. There were no coke parties after shows at this point. My crew mate Thai even told me once that he absolutely HATED that shit. That gave me even more of a reason to keep my use a secret. I hadn't landed a job yet, so I was pretty free and clear to party. And that's honestly what I was doing at this point: partying in a way I never did in college. I'm such a late fucking bloomer.

Driving from the upper-middle-class, historically Swedish, and wildly commercial neighborhood of Andersonville on the northwest side of Chicago all the way to the yuppie-boomer capital of Warrenville wasn't exactly working for me. It was more than forty miles of highway driving. So, we eventually brought the party to Warrenville. With parents who were often on holiday and the seclusion of the suburbs, we got quite cozy blowing lines and going to local bars to drink and talk and plot on how I was gonna get a job, then eventually rap again.

One night I was a particularly impressive mix of boozy and high, and it felt as though my words were literally shaping my world. I could *see* everything I was talking about and becoming more of myself, or so I thought. My punches landed and my sweet nothings were somethings. I had Meg swooning and the music in the background was part of the seduction.

We'd been bumping the albums *Just Tryin' ta Live* and *God Loves Ugly* by Devin the Dude and Atmosphere, respectively, over and over. I would obsess about the music. Most of my friends were NOT into cocaine, and my crew, Nacro, who was helping me a little with my music career, would certainly not approve. But Meg would get high with me and talk for hours and hours about the tiny nuances of sounds and lyrics that would rock my soul—and my nose. She was a complete nerd for Morcheeba and Portishead. She was really into Nas, too. And Psalm One, of course.

We were sitting in her 2001 black Honda Civic in the large driveway of her parents' ranch-style home with *God Loves Ugly* blasting at full volume. And she was starting to talk shit about herself. She had always struggled with her weight, which was something we both had in common. But this night she was being particularly rough on herself. Being equally tuned into this groundbreaking emo-rap album—from a label I would eventually cross paths with—along with her insecure musings stirred something in me.

"Get out the car."

"What?"

"Get out the car—now!"

"What are you doing?"

"I'm showing you how beautiful you are."

The sinful drip tasted like the best rap I ever wrote, my eyes bouncing like Drake streams. This chemical gall was taking me and sending me, and I was feeling things I hadn't felt before, which was really just my brain being destroyed. I mean, let's be serious. But in these early nights of cocaine, music, and lovemaking, I felt invincible. Like my words could not only change her life, but the lives of others. I was high as shit and so fucking arrogant. I reached out to grab her hand and swung her into my adoring arms. She really was a thick, beautiful, and intelligent woman. With a hint of crazy.

"You're crazy."

"You think you're fat and ugly, and I'M the one who's crazy? What the fuck are you talking about? Do you even ever SEE yourself, Megan? You . . . are . . . fucking . . . gorgeous!"

When I hit her with the gorgeous line, I held her so tight, making sure to let go only to let her feel the weight of my words. And with Atmosphere blaring in the background, in all their suggestive emo-rap glory, the stage was set. Her eyes welled up and it was like the night sky changed hue or something. It was such a beautiful moment, and we were so in love we couldn't stand it. Yeah, we were high as fuck. But the way we spoke that night, the bond we shared, the soundtrack we heard WAS the drug. It's a feeling I'll never forget. Whether on beat or a frenzied whisper in a lover's ear, RAP is POW-

ERFUL, mane. I knew one of those days I'd have the right words to change both our lives. I could feel this. I was captivating. I was honest, or so I thought. I was a fucking emcee.

Enter Silliker Laboratory. This indie lab no longer has that name and is not at the same location it was when I was working there, but in early 2003 it was a modestly sized independent food-testing laboratory working with local stores and food retailers. In college I'd desired a job in food or fragrance, so when I got offered the role of food microbiologist eight months after graduating, I promptly accepted. I stopped partying with the hard stuff when I accepted the job. I just did the occasional weed smoking; drinking alcohol was a constant.

I buckled down and showed them my pure drive, talent, and skill in the laboratory and was quickly promoted to the role of chemist, which is what I'd wanted all along. A JOB IN MY FUCKING FIELD. I was responsible for testing mainstream food products for nutritional facts. You know when you look at the back of items at the grocery store and the label tells you how much fat, calories, carbohydrates, etc. are contained within? I tested your favorite foods for that. I found out some really gross shit about fast food. That's a whole *other* book, though.

Now, we were adulting. I had a job, Meg found a job in her field, human resources, and it was time to move into our first apartment together. Now, the player in me did NOT want to move in with my girlfriend, but her parents made an offer we couldn't refuse: They would pay our apartment lease for ONE YEAR, given we didn't move somewhere "undesirable." This was some low-key racist shit, cuz they didn't want us moving too far into the city, where they knew their daughter loved to go with her rapper girlfriend whose family still lived in Englewood. At the time it didn't seem like a controlling action or a negative gesture. It was a year of free rent while we got on our feet. Who would refuse? We moved into a two-floor beauty of an apartment in the village of Oak Park.

The Oh Pizzle is just west of Chicago's city limits, but for all intents and purposes, ya girl was living in the burbs with a job working in her field. I was grown, assholes. Now it was time to try and fold music back into the recipe.

I was thriving at the lab. I went from microbiologist to chemist very quickly and was trusted with way too much responsibility after I demanded a modest raise from $9.50 an hour to $11.25 an hour. I handled almost a dozen separate tests and procedures, and I was working long hours.

I'd figured out a way to do music AND chemistry, just like I'd done in college, and it was the most tiring and wonderful formula to develop. It wasn't sustainable, though. On a typical day, I would leave for work around three o'clock in the morning and get to work around four. I'd work until around one in the afternoon and head home for a nap. Around four o'clock, I'd wake up and start working on music. I'd either write raps all night, have beat sessions with producers, or rehearse for shows. If I was fortunate enough to have a show that night, I would get home from work around two in the afternoon, sleep until eight at night, do the show, and then stay up all night and go to work after washing the hip hop from my body. It was brutal. But it was starting to pay off.

CHAPTER 5

THE PERPETUAL ONE TO WATCH

She wakes up 'round four a.m./
And then rolls with the snooze so she can snore again, you see/
She's sleepy from the night before/
Was on the porch since ten with a gorgeous pen, ya know?/
Another sun, another bill to pay/
Another cynical squeal to golden seal your fate/
It goes, C to the R-I-S-T-ALLE/
Got a few private poems, but the rest are for sale . . .
—"The Living"

An old-school laboratory is kinda scary first thing in the morning. The sun isn't even close to rising and lights flicker in the lobby. Industrial-freezer doors swing heavily as you enter the eerily quiet building. You wonder if that rustling behind the many refrigerated corners is vermin. You begin to smell things. Once you become accustomed to the smells, you can predict how the day will begin.

Some days the smell would be rotting meat. For months at Silliker Laboratory, in Chicago Heights, the microbiology sector was

53

testing local beef for grilling season. Huge containers were filled to the brim with decomposing cows swimming in testing brine. It smelled like shit. The beef was being tested for contaminants like E. coli. Upper management loved these tests cuz they were expensive. When the lab smelled like shit, the lab smelled like money. I knew overtime was inevitable.

Some days the lab would smell like cheese. When I turned the corner from the lunchroom to the main laboratory and it smelled like baked Kraft Singles, I knew someone was in there overachieving as well. Great minds. A big part of food testing is setting up a test and waiting hours for the results. Kinda like a Crock-Pot. The sooner you started, the sooner you could leave. I always had that place smelling like cheese.

Kraft Foods was Silliker's bread and butter, so to speak. Its headquarters is in Chicago, so the lab got a lot of business from them. I got a lot of business from them. After gaining employment, I was trying to get in the lab to work as much as possible so I could go home to the lab and make music. I finally started imagining a new album.

One morning, I turned the corner and walked down the hallway, yawning as I approached my testing station. It smelled like cheese, so I knew someone else was there. I was running an hour later than usual, so I got there at around five o'clock. This was still much earlier than when most scientists would arrive, but a few of us liked getting off right after lunch. I was stationed in the very front, so I was one of the first scientists you would encounter upon entering. A sitting duck.

I got to my station and there was a *Chicago Tribune* clipping taped to my computer monitor. It was an article that named me as well as Nacrobats as some of the new Chicago artists to watch. In bold red Sharpie, the words IS THIS YOU, CRISTALLE?, with multiple arrows pointing at my picture, caught my stare. It was a black-and-white picture, so those red streaks made my face even more noticeable. I was shocked. I didn't realize I was an artist to watch. I didn't know I was gonna be in the newspaper for anything.

But more importantly: I DIDN'T WANT ANYONE AT THE LAB KNOWING I WAS A RAPPER.

All of my rapper friends with jobs told me to keep that bit a secret, because bosses hated knowing their employees might leave soon, or go on tour, or mentally be somewhere else at work. All of these were true for me, but I needed a job. I wanted all the rapper business far from the chemistry business. But I got caught up with actual publicity. I was awesome. But uh-oh.

As I turned around, one of the other chemists walked up, cheesing like she'd won the lottery. Her eyes and teeth gleamed with my secret on her lips. Her name was Marie.

"Is this you, Cristalle? Are you, like, a rapper?"

"Well, kinda . . . "

"KINDA? You're damn near famous. You're in the PAPER."

"Marie, I'm definitely not famous, and I definitely didn't want anybody around here knowing I rap." I looked around guiltily.

"Well it's too late now. Shit. It IS you. Damn."

Marie looked equally puzzled and disappointed by my response, like I'd suddenly become this different person. I was never into making friends at work, so when folks wanted to link up and get strawberry frozen margaritas at happy hour, I'd always declined. What the fuck IS happy hour, anyway? (Full disclosure: I went with them one time to happy hour. It was super awkward, and the nachos were TRASH, so I never went again.)

I was brainstorming a new album. I had a new crib in Oak Park and a girlfriend at home I was in love with. I never disclosed anything about my personal life, really. I didn't want or care about having work friends. Marie just kept looking me up and down and smiling because she knew I was gonna be the talk of the lab that day, and she knew I wasn't looking forward to it. She also may have considered my days working there were numbered. I told her I just wanted to get through my shift and go home. She got weird after that.

Everything got weirder when I started getting press.

Although 2003 to 2005 wasn't a golden age of hip hop, it was a time when CD-Rs, mom-and-pop shops, consignment, college radio, and the underground were so booming any press for an independent artist was considered a huge step forward. Local press was tuned in to the Chicago scene, but nobody could truly cover the vast output of so many interesting artists around that time. I was fully prepared to be overlooked, especially considering how women artists weren't really getting shine.

Shawnna, of Ludacris's Disturbing tha Peace crew, NewSense, Infamous Syndicate, and Ang13 come to mind when I think about the women in Chicago making moves during those years. There will always be more voices in the streets and in the know than on the screen, and this era was no exception. Getting shine as the only woman in the Nacrobats crew, which wasn't true—it was a piece of the narrative I fought against—was happening to me. I was becoming a "real rapper," but I was also finally working a chemistry job commensurate with my experience. I still had work to do.

My chemistry background and relative newness, considering I'd been downstate at U of I, made my hip hop backstory a breath of fresh air to the locals. I was one of a few women getting noticed, so every time I did a show it was like I was exposing SOMEBODY to women rappers in general. To this day, I have a good rapport with journalists and publicists because of my mom's discipline to the craft—which is why I have the utmost respect for good journalism—my background, and my ability to ramble incessantly. All these things came together to make me not only a viable solo story but also a person to highlight in any press about Nacrobats.

I am proud to be a member of one of the most legendary crews Chicago has ever known: Nacrobats, aka A in the Square, NOS, Network of Stars, Nacro, et al. Yo' girl was definitely the new chick on the scene but had the backing of a big citywide crew. Once boasting more than a thousand members, in the late '90s this celebrated outfit, fronted by Pugslee Atomz, was open to Chicago kids wanting to represent hip hop.

The sound was traditional hip hop beats with not-so-traditional rapping styles. With so many interesting rappers in the crew, the sound had many flavors. It was almost like listening to free-form jazz, hearing Nacrobat songs. You never knew what you were gonna get. One rapper might have an aggressive style, and in the next few seconds you'd hear a rapper floating blissfully over a track, melodies in tow. Freestyling was a huge part of the music. Heading into the early 2000s, the crew self-released a ton of tracks and took over events and public spaces around the city. Numerous members were taking their various talents worldwide. Pugs asked to put one of my tracks, "Simply Beautiful," from my first EP, *Whippersnapper*, on one of the early Nacro tapes. The rest is history.

When I officially became a member of the crew, I got word of it by seeing my name in the paper as a member, which is wild as fuck. It was a delightfully weird initiation and I'll always be proud of it. Pugslee is a true pioneer of Chicago hip hop. Nacrobats has too many raw and powerful people affiliated with it to name each one individually, right here. If it's still in print, I suggest you grab the Nacrobats book. Our crew definitely changed the narrative in Chicago hip hop. Nacrobats is a saga.

In 2003, I am twenty-three years old, and hip hop is around thirty years old. This was a pretty innovative time in the genre. The do-it-yourself aspect dominated, so a lot of artists were becoming known in true homegrown fashion. The underground was bursting with talent that, depending on where you lived, you may or may not have heard of. Regional acts were thriving. Detroit was carving out a bigger spotlight, thanks to Eminem. Minneapolis was becoming more of a hub, thanks to Rhymesayers acts like Eyedea crushing it on the battle-rap circuit. Scribble Jam was an annual hip hop festival in Ohio that brought thousands of kids from around the country to drown in underground rap. The Midwest was still behind the coasts in terms of popularity, but we were bubbling. It's crazy to think of having any involvement with some of the bigger acts of the moment, but eventually that became the case. Music was starting to become this twenty-two-hour-a-day obsession for me.

I could write a whole book *just* on the biggest hip hop acts that popped between 2003 and 2004. Instead, I've listed some below. I'm sure some readers will find glaring omissions here, too, but keep in mind these were SOME of the albums and songs defining MY '03, when I was in the lab, desperately trying to get out of it. I didn't hate working, but I loathed the ennui that came with it. The repetition. The small talk. I'd seen what a life in music might look like. This is the great music that inspired me while I was plotting my great escape.

Canibus, *Rip the Jacker*

Many claim that Canibus is one of the greatest rappers ever. Canibus is known in the battle circuit for allegedly dissing LL Cool J on *his own song*, "4, 3, 2, 1." Dissing an iconic rapper in his own house? That's unheard of—and kinda insane. Canibus is a legend for that alone, but his other raps are the stuff of legend, too. His 2003 album is a bible to technical emcees. It's a master class in complex rhyming and a testament to one rapper's ability to navigate the big stage without having crazy commercial appeal.

Canibus is a rapper's rapper, having, as of late, become less of a household name. But it's still a name that comes up when speaking of the greatest ones to ever do it. The craziest part about *Rip the Jacker* was that Canibus didn't even hear the finished product until he came home from the military—he'd sent his vocals to the label after joining the US Army.

Fun fact: I did a song with Canibus in 2010 for his album *Melatonin Magik* and didn't even get a chance to meet him until way after the album was released. It's a song called "Ripperland," and it remains one of the oddest features I've ever done—from the way it was conceived to the fact Canibus lists me as "The Goddess" Psalm One on the credits.

Little Brother, *The Listening*

Little Brother (LB) is one of the most influential rap groups ever, and in my opinion they didn't make enough albums. They recently reunited, so something is right in the world. When the LB debut dropped, you had to be living under a rock if you loved hip hop and didn't know about it. The sound hit my ears so differently. I was floored more by the lyrics and the style of these two rappers more than the beats. This was a new perspective. Southern rap that didn't feel overly draped in drawl, drugs, and gangsta, it felt good and more relatable. You can hear the LB influence all over hip hop, and Phonte is one of my favorite rappers. There would be no Drake without Little Brother.

Fun fact: I got to tour with Little Brother in 2007, and we remain rap pals to this day. Shout out to Phonte, Rapper Big Pooh, and Big Dho. Great guys.

Vakill, *The Darkest Cloud*

Chicago hip hop was gifted a major moment when this album dropped. As far as battle emceeing and hardcore, technical rhymes are concerned, few do it better than Vakill. He was, like, scary. Great in stature, heavily respected in the scene, and backed by the legendary production crew Molemen, Vakill's *The Darkest Cloud* is simply an amazing hip hop album. It was a highly anticipated offering, but it didn't do the numbers outside of Chicago a lot of us were expecting. Vakill is also one of the greatest Chicago battle emcees. Do some research on him today.

Fun fact: I got a chance to work with Molemen on a few tracks and even flirted with the idea of signing to their old record label. Getting the respect of artists on the Molemen label meant a lot to me. A rapper's rapper liking your raps was monumental, and everyone affiliated with Molemen meant business.

Eyedea & Abilities, *E&A*

Before I continue, REST IN PEACE, MICHAEL LARSON (AKA EYEDEA). His death still hurts a lot; we lost one of the brightest and most innovative rappers in the world when he passed on. I just got into a debate the other day about the best freestyle rappers, and many people mentioned Eyedea. The young prodigy made a name for himself in the legendary Rhymesayers world, and he really delivered on this joint album with master DJ/producer Abilities. Known for rapping off the beaten path and lending his voice to some head-scratching beats taught fans to expect the unexpected with *E&A*. This album is TIGHT. Rappers can't fuck with this album. Even if you weren't in love with his style, you couldn't deny Eyedea's ability.

Fun fact: Eyedea was the only rapper on Rhymesayers who ever gave me any feedback or tips on how to navigate becoming a better performer. He complimented my music early on, and my very first show in Minneapolis was with Nacrobats to support his debut album, *The Many Faces of Oliver Hart*. I miss him. R Eye P.

Jay-Z, *The Black Album*

The Black Album is my second-favorite Jigga album, right behind *4:44*. This album was *supposed* to be his last. Shawn Carter screamed from the mountaintop that he was retiring after the album was released, in November 2003. This LP features some career-defining songs and tear-inducing sentiments, and I couldn't actually imagine what the game was going to be like without him. Luckily, he was lying, but this album did give me everything I needed in a last project. I wore this CD out in my car. We couldn't believe Eminem produced a track on there. "99 Problems"? "Dirt off Your Shoulder"? "Public Service Announcement (Interlude)"? Come thee fuck ON, man. This album is an official classic.

Fun fact: I never bite rhymes. I really don't. But if you listen to the outro song on *The Black Album*, "My 1st Song," and then listen to my song "Macaroni and Cheese," you'll swear you've heard that flow before. I just HAD to take it.

50 Cent, *Get Rich or Die Tryin'*

This album had me in a frenzy. OMG, what a ride. What a rap moment. So many bulletproof vests. This is a monumental hip hop album, and I was a huge fan of G-Unit. When 50 broke through, he seemed more street than any street rapper before him. This was such a big album, I would be hard pressed to find many people over the age of thirty who didn't love it.

I was still so wet behind the ears at this professional rapper shit. But I was starting to believe I had what it took to become one. I was a standout in my crew, I was getting press, I had done a couple of out-of-town shows, and Meg was even helping me with logistics. Local press and a few memorable performances gave me access to a lot of "cool" rap people in Chicago. I also had more songs I was recording and I was getting better at writing.

At this point, indie–hip hop crews and labels, like Molemen, Galapagos4, Definitive Jux, Hieroglyphics, Rhymesayers, and G-Unit, were making a killing. It felt like little movements were happening all over hip hop, all over the country. And maybe, just maybe, little old Psalm One could begin making a true splash herself.

CHAPTER 6
MY BIO *IS* CHEMISTRY

Heterosexual men stop being nice about two weeks into a tour leg. If they're getting laid, they're being very graphic about these details and trying to figure out how to get MORE laid. And if they're not getting laid? Watch out. Everything is coming up pussy.

"Yo, what time is it?"

"Pussy time."

"What city are we headed to?"

"Pussyville."

"How many CDs did you sell last night?"

"Pussy five."

If these spaces were safe, these sentiments could theoretically be comical. I have a nasty little mind and I love a nasty little joke, but as I get older, I wonder about who's benefiting and who's getting violated by these ha-ha, boys-will-be-boys moments. How safe is a space when the token woman is pretty much constantly exposed to the creepy, verbal side of rape culture? Being that woman on *every* early tour wasn't ideal, but it did teach me a lot about the male (rapper) psyche. Most feel entitled to women's bodies, especially if the women were at a rap show. In a lot of minds, if a woman had the balls to show up at an underground–hip hop show, she'd better be prepared for all this dick talk.

Most rappers will go their whole career without ever sharing a tour vehicle with a woman artist. I've been touring for well over a decade now, and on 98 percent of the tours, I wasn't only just the lone woman, but the *first* woman many of these guys had toured with. As recently as 2018, I was on tour and a dude had the nerve to exclaim, "I don't like touring with females because we can't say what we wanna say." I begged him to speak his mind. He had a very weak, very incel-like mind. The president of a label I'll be discussing a lot in this book is infamous for allegedly saying women don't belong in rap, or on tour. We can all make educated guesses as to why anyone would say something like that.

More to the point, many rappers only invite women to their tour vehicle if they're fucking. So, as you can probably imagine, I've spent more than a few uncomfortable hours traveling in cramped spaces with varying levels of creepy dudes. I blocked out a lot of the sex talk. That's what headphones are for. And weed. It's wild to me to know some of these dudes I've shared vehicles and stages with have even been accused of rape. I was spared the sexually violent side of hip hop on tour, but I was exposed to the sentiment. I won't say all the men I've toured with have been disgusting, only a portion. But OMG, what a portion.

> *Britney Spears toxic, rap ain't got no conscience/*
> *Fuck them and they boys club, TLC, yeah, no scrubs/*
> *Really weird profits/*
> *Rap is Britney Spears toxic ...*
> **—"Britnee Speerz"**

You truly find out so much about people when you travel with them. I've developed some of my closest friendships with men by touring with them. Wonderful, insightful, nonviolent men. And I can say with a straight face that I've slept with tons of midlevel rappers—not sexually, though. Like, we were in the same bed and went to sleep.

I've never felt physically threatened by a man on tour, but I've never felt 100 percent safe either. That's a terrible reality lots of women artists endure on the road. The price of admission is way too fucking high, but how else was I gonna blow up? This was the way to do it as an indie artist. Hit the fucking pavement.

My early tours were such a mind fuck. We would go out for a week or so or do one-offs, traveling to do one show then coming right back home. I found myself drifting so much at work after getting a taste of that life. Being back at the food-testing lab with its omnipresent smells of baking cheese and rotting beef and the occasional new fast-food item—we tested Mickey D's McGriddles before they entered the marketplace as well as a new mayonnaise recipe Burger King was trying out—was losing the luster it once had.

I wasn't making nearly as much money touring at first, and my pay at the lab was good, but my postcollege goals were rapidly morphing from beakers into beats. From solvents to stages. I started to get it real bad for the road.

Working diligently with Nacrobats on the moonlighting tip gave me access to a lot of other like-minded creatives. Overflo, a producer, along with some Nacro affiliates had given me beats during my last semester at U of I. Everyone I knew wanted Overflo beats. And he and I quickly became friends. We were both complete goofs and had a blast working together. We would also nerd out on music often, hang out with our partners together, and have long talks about what we could accomplish if given the chance. His ambition was attractive to me, and his approach to production and different soundscapes made me a quick believer in his ability to take my art to the next level.

Overflo was a godsend. He just wanted to make the best song. That was it. He truly wanted to craft the best beats and help musicians thrive. It wasn't all competition and machismo with him. He *never* made me feel unsafe or uncomfortable. God really looked out for me by aligning us. He pushed me to think about the movement of a composition and the creation of a full body of work. He also challenged me to never go into the vocal booth with notes or lyrics. He wanted me to always have my shit memorized. He wanted me to work on breath control and presence, always. He was really a hip hop A and R (artists and repertoire) guy without the title or the pay.

Circa 2004 we started working on my first full album since *Bio:Chemistry*. Because of my minibuzz, we decided to give fans some new music while we took our time on this new album. I was about to sell out of the one thousand copies of *Bio:Chemistry* and would then have no more music to sell. And I wasn't close to finishing my new shit. Overflo suggested we make a deluxe-ish, updated version of the album and call it a sequel. At the time I thought it was a brilliant idea. Streaming was not a thing yet, so the only way people got to experience the album was if they bought it. It was time for new tunes.

We ended up taking *Bio:Chemistry*, removing our five least-favorite songs, and adding five brand-new songs. I called it *Bio:Chemistry II: Esters and Essays*. At that point, my life consisted of going from one lab to another. An ester is a chemical compound, and certain types of esters are used in synthetic flavors, cosmetics, and perfumes. The title was fitting. The chemistry degree and my work at the food lab were fully present in my music.

These themes pop up here and there in my music, along with glimpses into my spirituality. I guess you can call me one of those church kids. So many artists who grew up in church, practicing Christianity, have a running theme of God in their music, even if it's not fully intentional. Even if we were full-on "sinners," God has a sneaky way of popping up in our lyrics. Another running theme in my music is ambition. I always have something to prove, as if being a good artist just isn't enough for me. As if having fans who love my shit isn't quite enough. I don't know why that is. It just . . . is.

It felt like Overflo and I were creating music at one hundred miles per hour. He was making a ton of music at the time and starting his own rap label. We were a lot alike in that we'd both rather go to the studio than the club. We'd rather argue about music than anything else. He'd promised me, during a blood sacrifice, that he'd give me his best beats. True story. (Just kidding about the blood sacrifice part, though. It was probably more like a beer sacrifice.) I really wanted to have an edge over my peers with this next album. That was always in the back of my mind. So, we promised each other we'd always put our absolute best foot forward with these records.

"A Girl Named You" came about like many other songs. I would climb the seemingly endless, narrow staircase up to Overflo's top-floor, two-bedroom spot in Uptown, a neighborhood on Chicago's North Side. In the summer it would be sweltering and, in the winter, WE would be melting because of all our seasonal layers of clothing. Needless to say, it was usually hot in his home studio.

He'd be playing beats; I'd be smoking weed. He had this thing where he would play a particularly cold beat, but only like four seconds of it. He would tease the shit out of me with the music, making me virtually beg for more. When he played the instrumental to what became the intro track on *Bio:Chemistry II*, there was no shame in my game.

"Whoa, whoa, play that again. What the fuck was that?!"

"This beat was for Slug, but I never heard anything back from him."

"Ok, so I can have it. Play it again."

Overflo played a quick snippet and immediately shut it off, laughing the whole time.

"Asshole, I need that beat!"

"I don't know, Psalm. What if he calls me back?"

"Overflo. He's not calling you back. Give me that beat and watch what I do with it."

A soulful bassline looped under these airy, church-boy synths and took me right back to Sunday and wooden pews. And I don't mean the church days when I was in the closet and questioning everything. I mean the church days when I couldn't wait to dress up and praise Jesus. My name ain't biblical for nothing.

A young Psalm One ready and excited for church on Easter Sunday, circa 1986.

Jesus is my homeboy. I remember being so spoiled as a tiny kid. My mom and aunties always bought me nice, expensive dresses, and I needed somewhere to wear them. My mother's mother, Pinkie, rarely missed church, and on my father's side the story was similar. It's interesting to note that both my grandmothers lived *right next* to their respective churches. Like, you could look out of the window and see church. It was never far away. My first rap name was Kizzie Tangents, but I got my first press as Psalm One. So, I ran with that. In the Bible, *psalm* means hymn. I think it's a beautiful name. At my most arrogant I think my songs are personal hymns. It fits, see? Church is never too far away. I can be such a Christian.

The church-influenced "A Girl Named You" is the perfect beginning to *Esters and Essays*. The first sound you hear is my emphatic and melodic request for y'all to "wait a minute" cuz I'm gonna "bring it on home." The feeling I get when this album starts is joy. I try to capture that feeling with a lot of my intros. But this one was so special to Overflo and me. After the request, I launch into a story about the first time I got saved during Sunday service at my uncle's church. At the time my uncle, by marriage, and my aunt, my mother's sister, were full-on pastors at a church I attended as a teenager.

Getting saved basically meant you believed Jesus died for your sins and then told everyone about it. It meant repenting and rejoicing that your soul was rescued from eternal damnation. It meant a long day on the pews. My uncle and aunt were very persuasive. This sounds crazy, but those two could really preach their asses off. Forgive me, Lord, but that's the only way I can describe it.

One particular Sunday, in the early 1990s, my uncle was on a quest for souls at this tiny storefront church on the far South Side, near Corliss High School. There were folding chairs instead of pews at this church (but we still called them pews), and God was definitely in the house. I had a handful of cousins I sat by every Sunday, and we were captivated by our uncle's sermon. His cries for us heathens definitely stirred my insides. I wanted to accept Jesus as my *personal* lord and savior. I wanted to turn away from sin and live a holy life.

As the call for miscreants rang out through the hall, I felt compelled to stand up and give my life to the Lord. I walked up to the altar, with tears streaming down my chubby cheeks, while the congregation exploded in wild, approving yelps.

"Yes, baby! Give your life to him!"

"Amen, amen, amen, amen, amen, amen! Praise JEEZus!"

"My God is GOOD!"

The elder church mothers surrounded me as my uncle palmed my head firmly yet lovingly. He prayed for my soul as my mother stood in the audience clapping and nodding. Elaine was never one to scream and holler in church, but she was a crier.

She was crying more than I was as I surrendered to this Baptist ritual. It felt good in my soul and the love I felt by the congregation after church was something inexplicably awesome. My family was super proud of me, and I was glowing with that Jesus glow.

I buckled, I gave it all to Him full of sin with a grin and my childish ways/
I chuckled, paved the way for grimacing when I couldn't sit with my
Bible, wait/
Wait a minute I, forgive me, Father/
I've altered from the true calling of a good Christian/
I sin and I don't bother . . .
—"A Girl Named You"

Though this feeling didn't last and it wasn't the last time I got saved, the first verse of "A Girl Named You" describes this particular Sunday and how it felt. When I listen to it, I can close my eyes and be in that folding chair, my virgin soul weeping for acceptance. The second verse is the acknowledgment of divine protection throughout my life. It's also the acceptance of constantly falling short of the glory of God. I have been a liar and a sinner and a fornicator. By 2004, I had plenty to repent for. So, I figured I'd do it in a song. The track adds religious depth for the first time to my catalogue and thickens my overall plot. Praise God.

Little miracles were happening in my career, and I was getting the opportunity to take my show on the road even more. A couple of out-of-town rap excursions proved I had what it took to please hip hop fans outside of my comfort zone. A few pieces of great local press proved I had what it took to at least go beyond the city limits of Chicago. I wanted to quit Silliker so bad.

On the surface, my relationship with Meg was doing ok, but my ego was out of control. What I now recognize as very real anger issues started popping up more frequently. I was always just so anxious about music, money, and stability. I wanted it all—now.

Meg was a down-ass chick, but even she would get sick of my shit, and we would mouth off at each other. She had a spicy way with words and was a bit of a control freak, so arguments were inevitable. She was also simultaneously frightened and fascinated by my trajectory. I was a nightmare to deal with when I was intoxicated, and I talked about my career ALL THE TIME. I was also frequently absent.

Weird hours at the food lab plus my moonlighting gave us less and less quality time together. I was taking every show or recording session I could in my spare time, and when I did stay at home, I was getting high. My "normal" vice was weed, but at this point I was slowly reintroducing a bit of cocaine. It wasn't close to being an everyday thing yet, but I would occasionally get up with my old pal Suzy and we'd party all night. Or Meg and I would throw a "fancy" dinner party and invite people to come melt their faces off with drugs and alcohol after meals were consumed. Meg always had a better handle on her vices than I did. While I would get obliterated at parties, mostly for lack of knowledge of my tolerance levels, she would be seemingly ok. Our bond was stronger than the party and bullshit, but little did I know the partying and bullshitting was gaining traction in my life.

Towards the end of my career as a food chemist, I had all but checked out. I wasn't as meticulous with my testing as I was at the beginning of my employment. I never got written up, but I was called into my supervisor's office a time or two. Everyone at work knew I was a rapper, and it was awkward. I reassured lab management I wasn't gonna quit, but I was planning my escape every second. I didn't know how or when, but I couldn't wait to leave that place. It was only a matter of time before I burned my lab coat and gave the biggest middle finger to that job. My days were numbered.

Those early tours were some of the happiest in my life. Looking out into the vast expanses of the US, from strip malls to corn fields to mountain ranges, eating gas station snacks, and putting my stamp on indie hip hop with my rap pals was a dream come true. Thinking of words, putting them to beats, and being able to grab a mic and recite those words onstage in front of hundreds, or thousands, of people is an insane concept. Many artists say the most addictive drug is fame, and I fully understand why they would say that. You can be someone different, if that's your thing. People love you. Nobody knows who you really are; they only know what you rap to them. And they're mostly paying you to rap. Depending on the person in the audience, their feelings about you being onstage in front of them can range from indifference to worship. And I *do* mean worship. I've been called a deity for simply rapping. While I deny anything of the sort, if an artist isn't careful, all the adulation can get them into trouble. But for now, this was some good trouble—some dreams being fulfilled. Even if some of the guys in the vehicle were complete dicks, that was a small price to pay. At least I had Overflo in my corner.

One of the earliest Psalm One photos taken for potential press. Taken by Over-flo, his wife graciously lent the shades for a cooler look. Taken circa 2005, but this press photo was used for a few years.

CHAPTER 7

THE RHYME SAYER WITH THE VAGINA

Come join my mighty crew/
And even though they rarely play her/
I'm a player . . . the Queen of Rhymesayers . . .
—"Kan of Whoop Ass (Reprise)"

Psalm One press photo number two, taken when we realized this rap shit was gonna happen for real. The image left something to be desired, but it was the

best that could be done at the time—haha, circa 2005. Photo credit: Thaione Davis of Nacrobats.

They didn't have to tell me there was no crying in hip hop. They should have told me there was no human resources. I knew there was no crying, but I did that shit nonetheless. As I pressed the landline—yes, landline—phone receiver to my glistening cheek, I couldn't believe I was being so vulnerable. My anxiety was on permanent tilt, and there was little to be done about it. A lot was at stake.

I'd had a few deals on the table for the follow-up to *Bio:Chemistry II*. After touring a little on my own and establishing an online presence, I was beginning to get some looks. I had also impressed a few very respectable rappers. One of these rappers hailed from the West Coast and even dug around to find my phone number after hearing a few of my tracks online. He eventually found the phone number of Overflo's assistant, Adam. That day was weird as hell. Adam called me and said I should be expecting a call any minute.

"Hello?"

"Hey, this Psalm One?"

"Uh, yeah. Is this Casual?" I waited in thrilled silence.

"Yup. You raw."

"Damn, that's crazy. But, excuse me?"

"You raw. Your raps are raw. I want you on my next album."

"You want ME . . . on your next album? Are you serious?"

"I don't really call people out the blue like this. Yes, I'm serious, girl."

Time to call his bluff—or so I thought. "Well, if you're REALLY serious about getting me on your next album, you'll fly me out there to record it."

There was a long pause. Then he said, "I'll call you back in five minutes."

Click. And silence. And then the longest fucking five minutes ever. As I paced my Oak Park basement in my underwear, I let all the negative thoughts consume me. (There's that low self-esteem again.) I thought about how undeserving I was, how this must have been a mistake, and how he was never gonna call back. Like, maybe he'd called the wrong person.

But hell no, he didn't call the wrong person. He wanted Psalm One. He'd called all around the city and used his Midwest contacts to hunt me down, and it was *me* he wanted to work with. This felt like an updated version of when I was recruited to rhyme when I was in college. People would get word of me and sometimes, just sometimes, we'd build something.

The phone started ringing again and my face exploded. I ran to pick it up.

"Hello?"

"Give me your full government name and date of birth for this plane ticket to Oakland. I told you I got you, girl. I'm a BOSS."

My jaw had to be lifted off the floor in order to give him my information. I wasn't easily impressed, but this was fucking impressive. This might have been the most impressed I'd been by a rapper up until that point. A highly respected artist was willing to fly me out to California just so he could vibe with me and get a song with me on his album. Now, if a rapper called me out of the blue for a verse today, I'd be less impressed. But then, at the beginning of my pro career, I was flabbergasted.

I'd never heard of such a thing, and when I told Overflo about it, he couldn't believe it either. I was getting my first real placement on a highly anticipated album and was being flown out to get it done. I hadn't even known this was a dream of mine, but it was certainly a mothafuckin' dream come true.

Meg seemed cautious yet proud of me. She just kept assuring me my time was coming and to make a good impression. She reminded me to listen more than I spoke because I was going to meet legends and I sometimes had a problem with talking over people. She also told me to believe in my raps and roll with the punches. I had some pocket money, a hotel room, and a credit card if I needed it. Baby's first studio excursion away from home, a feature of the indie-rap starter pack.

When you're getting hosted by a legend in their hometown, the trip is a little different. Instead of tourist attractions, you're getting tours of the turf and schooled on where and where not to go. You'll probably hit the strip club, of course the studio, and if you smoke weed, you're gonna smoke a ton.

As soon as I stepped off the plane and grabbed my shit from baggage claim, I was texting my new rap mentor my whereabouts on a now-ancient flip phone. Casual told me to look for the green Jeep. His California accent was so thick I had to listen extra close to understand him when we first became friends. But I bent my ear to his twang quickly and it eventually became soothing.

"Ay, Psalm, you smoke weed?"

"Yeah."

"Oh yeah? I'm sure you ain't never smoked like this before. I'ma show you something. I'm pulling up now."

The green Jeep pulled up to arrivals and I was cheesing ear to ear. This was weird and new and something I could have never imagined. The cool shit about rap dreams is sometimes you are blindsided by them. I went from fighting sleep in my basement to flying across the country to rap with legends. I'd been sleeping in the basement a lot of nights because of the long hours I was pulling, not to mention some increasingly bad arguments with Meg. But now I was in Oakland. Things were getting interesting.

"Welcome to Oakland, Psalm. We about to make some slap."

"Ah shit, hey, man. This is so cool I don't even know what to say."

"Let's roll. I'm sure you'll figure it out. But first we gotta get some more trees. I'm about to run out."

The whole Jeep smelled like a dispensary. There were traces of it everywhere, even a couple of beautiful purple nuggets seasoning the console of the vehicle. This dude had to smoke on the way to smoke. At the time, California was one of a few places in the US where recreational weed was legal. The vast majority of my weed smoking had been done illegally, so I think I speak for many people when I say I wanted to overindulge in legal weed JUST because I could, even though we were still going to the block to cop it the old-fashioned way.

We went straight from baggage claim to baggage claim, if you get what I'm sayin'. We parked on the block and debated multisyllabic verse structures while waiting for our flowers. We also started learning each other's musical backgrounds. Turns out I was a bigger fan than even I had realized. I'd heard and enjoyed quite a few songs of Casual's without knowing it was him. This was before Shazam, YouTube, and Google, so sometimes you heard songs and never knew who did them. I was learning so much by just being around someone with this kind of résumé. He'd been on a major label, left, gone indie, and was now enjoying great success doing things his way with his group, Hieroglyphics.

He showed me platinum records, gold records, and a warehouse of his creations—and he treated me with rap respect. He didn't want anything from me other than the best bars, and there was no ulterior motive. That was so empowering and refreshing. Another person, infinite levels above me, really just wanted to make a dope song together. No grooming; no funny business. Pure hip hop.

We are always made aware of these terrible stories where the woman artist gets "flewed" out and taken advantage of. A Future-like "I'm good, luv, enjoy" moment where the chick doesn't wanna fuck the dude, and therefore never gets to work on anything. Or the chick who takes the bait of a male artist who says he wants to work with her but has no intention of actually working with her—he's just scheming to get her in a dark room and prey his way into her panties.

Later in my career, I would learn more about grooming and rappers being used for bait and marked for prey. Rappers being love bombed, then manipulated, then being scared into submission for fear of losing their spot on the roster. At this point, I was part of one roster, with Overflo, and he was a saint. Casual immediately made me feel comfortable. There was no creepiness, only hip hop and laughs.

Throughout my four-day course in all things Oakland, I stayed at a hotel. We'd meet up in the mornings to catch vibes and discuss what we were gonna rap about. The first night we rode all over the Town. I got to experience the off-the-beaten-path Bay Area, and I was able to meet Casual's friends, who were, coincidentally, also rap heroes of mine.

The second and third days we locked ourselves in his crew's legendary studio space and worked on what would become my first indie placement. The process was something I still have never duplicated fully. It was flowy and somehow still brimming with technical energy. It was challenging and it was lyrically something to marvel— IF you're a stickler for words.

Let's get into some lucid dreamy rap stuff.

My favorite rapper of all time, Black Thought of the iconic Roots crew, allegedly said in an interview that he raps so well because he naps in the studio. While he's wading in the waves of sound, he begins to subconsciously tap into the music in a way that is unmatched. He's the best rapper of all time, no disrespect to any of my mentors. Thought is always so fucking sure of his raps. There are never too many words, but there are always SO MANY WORDS. His freestyles are glorious, and I am always blown away by his pen. The idea of Black Thought expressing how his lucidity was the practice of writing in that sweet spot of time between being fully asleep and fully awake is instructive and inspiring.

My Oakland mentor and I were locked in the studio, doing our best chimney impressions, and picking beats. Once we decided on what soundscape to use, we started building the structure of our song around the theme of freaking. *Freak* is slang for synthesis, for taking something from its usual place to somewhere so much greater than what it was originally intended for. You can freak a beat, a flow, a piece of clothing, a meal, a lifestyle. If you can freak stuff, you're winning.

We wanted to freak each other's rhymes, syllables, themes, and even cadences. He wanted to bring a technical symphony out of my rhymes while he challenged himself. It wasn't biting. In the era of hip hop I grew up in, biting, or taking someone's rhymes and expressing them as your own, was the ultimate sin. It was sacrilege. Within our song, we mirrored each other's sentiments and the technical aspects of each other's words. The trick was the cadences. Writing like this was exhilarating, but exhausting.

After writing for a few hours and consuming the obligatory copious amounts of weed, I was wiped. By the second day of the session, I was pushing my brain so hard and smoking so much I just started taking naps in between takes. I really believe that's why the song "Bitin' and Freakin'" came out so dope.

Lucid dreaming is a term coined by a Dutch psychiatrist to describe the dreams in which you *know* you're dreaming. You can sometimes even "steer" the dream because you are aware of the events inside the dream. It's been studied for centuries. It doesn't suggest your subself is fully asleep, though. Maybe it's because we are microawake? Half enlightened? I'm certainly not an expert on this stuff, but I've experienced lucidity in my dreams.

I've even been on my Black Thought and rapped in my dreams. But 99 percent of the time, when I woke up, I didn't remember the raps—only little pieces of them. One hundred percent of the time, the raps were SUPER FLAME INFINITE FIRE EMOJI RAPS that will never get heard because they're trapped in my dreams. (Bum-ass raps.) One day I'm gonna rap in my dream and be able to grab my phone in my sleep and transcribe them. Maybe they'll make an app or an injection for that. On second thought, I don't want that. Too *Black Mirror.*

Anyway, at the Oakland sessions I was able to drift in and out of my subconscious and retain the raps. I was able to sorta wake up, write these super technical bars, and record them. The performance in the booth was the most difficult part because I was so drained.

The writing was an extremely challenging exercise in homophones, syllables, and homonyms and of cadence, bar structure, and the fly shit only a really skilled rapper can provide.

> *I said I pause for a second, so calm your perception/*
> *Sissy, Psalm's in the session, so strong it's refreshing/*
> *Let the dogs in the kennel, I'll be tender with the rendering/*
> *Let 'em sing/ I freak a bar, bitch, you been a fiend . . .*
> **—"Bitin' and Freakin'"**

My mental was on fire. But the song came out incredible, and by the end of the trip I'd made a new friend. Most exciting of all, I was also offered a recording contract.

Holy fucking shit. My first deal.

By the time I'd settled back in Chicago, I had not one but two potential deals on the table: one from Casual's Hieroglyphics Imperium Recordings and one from Rhymesayers Entertainment (RSE). I had no choice but to weigh the options of a full-time rap life. Both labels were sans purely women rappers at the time, but Hiero had introduced the world to Goapele, an amazing multitalented singer, artist, rapper, and performer. With her success, Hiero was sure they could have similar success with me. But the other deal on the table, with Rhymesayers, intrigued me so much.

Here was an equally legendary label with legendary artists who'd shaped my young adulthood. In college, everything I knew about them I'd learned from an early crew tape and seeing members of the label perform down at U of I. Some of my first extremely fun rap shows were those giants invading our little college town and giving all the locals hope for the future. The world was a shit show then, too, and there's nothing quite like seeing your favorite rappers wax loud and poetic, dripping sweat, and screaming with youthful, hungry angst to distract you from that reality. Then, it was George W. Bush. Then, it was a recession. Then, it was chat rooms. Then, it was dick and pussy. (It's still dick and pussy.) Then, the antidote to all of this, for me, was hip hop.

But then, I didn't know that a few years and one Nacrobats performance opening for Eyedea (RIP) later, I'd be offered a deal with that same label.

Rhymesayers is a big Midwest indie label, based in Minneapolis, a city smaller than and about seven hours northwest of Chicago. Many of their artists had been touring for a while, so I was sure signing to them would ensure the same for me. I would soon find out how little is assured in this business. But my buzz had brought me this far.

How I got the RSE offer was probably—and this is my opinion—due to a combination of my buzz, gender, and proximity to Minneapolis. Psalm One came seemingly out of nowhere to the Chicago/Midwest scene because I'd paid my dues down at U of I. When the head honcho at RSE caught wind of my Hieroglyphics deal, I believe he felt he had to act. So, I think his offer was a reaction. It was quite a chess move, one that I am still dealing with to this day. The possibility that I was signed only so they could boast having a female rapper is real. But at the time, my head swelled from the attention—and the vast possibilities of it all.

Between Casual sending in the Hiero paperwork on what turned out to be a pretty good deal and RSE putting their name into the proverbial ring, I got the opportunity to do a song and a few shows with Brother Ali. Having two deals on the table had me all but Jerry Maguire-ing my job at the lab but I couldn't quit just yet. I was running around and trying to get industry advice.

In retrospect, how I responded to news of the record deals was probably the beginning of some pretty rough anxiety. I would often get these knots in the pit of my stomach and lie awake at night, obsessing about life on the road and in the studio. I was smoking every moment I possibly could. I didn't know what to do, but I had a handful of smart people in my corner.

Meg had a few power connections via her parents and privilege, and introduced me to Snoop Dogg's then lawyer. (You read that right.)

We met at Bar Louie in the bad and bougie neighborhood of Hyde Park and discussed my future very generally. To me it felt like I was gonna blow up any minute. Here was Snoop's fucking lawyer talking with little old me, telling me he loved my music and wanted to work with me. I'm sure all of this caused my ego to increase several sizes. And all of it seemed to perturb Overflo, who I'd practically been living with at the studio, which brings me back to the crying on the phone.

During this process, Overflo and I had been having these incredibly long conversations about what getting signed meant. One time, I was in my woman cave at home at about three in the morning when my landline rang. It was Overflo, telling me, in a very stern voice, that he wasn't interested in just watching me, as an artist, slip through his fingers after being so involved with my career. He expressed his fear that I was gonna just up and move to California or Minneapolis and stop working with him. I thought it was the craziest shit I'd ever heard. I'd never considered that, but I also wasn't considering him in my decision-making process. When the offers came in, I'd gone straight to a big-time lawyer and people in the Chicago industry who actually didn't have my best interests at heart. Although Meg did, she was a master at human resources, not the music industry.

It was a rough conversation.

"I mean, Overflo, I don't know what the fuck to do. I just know I wanna tour and I wanna rap and I wanna quit my job and make music all the fucking time."

"Well, I wanna help you do that. People up and leave Chicago all the time or they go away. And I'm proud of the work we do together. I don't want you to just up and leave."

"I don't even know what the fuck to do. How can you help me with paperwork and meetings and all this extra stuff while finishing the album? I'm confused."

"Make me your manager."

Through sniffles and chokes, I stopped dead in my sobby-ass tracks. "You mean, like, an artist manager? Like my manager?"

"Yeah. I'll talk to people. I'll make sure you have help with your music."

At the time this seemed like a brilliant idea.

Overflo had been running an upstart indie label, Birthwrite Records, when it wasn't the thing to do. He'd found and worked with so many artists in Chicago with the simple mission of making great music. He cared about quality and musicianship and collaboration. He was kind and thoughtful and ultra fucking talented. I found him to be quite sharp. Yeah, this seemed like a brilliant idea.

"Damn," I sniffed, "my manager. Ok, man. Yeah."

And thus, a page was turned. I had lawyers and managers and deals on the table, but nobody I rapped with had experienced what I was experiencing—or at least I wasn't aware of anybody's brush with these things yet. And here was Overflo. He and I didn't have any paperwork to formalize things between us yet, but he went to work for me the very next day.

Artists, here's a pro tip: When you get offered a recording contract with a label, acquire your OWN lawyer and have them navigate you through the signing process. The record label will offer up THEIR own legal assistance, which seems great to the untrained artist, but get your OWN representation. A label lawyer works for the label. YOUR lawyer will be on your side.

I'm happy to say both offers had decent terms, even though I only had Snoop's lawyer look at one of them. He was so fucking hard to get ahold of. After that first meetup, I think I may have spoken to the guy five times via email and once on the phone. I eventually had to let him go. That was a funny-ass phone call. He was a little too amicable about being fired for my liking. Then again, he'd done million-dollar deals, so how could he prioritize my multithousand-dollar deal? So, I had the label's lawyer look at the other deal and, thankfully, I wasn't getting *completely* jerked in the agreement. A blessing. I would come to find out contract terms aren't the only things to consider, but I wasn't signing some death note.

This was way before the advent of the 360-degree clauses a lot of artists unfortunately sign now. A 360 clause is, to put it very simply, a deal that gives the agent, label, or whoever a percentage of EVERY FUCKING THING an artist makes. It's a multirights contract that is all encompassing. Before this 360-deal stuff was a thing, *most* indie record deals would give the label rights to a percentage of record sales and certain costs they accrued while making the album. Most of these deals wouldn't give labels any rights to an artist's show fees, merchandise, or sponsorships. Not with a 360. To be fair, any label offering a 360 deal usually agrees to help with the business side of everything. So, they're entitled to a percentage of everything. But that can get tricky and sticky real quick. Fuck all that. If I make a cat video as an artist, I need *all* the money from that. The label shouldn't be able to get a percentage of my cat-video money. But that's just how I view things.

Neither deal offered a huge amount of money up front. But both gave me an opportunity to get music out on a reputable, respected label and possibly tour for the rest of my life. Well, maybe not that last part, but it was an opportunity to put out a commercial album and tour that album. Plus, a little bonus money for yours truly.

The Hiero deal's bonus would have given me the equivalent of a semiluxury new car. The RSE deal's bonus, after paying for recording fees, would be about the equivalent of a very nice used car. But RSE's artists at the time were touring more than Hiero's. Hitting the road again was everything to me. All I wanted to do was stay performing onstage for a bazillion fans. I was warned about how harsh a life on the indie circuit could be at the beginning. My mentor described it as "four niggas in a car sweating and smoking and telling bad jokes for hours to perform for an hour and maybe get paid what you're worth for it." It sounded like the best shit I could fathom.

After losing a personal lawyer, gaining a label lawyer, taking a few meetings, and crying some thug tears on the phone with my new manager, I decided to go with RSE for my next album. It would be my first commercial effort with national press, touring, and a budget. I had every reason to believe if I'd gone with Hiero, I would never be able to work with RSE. But I had gained a friend and a mentor in the Bay, and I knew if I went with RSE I'd still be able to work with Hiero. But I still needed to tell Casual I was turning down his offer. At that point, it was one of the hardest phone calls I'd ever made.

Ring, ring.

"Hello, what's up? You look at the contracts and figure out what you need?"

"Yeah, man. I've been thinking about it for weeks, and I've decided to go with Rhymesayers."

"Oh, shit. Damn, ok. Well shit you gotta do what you gotta do. It's still all love."

Psalm One and Casual during a stop of Hieroglyphics' 3rd Eye Vision Tour, St. Paul, Minnesota, August 2019.

And that was that. What a fucking player. I was so afraid he was gonna maybe cuss me out, but I wasn't remembering how many deals their collective had seen. He had plaques; a loss of one potential artist wasn't gonna fuck anything up for him. Plus, we had a genuine bond and he reacted like a friend would. I was so relieved. I'll never forget the kindness and fairness he's shown me throughout the years. To this day I honor Casual for a magical session, a one-of-a-kind look into an independent-rap empire, and just pure California love. Deal or no deal, that trip to the Bay Area helped shape my career. That was pivotal and important for a new artist to experience. It was everything to me.

Now, it was time to lock in the paperwork with RSE and quit my fucking job—soon. I hadn't told my bosses I had a record deal on the table that would require me leaving. The terms of my deal weren't completely worked out, but I was indeed absolutely and completely checked out at work. I'd even been called into my supervisor's office to discuss my morale. She'd noticed my fervor for the job was waning. She wanted to know if there was something she could do to help which, to me, was code for "get your shit together or we're gonna get rid of your ass."

I had no idea the paperwork was gonna take several months. I had no idea I was gonna have to wait months for artwork for my album or that I was gonna have to have an idea on imaging and sequencing and overall packaging for my shit. I had no idea my job didn't start and stop with rapping to beats and that I would have to help with all the other shit. I had no idea I was gonna have to hurry up and wait so much.

The deal was done in the late summer of 2005. We were aiming to release my commercial debut, *The Death of Frequent Flyer*, in the spring of 2006, but it got pushed back a few times and was finally scheduled for a July 2006 release. So, for a year and change I was trying to prepare and I was nervous as shit. The head honcho at RSE had told me not to quit my job until it was completely necessary, but by early 2006, I was over that. My signing bonus check had cleared, and I was doing shows, so money was coming in. I thought money was always gonna be coming in. I didn't care about the food lab anymore. I pretended to, for a little while, before I dropped the bomb on them.

The day I quit my job was glorious. There had been rumblings of my rap career and a few people were hating on me, so it wasn't too surprising to upper management that a resignation was forthcoming. What was surprising was their counteroffer: lab management.

Chemistry's feeding me, cuz I charge much less for my two EPs/
Gimme a tour so I can do me thing/
And feed my mama through rap and let me prove these things . . .
—"The Living"

By now, Marie had been promoted to supervisor. And *her* supervisor told me they knew I had other prospects, but they really appreciated my work and efficiency at the lab. They said they were restructuring and hoping to promote me, too. This came after I gave them my two-week notice. I was floored, but I was done. I'd never had a salaried job in my entire life, and here was one staring me in the face. It's what they tell us we should want: a salaried position in the field we study in college.

I told them I was flattered but turned the offer down with a rap-eating grin on my face. I also told them I was going on tour and releasing an album. I was following my dreams and literally two people in that entire lab congratulated me. There were at least two hundred people in the lab and several dozen in my actual department. Most people responded to my departure with a stoic "oh." Some literally frowned in my face. One interaction always stood out:

"Damn, you're about to be a rapper on tour, huh?"

"Yeah, man. It's kinda crazy to think about."

"Yeah, you're about to be better than us."

"Well, I don't know about *better*. It'll definitely be different."

"Much love to you. Hope I see you on the TV one day!"

"You never know!"

Lovers and haters gon' love and hate. I hated the thought of normalcy. I didn't wanna just go to work and come home. I had gotten a taste of rap life and I wanted more. I had an opportunity to do it, and for fuck's sake, I was gonna do it. I ran out the lab doors for the last time and literally laughed like a villain who'd gotten away with the stash. I was free.

I could always go back to the lab. But I didn't want that. Thirteen years later, and even though in my most recent years I've taken jobs to supplement my income, I haven't had to go back to the lab full time—yet. It isn't off the table, because that was another professional dream of mine. In fact, it was my very first tangible professional dream. But rap has taken up every corner of my adult existence. And every time I try to leave, it keeps pulling me right back in. So for the most part, I left the lab and didn't look back. It was time to drop my first commercial album.

Putting an album out during the Myspace era was interesting. Myspace was the premiere social-networking service between 2005 and 2008. Being on someone's top eight was everything, and that friend count was my first taste of social-media chum in the water. My friend count was massive and my page was popping, thanks to that lightweight coding everyone with a dope Myspace profile was doing. After promo for my album started, my page exploded, and that ended up being where most of my digital press went. That, and rap forums. The rest went to good old-fashioned physical print, hitting the road, and college radio. The good ole days of independent music.

I went from obscurity to relative obscurity to an extra-medium buzz in a matter of a few months. I toured with the giants of the day: People Under the Stairs (RIP, Double K), Del the Funky Homosapien, MF Doom (RIP), Gym Class Heroes, and almost every artist on the RSE roster. I was in local Chicago publications so fucking much that a bit of hometown celebrity was starting to kick in, and I was featured in all the big national publications, including *Rolling Stone* and *Billboard*. I wasn't bound to a regular schedule anymore, either. That allowed idle time to show itself. That allowed my shadow side to become more pronounced. That allowed me to smother my anxiety with substances.

When I was off the road and not in the studio, I was giving my girlfriend hell. My obsession with rap and my upgraded career kept me anxious and thereby drunk and/or high most of the time. I was battling the notion that I wasn't good enough. I was overpersonalizing the growing pains everyone faces when tackling new career paths. It's a new language, and even though people love to wax poetic about what they would do if they were famous, even the tiniest bit of fame can make some people go absolutely insane.

Meg and I did not make it through my album release. We did not make it through the Myspace era. I cheated on her, on- and offline. She definitely tried to tie me down with conversations of kids, marriage, and the like—A LOT. She was definitely controlling and had a bit of a manipulative turn during our relationship, but I believe it was because I was becoming unhinged. She was afraid for me, afraid for my ramped-up substance abuse, and afraid to lose me. I was becoming more and more comfortable with the thought of not having her.

The cocaine use had gone up a bit, in secret, so I was high on that shit more than she knew. I was smoking every day, and after a few tours I had picked up some lightweight alcoholism. I needed a girlfriend who was gonna let me party the way I wanted. She needed someone to be loyal and ready to settle down. Oil and water. Peanut butter and cheeseburgers. I loved her so much and we broke up so many times before it actually stuck. But when it did, boy did I take advantage of not having anyone to come home to.

When I moved out of our Oak Park spot, I moved in with Suzy. Rent was cheap as fuck. I could get shitfaced every night and it didn't matter. I was gonna go back on tour soon anyway. And on tour, getting shitfaced was low-key encouraged.

Even though I currently practice polyamory, I was a serial monogamist for a really long time. I was also very careful about having sex with groupies. I was never fully into it, even though I'd indulged a few times—and I was afraid of sexually transmitted infections. I'm a cuddly person who likes whispering sweet nothings and raw, consensual genital play, so I guess I can be pretty picky with who I fuck. Most guys are a #MeToo moment waiting to happen at shows, and sloppy chicks can be annoying and kinda sad. Going from the fat kid in school to an awkward fetish was wildly confusing. Being Psalm One meant some people wanted to fuck me just because of that. Cristalle Bowen wasn't too shabby, but Psalm One? They wanted to invade my bed.

Professionally, touring was going smoothly and I was leaving an impression, but I didn't have the god-like command of audiences yet. A lot of acts I was supporting on tour were like Sherpas to fans. Even if the music wasn't knocking me in the puss, the fans would lose their minds nightly when the headliner came on. I supported a lot of rappers with cult followings, so I took more than a few pointers on emotional manipulation and the power of a good chant. I was learning, I was becoming a student of the road, but I wasn't recording a ton.

Being at the studio was becoming more of a party than a place where we actually got work done. New artists, if you're reading this, make sure that when you start gaining a little buzz, you're well-rounded in your approach to staying relevant. It's not all online, on the road, or in the studio but a delicate combination of all three. And watch your studio time. Are you being productive? I could churn out raps as fast as the fastest writers, so I wasn't particularly concerned with my next musical offerings. We had also released my first two mixtapes, volumes one and two of *Get in the Van*, so I had new music out there. And at that point in indie rap, you could tour an album for at least two years before the fans started bugging you for new shit. I had time. But honestly, I should have been more concerned with my next album. If you're an artist reading this, learn the lesson I just explained above. I learned the hard way.

I was a woman about town now and doing a lot of shows, but in the studio, I wasn't working on the follow-up to my first commercial album. My CD was in Best Buy now, but in a few years who would care? When I wasn't on the road, I was a hometown darling. Yeah, I got drunk a lot and got high more and more. I smoked a ton of weed.

Nobody said shit. And I certainly didn't have the discipline I can brag about having now. My friends and peers were carrying their own monkeys on their backs. Normalcy was out of the fucking picture.

Enter Tania (not her real name, because I wanna protect her a little bit). Tania was a Mexican lawyer who loved light rum and dark raps. And cocaine. Boy, did she love cocaine. We were a match made in hell. She was very much into the idea of dating a "real" rapper. She even insisted I live with her when I was off the road. Rent-free. Another person willing to absorb a huge life expense. I had no idea this was a control tactic. I just knew with no rent to pay I'd have more money to spend on bullshit. And I DID.

We partied EVERY FUCKING NIGHT. She taught me how to mask a hangover; I taught her how to be even more obsessive about a partner's life on the road. This would become my least-healthy relationship to date. She was also my first violent partner. Before dating Tania, I was usually the one who lost her cool first. I'd pushed Meg twice and felt so bad about it the second time—because she fell down, hard—I'd never considered putting my hands on her again. I'd also never considered I'd have an issue with domestic violence. Tania was a Roller Derby chick. She got bumps and bruises for fun, so violence was second nature for her. We were in for a bumpy ride.

The whole Kurt-and-Courtney, Sid-and-Nancy thing is real. It's not some glorified druggie fairy tale. You can really get caught up bad in a relationship when the drugs make it a threesome. Add a little fame, and things can get downright spooky. A good year and a half into a full-time rap life, things were starting to take the plunge into troubled waters. Toxicity was everywhere. If health really is wealth, I would've been impoverished. But, the music career? I had that.

CHAPTER 8

A SUMMER
IN SAN FRANCISCO

Psalm One press photo from (now out-of-print) SPIN *magazine, summer 2006. Used with permission.*

A t the time, there seemed to be something both dark and poetic about roaming the streets of Chicago near West Town at 2:45 in the morning, deciding whether or not I was gonna go back to my girlfriend's house to blow another few lines, or if I was gonna go to Duk's Red Hots for a cheeseburger and fries to help my high come down, or if I was gonna go lay in the bathtub until I woke up.

I was getting floaters in the corners of my eyes because I hadn't been to sleep. The police passed, and I tensed up—but they were just looking for a different asshole.

I decided to go back to Tania's house with the burger. Then I put on *Dave Chappelle's Block Party* and passively masturbated so I could eventually relax and go to sleep, just as the sun was coming up.

Tania woke up soon afterwards and ran through the shower. She gargled mouthwash for what seemed like an hour, ate spoonfuls of peanut butter (she championed it as masking the smell of booze), and guzzled Gatorade AM to get ready for work.

She still smelled like a distillery when I got really close, but she was MY distillery. And, like the careless rapper I was at the time, I would drive her to work and back home so I could use her whip for whatever. I was mostly idle.

I sure do love the road. Between the summer of 2006 and the end of 2007, I'd been to Europe and all over North America, rapping in the faces of all who would listen. My favorite tour stops were always in Europe and on the West Coast. They were so far from Chicago and so different. My album was out. People liked it. But touring had begun to slow up after about eight months, and I wasn't producing anything close to a follow-up to my commercial debut, *The Death of Frequent Flyer.*

I wasn't sure what my next move was going to be, and to be honest, I felt a lot of my rap peers were overly competitive about, well, every-fucking-thing. It was less camaraderie and more let's pretend to like each other while competing to outsell one another. I know that's the business, but I still needed musicianship. Music had always

been fun for me and about collaboration, but I felt stranded and iso-
lated in Chicago. I also didn't feel very welcome in Minneapolis, the
home of the RSE, for the same reasons.

It felt like I'd waited my whole life for my first commercial album
to be released. I'd quit my job, signed the deal, finished an album for
a major indie label, and rapped on stages. I'd toured the tours. I'd
done the things. But in the blink of an eye, rap work began to slow
down. This was happening just as I was getting used to a faster life.
My peers weren't as nice about making music anymore. I was now
competition. And my acquaintances were less into music and more
into partying. At least when I was partying with nonrappers, people
were still rightfully impressed and I didn't feel like a target.

Up until that point, I'd always made stuff with others. From my
crew affiliations through the making of *Death*, I'd always had friends
and feedback. But things changed, quickly. Many of the producers
I'd worked with on my first album were strained and overcommit-
ted. Overflo, while trying his best as a manager, was never able to
maintain a good relationship with the powers that be; I was advised
by a label mate to fire him. I was told I'd be managed by the label, and
that turned out to be a lie. It was a huge mistake listening to that bad
advice, and it would be years before Overflo would trust me again.
I was truly alone and unable to even get beats from him. He'd also
decided to move to San Jose, California, to be closer to his family,
sometime in 2007. So for the few months, before we parted ways,
he was working with me remotely. My rap relationships were all but
falling apart. I wasn't getting the pick of the beat litter anymore. I was
feeling pretty stifled, not to mention my relationship with Tania was
reaching new lows. We were both increasingly toxic.

But we were having so much "fun."

I was living rent-free and driving the car of someone who was
making over $120,000 a year and living well below her means. There
was a lot of (her) money to spare, and even though I was making less
and less money on rap shit, I didn't really feel a shift in lifestyle.

I didn't know how poor of a rapper I was actually becoming, because I was still making money. I didn't have any huge bills, and my credit card bills were being readily ignored. I was living the dream, and ignorance was bliss. I spent my money on personal entertainment, like lavish dinners and nice shoes.

But I was supposed to be making money as an entertainer.

Feeling creatively claustrophobic and tired of Chicago allowed me to agree to a change of pace. A relocation. After a few insane declarations about my mental state, the planet, and Chicago, I decided to move to San Francisco with Tania. She was a litigator for a major health insurer and was starting to feel like the devil. I imagine that feeling helped fuel our drug and alcohol binges.

Every one of her work friends was a rager, and lemme tell ya: Lawyers can PARTY. Probably more than entertainers. And they could afford the lifestyle. Disposable income and nice outfits can get you pretty far in the party zone. Tania wanted to pursue her dream of becoming a defense attorney for undocumented people and had actually been looking for employment in that arena. She was eventually offered a position in California.

Given my history with the Bay Area, I was down with the idea. I'd always gotten a lot of love when I performed there, I had a few friends there, including my mentor, and it was known for being gay friendly. The Bay Area is beautiful and diverse, and the weather was usually beautiful. I had never imagined living anywhere other than Chicago or New York City. College didn't really count, because it was so close to home. My aunt and uncle lived in North Bergen, New Jersey, just across the river from New York City, so did an ex-girlfriend of mine. I love the pace and the thickness of New York. You could get so much done in a week there, things that might've taken a month elsewhere. It's the capital of the universe. The labels were there. The agents were there. Many musicians moved to New York to jump-start their careers. Living there wasn't so far-fetched.

But Cali? Casual lived there, and we'd worked on "Bitin' and Freakin'," which was very well received. I was excited at the possibility of reconnecting and getting to work with more folks from the Hieroglyphics label. And since Tania was hell-bent on starting a new chapter in her own career, in February of 2008 we packed up her Nissan Altima with all of our shit and drove cross country to San Francisco to begin life anew, her two cats (yeah, we did the whole traveling-with-felines thing) in tow. A lesbian dream. My mother was worried sick. And my friends, especially my homies Suzy and Dustin, who'd seen Tania and me get shitfaced and fight often, were not very happy to see me leaving with her. In the pit of my stomach, I knew it might be a bad move, but I was pretty sick of being stagnant in Chicago.

> *Something like a road cat, something like a flea/*
> *In the ear of the big dog/at times I'm a bit lost/*
> *Year of the frequent flyer, year of the screwy/*
> *Ran away so fast, I swear I never knew ME/*
> *Didn't look back, just getting to that/*
> *Moved six times in three years, fool, YOU unpack . . .*
> —**"Better Than My Last (Dirty)"**

I'm so convinced I have angels watching over me, and they kept San Francisco from swallowing me whole. It is so much more expensive and classist than anywhere I've ever lived, and I quickly realized how little I actually had. My girlfriend was making good money, and I was making close to none.

And yes, San Francisco is known as one of the gay capitals of the world. It's awesome if you're a thin, gay, white man. I ain't that. And it's not lesbian friendly. When I lived there, San Francisco had two lesbian bars and what seemed like a million gay ones. Even in 2008, before the tech sector occupied the city and lives of most people remotely close to Silicon Valley, the cost of living there was much higher than in Chicago.

For $1,750 a month we were living on the edge of town, over-looking the Pacific Ocean. At face value it was beautiful, but if you live in San Francisco and you can *see* the ocean from your home, that means you live far as shit away from everything. And if you don't live in a house, you live in a SMALL-ASS apartment. We had one and a half bedrooms, a bathroom that wasn't big enough for anything but a small standalone shower and a tiny sink, and a kitchen that was only big enough for a hot plate and a tiny fridge. I actually think half the place was part of the garage, but that's neither here nor there. It was home and we treated it like shit.

Rap shows had come to a major halt. After playing just a few shows in Chicago after four major tours, when the dust settled in San Francisco, I realized I had exactly two shows lined up over the next three months. I had no savings to speak of. I'd spent it all on mov-ing and the first few weeks of groceries. Tania and I quickly started fighting every single day and the trust was fleeting. I was extremely alone. Those last two shows put a little bit of food on the table, but I could barely do any shows after that because my booking agent was nonresponsive. My label head was also very hard to get ahold of. For the life of me, I couldn't figure out why.

For the first time in what felt like forever, I realized I had to get a real job—or four—again. Tania was no longer down for paying rent for the both of us. She was also not cool with me driving her car any-more, which was insane to think of as we were living in fucking San Francisco. Every place of interest was so far away and public trans-portation was not that great. I guess that new rapper-as-a-lover sheen had worn off. It was time to shit or get off the pot. I was sad as fuck.

Our little home was in a shared duplex with our landlords, a newly married couple who needed to supplement their incomes to survive the astronomical housing prices. Tania and I were cramped and we treated each other like shit. We pretended not to hate each other for the landlords. I was becoming very angry and confused with life on top of needing to get a few jobs. Where was this rap career? I was feeling very ignored by my record label. None of the producers on the label wanted to work with me because of commitments to bigger artists. (Or maybe something else?) Bookings were gone. Anytime I was onstage, I felt great. Shows were my happy place. But I had no shows. The business of Psalm One was indeed NOT booming.

For context, this was still the era of hip hop where you could tour an album for a few years. You could have ample time between releases, years even, and still have loyal fans. Not like now, when, if you take even a year between releases, some fans will say you've fallen off. Insanity. My debut came out in 2006 and I had mixtapes. It hadn't quite been two years yet, so I was still in a decent space with releases. People hadn't forgotten about me or anything. Fans still let me know how much they loved my music. But I was getting fucking antsy.

Right before I'd left Chicago, I'd picked up a short seasonal position at a charter school, helping with after-school programming. It was a good monetary cushion for my upcoming move, and it looked great on my résumé. My experience at the charter school back home helped me gain employment in education in San Francisco. Plus, it helped me realize I'm pretty good with kids. They listened to me, I think, because I was patient with them. Being lonely often as a kid made me very receptive to the little homies. I especially connected with anything regarding reading, math, science, or just plain small talk. Having so many people in my childhood who cared about my schooling rubbed off. I really want young kids, especially ones that grow up in impoverished neighborhoods, to have the tools they need to succeed.

A very slow career shift was happening in San Francisco, and it started with an after-school program close to where I was living. I'd applied to be a poetry instructor for America SCORES, an accredited organization with an emphasis on team building through the combo of soccer and poetry. Poetry I could do easily. But soccer? Hell nah.

Luckily, I was able to find a sports-medicine student from San Francisco State University to help me coach soccer in exchange for college credit. I had the skill to help the kids with poetry, and having help on the soccer end gave my whole squad a boost. The kids were not able to do one activity without the other.

But the hours were so sparse I knew I needed something more in order to afford to breathe. My second job was doing ACT-prep classes and tutoring at local high schools. I was also doing some private tutoring. I really loved the latter because of the one-on-one connection with students. School can be really pressure filled. Sometimes even the most dedicated student can become less dedicated because of their friends. They'll be led by the behavior of other kids and take their cues, good or bad, by what their peers are doing. With private tutoring, there is no threat or risk of being "uncool." It's just the student, the tutor, and the lesson.

Generally speaking, any parent who was paying for the tutoring I was providing had some money. My services were not cheap. I'd be tutoring some kid in math or reading comprehension for seventy-five dollars or more an hour, daydreaming about what the fuck it must be like to be that papered up. It reminded me of how much my mom sacrificed for me to have the tools I needed to be a good student. Maybe all of those parents weren't rich, but all of those parents wanted to give their kids an extra push. That inspired me to do a good job. And since I was on public transportation in San Francisco, I was getting a helluva workout. Hills upon hills kept my leg muscles on point. I would trek on foot to some mansions in Pacific Heights or Nob Hill. I was really going through an identity crisis, so you can imagine my surprise when one day I got identified by my student Michael.

We were sitting in his parents' massive kitchen, whose windows looked out onto a chicken coop, going over some precalculus. Michael seemed preoccupied. Then he said, "Hey, Cristalle, can I ask you a question?"

"Yeah."

"But, it's not a math question."

"Uh, ok, shoot."

"Are you the rapper Psalm One?"

"What?"

"Do you rap? Are you a rapper, too? Are you Psalm One?"

It was just like in the lab. Spotted. Only this time I was embarrassed. It was a mind fuck having to have a job but still having enough rap cred to be detected. My face flushed red as I sat at the table with my mouth on the fucking floor. This high-school kid knew enough about indie rap to know and recognize me? I didn't even have a music video out, which was a gripe I'd always had with the label. So how in the whole fuck did this kid know who I was?

"Uh, yeah, haaaa. I am Psalm One."

Michael shot up out of his chair and started running around the house screaming, "Psalm One is in my house! Psalm One is in my house teaching me math!"

I didn't know what to do, so I just laughed. The kid was elated, and his mom stood there just as shocked. She definitely didn't know shit about indie rap. All she knew was her kid was really fucking excited and I was teaching him math. We finished up the lesson eventually, and before I got home there was an email in my inbox from Michael's mom.

She said I was the best tutor her son ever had and he wouldn't shut up about how glad he was that Psalm One was helping him with his schooling. She told me they'd gone through no less than four tutors and the kid ran them all away; he hated them all. I guess there really was something special about having a tutor he already thought was cool. She asked if she could hire me for even more sessions and possibly recommend me to some other families. Could you believe it? My degree was actually fucking paying off. Of course I said yes.

Cha fucking ching. Did you know there's a whole industry of independent tutors, and some even make their whole living tutoring rich kids? Well, I was thrust into that world by being a broke rapper with a chemistry degree. I was really good at it, too. I spent my first cold-ass summer in San Francisco tutoring a handful of kids in a variety of subjects in order to prepare them for college. I tutored one young lady who really didn't need it. Her mother was newly widowed and had been left a substantial amount of money. She overspent to make sure her kid got into the best schools. Well, this girl knew *everything* she needed to know about high school–level chemistry, so for $100 an hour we did kitchen experiments and talked about what it was like growing up without a dad. We bonded on having overprotective mothers and only liking science-based math problems. It was definitely one of the easiest, yet more meaningful jobs I ever had.

My third job was by far the funniest and also in the education sphere. I worked at Gymboree, a chain of kids retail stores and instructional facilities that filed for bankruptcy in 2017. I worked there as a music instructor for kids ages one through five. Imagine me blowing bubbles and teaching tiny children how to play fake instruments and crawl under huge, colorful parachutes. I would do all of this while playing ABBA and keeping an award-winning smile on my face. Now, with multiple paychecks coming in, I could better afford to live in the Bay.

I cannot overstate how expensive and therefor classist San Francisco is. Most Black people were priced out of living there by the turn of the twenty-first century and were residing in Oakland and neighboring cities. People would really judge you based on how expensive you looked and what you wore. I was already dealing with low self-esteem and the sadness of not having my friends and family around for support. I wasn't rapping. I was alone at home a lot. I needed to stay busy and stack bread.

I had three jobs, making money coaching, teaching, tutoring, playing patty-cake, and giving seniors in high school real-ass pep talks when they needed them. I was boarding school buses, helping pack lunches, singing nursery rhymes, debating college choices, spreading sunshine by day . . . and getting into screaming matches and exchanging bruises by night. I was scared and escaping with substances. I didn't feel any love with Tania and I had no support from her. She probably felt the same about me. Occasionally, I was getting drunk at cheap bars, the only ones I could afford, and getting into MDMA (aka ecstasy, aka Molly, aka thizz, et al.) a little bit when I had extra money. The Bay Area is actually known for ecstasy. That up-all-night shit. It's all the same type of party drug, essentially. Cocaine was scarce and too expensive for me, but Molly was right there. And the Molly I was getting was pretty fucking pure. And cheap. A new chemical demon was lurking, simmering just beneath the surface. And I was making new nonrap "friends" too.

Tania was in a national Roller Derby league and had a built-in network of badass chicks in the Bay. I was never into scenes. I was into music. Tania was into music, too, but more as a fan of going out to shows. We were rapidly drifting apart. Her new job, life, new work friends, and Roller Derby gave her so many reasons to stay out later and later. We saw each other less and less. More than likely if I wasn't working, I was home.

With all my gigs and side gigs, I wasn't able to really go out and party or do restaurants or any of the shit I enjoy. Self-care was not a thing. I had enough to pay my rent, pay my bills, and put some food for myself on the table. Tania had usually eaten or at least drank enough by the time she got home, so I was really only responsible for my own food. I had budgeted money for a few party favors, but after all that, I was really stuck in the house. Tutoring and after-school stuff was usually in the evening, with the occasional weekend given to soccer games, poetry slams, and ACT proctoring. I wasn't really writing any music. Every now and then I'd write a rap but I didn't have any beats. Casual didn't live near me and Hiero was running a whole-ass legendary label with grown-ass men with families. Rap was definitely on the back burner, and I didn't like it one bit.

On top of needing to create and perform music, I needed more friends. The two needs are likely connected. Music and friends, friends and music. Music was my friend. Friends usually made music with me. But not now. Little did I know, I had a couple of childhood friends living in San Francisco.

I hadn't exactly kept up with everyone from my earlier years. College put me on a whole different path, and I only had a few friends from high school left. So imagine my surprise when I found out I had some old Chi City friends who'd moved to the Bay for work. I casually and quite literally bumped into an old chum, Matt, while visiting a skate shop with Tania and her Roller Derby friends. I was only there for the free beer and tortilla chips.

Matt bumped into me as I walked outside of the skate shop to smoke a joint. "Cristalle?"

"Matt? What the fuck?"

"What the fuck are you doing here?"

"I live in San Francisco with my girlfriend. I was just inside the skate shop hanging out. What the fuck are you doing here?"

"I've been living out here for the past few years for work. I live literally up the hill. Let's exchange numbers. Come by and hang anytime. You know we're always smoking Ls [blunts], too, so you gotta come through. It's great to see a familiar face out here!"

"Oh shit! You know it!" And you know I did.

Matt was a friend of a friend I'd known when I was younger, and we'd always gotten along. My group of friends throughout the years had always been racially diverse. Going to magnet schools and "smart-kid" schools meant diversity. It also usually meant I was one of a few, if not the only, Black kids in my circle. Matt was, and still is, a cool-ass white guy from Hyde Park, who I met when I was attending Ray. We got even closer when I'd come home to visit friends while I was still in college. We had the same interests: music and weed. We'd rapped together a little, so we always had a musical bond. His freestyle was always on point, too.

He wasn't so much into making music anymore, but he'd always remained a fan and student of the game, plus he was a really good writer to boot. You can't imagine how good it felt having a friend from home out there in San Francisco. I was suffering a low-grade identity crisis, and it was utter chaos at home. Being able to escape that nuttiness and let my hair down with folks I'd known for a long time was a godsend.

Matt lived with another friend from home and we instantly clicked. I was spending more and more time over there. All we did was cook good-ass food, watch TV, talk a lot of bullshit, and smoke. Since I'm a simple woman, that's all I need for a good time. In fact, I don't even need all of that. But they had all that, all the time, and we all had genuine love for each other. I had been craving this comradery.

It was also super refreshing to befriend people who did NOT like clubbing and going to bars. My girlfriend was a party animal, and even though I liked getting wasted, I wasn't as big on going out and spending a ton of money to kick it. That was another thing driving a wedge between us—money. It also didn't help that after exactly one hang, Matt told me he didn't like Tania and to keep her away from his crib.

"What? Damn, it's like that?"

"Oh yeah, it's like that. And frankly, Cris, when you and *her* are over, which I see happening soon, you'll have a place to stay. We'll let you live here when y'all break up."

I couldn't help but laugh. Stevie Wonder could see it: Tania and I were heading towards a stupid and violent finale. Matt assured me that when the time came, I'd have a safe space to bounce back. God was sending angels. But I was shocked.

"We're not just gonna gloss over the fact that you've effectively banned my girlfriend from visiting your house."

"I mean, she's a terror, Cristalle. And you know it, too."

I did know it. I had a tendency to enable my partners and apologize for their bad behavior. I'm sure there has been some apologizing for my antics by my partners, but I was particularly bad at thwarting abusive shit when it was directed at me. I know now, through years of therapy and shadow work, that I have abandonment issues and have historically put up with bullshit for fear of being alone. I don't have a fear of being lonely, because I actually like being by myself. I make myself laugh. I make myself come. I make myself better. But the idea of having nobody to talk to or come home to or love on when I needed it was scary to me. I really wish I'd had that insight years ago. But therapy is expensive and you know what they say about hindsight.

Anyway, Tania's drinking was at record levels and she made the worst impression on my new old friends from home. She'd gotten shitfaced the one and only time I took her over to Matt's house, and she actually poured water on his head during an argument about something dumb. WATER. She also cursed me and Matt's room-mate out at the dinner table—about two hours after meeting them. Needless to say, my homies quickly noted our dangerous relation-ship and banned her. Out of respect for me, they didn't cuss *both* our asses out. I mean, she was a raging drunk and she embarrassed the fuck out of me, but I was always trying to make it work. She hated me even more after getting banned from the guys' house. It kind of made me love them more. Water. I'll be damned.

By that point, I was throwing spaghetti at the wall, musically. I was making songs here and there with my rap mentor, but Casual was frequently busy with his own life. He had kids, his own label, his own career, and life in general going on. Even though he was really gra-cious with me and allowed me to come visit him at home often, I tried not to wear out my welcome. Plus, he lived far as hell from me. It took me almost two hours to get to his house on public transportation.

The Bay Area Rapid Transit (BART) is an efficient transit sys-tem, but if you live in San Francisco proper and commute by public transit, your options are limited when it comes to leaving the city. Seems kinda racist, actually. You can get to the bougie parts of San Francisco very easily by BART, but anything else is a trek, takes for-ever, and is not cheap. I'd gone to a few open mics and beat battles to find like-minded folks, but artists are so weird. We can be an untrust-ing lot. It was hard for me to make "rap friends." In the midst of my identity crisis with a little dash of impostor syndrome, I'd forgotten my name held clout. My bank account didn't exactly reflect that of a rap star. But my first album was critically acclaimed and I was still one of a few women who was rapping at that level. I was one of a few women who'd been on national and international touring circuits around 2006 and 2007. I'd touched thousands of people. I was forgetting that it meant something. My personal and romantic lives were suffering, but my rap life still had some gas in the tank. I just needed some reasons and the confidence to jump back in the car.

A local producer had started reaching out to me via Myspace after we'd played a bill together after I'd first moved to San Francisco. I wanted to make music so bad and I wasn't able to do it with any type of frequency, so when he started messaging me, I was extra receptive. Pat was a full-time artist and he loved my rapping. He also had a ton of weed and made beats all day long. To me, he was another godsend.

He wasn't like any other producer I'd ever worked with. And he smoked like a chimney, too, which is on brand for hip hop. Pat was also pretty eclectic, and he was dabbling in another form of the genre, a kinda morphed version of hip hop where electronic music, dance music, and chanty gangsta vocals were combined to take on a whole-new sound.

This was before EDM (electronic dance music). That genre and name hadn't been shat out yet. Nah, this was more like dubstep, super early dubstep that the mainstream hadn't gotten wind of yet. This was completely different to me. I needed beats, and he needed vocals. He knew Psalm One, and he was a fan. I quickly became a fan of Pat. He was silly as fuck. He was ecstatic to get me in the studio, and I was equally stoked to be in a creative space again. I had new friends and a new studio to go to that was in the city. It only took two BART trains, a bus, and a fifteen-minute walk to get to his spot. I was there as much as I was allowed. I was slowly finding my bearings, and my vices weren't choking me yet. I was almost breathing again.

CHAPTER 9

LEOPARD-PRINT PUNISHMENT

May sound grimy/you catch me onstage/
Can't catch me at home/Don't catch me off guard/
In the middle of the yard/Screamin' at the hoes/
Talkin' to my exes and I'm screamin' on the phone . . .
—**"Truce"**

When Tania and I did see each other, it was either on the way down from a bender or on the way out to a bar. She would get drunk, I would drive—which was the only time she let me drive her car—and we'd usually argue all the way home. Between bouts of alcoholism and light amphetamine use, we always found time for a screaming match. Those became occasional slaps to the face, which gave way to wrestling matches. It was only a matter of time before somebody called the cops.

When you're drunk as shit, you don't feel the punches you've taken until late the next morning. Blood tastes like snot that tastes like water and drips down with all the other poison you've been consuming that night. Off the beaten path in Oakland, in the back of a dimly lit bar, seething in anger and stewing in bitterness, I sat nursing rum and Diet Coke. I don't even know why I drank that.

SHE drank that. I needed a new drink.

When you're drunk as hell, the scrapes and scars don't hurt. Maybe you feel a quick jolt of pain, but it never lasts longer than your ability to say "ow." You keep taking what you're taking, and you dull the pain away with whatever the fuck is available to you. But in that bar, which was way too much of a hipster bar, I was numb. It was super dark for no fucking reason; you couldn't see shit except this small-ass circumference of a circle on the table made possible by an obnoxious red lamp taking up space. Little-ass tables and big-ass lamps and little-ass chairs and licks of MDMA in the bathroom. A few huge swigs of rum and Diet Coke, but not too much because you're driving.

Tania was pretending to celebrate her fellow athletes on their ascension to a new level of Roller Derby, but I knew she was mad. She was jealous because a lot of her friends were getting better and becoming all-stars. She wasn't. She was wearing blue when all the other girls were wearing pink. The way she was acting felt like high school.

Tania was a decent skater in Roller Derby, but her small frame got banged around a lot. She had the heart and mouth of a person three times her size, but at around three feet twenty and 103 pounds soaking wet, she wasn't exactly a physical threat. She also didn't practice as much as the all-stars in her league. She had a pimp hand that could stun you if you weren't ready, though.

Domestic violence in a same-gender relationship is something a lot of the mainstream doesn't consider. We always hear about some huge guy looming over a weak, sobbing woman. We see her black eye, her cuts, and her bruises. We see him seething. They always show us court cases about one person beating up on another. But what about when y'all are kind of equally yoked—at least physically? How about when you're a guy and your boyfriend is your build and you're just pummeling each other into the ground every other day because you're in the same weight class?

How about when the physical abuse is initiated by the smaller person in the relationship? Does size really matter? How 'bout intent?

What happens when you get slapped at least a dozen times, but when you punch back one time, your partner gets a black eye? What happens is, I'm a fucking abuser. (Well, not any longer. I'm reformed.) Takes one to know one.

I've been on both sides of the shit. I've gotten my ass kicked too many times. I've been in therapy for close to four years. Healing from many forms of abuse has now become a major point of focus. Dealing with my alcoholism and drug abuse has been another major point. But this wasn't until years after my relationship with Tania. I was an abusive partner to Tania; Tania was an abusive partner to me. I'm sensitive. And as much as I wanted to think I was in control of things, Tania controlled more than I admitted. My sometimes-altered reality made everything worse. I have anger issues and with my rap background, I was prone to saying wild things and getting positive reinforcement. Or a battle partner.

When I wasn't in control of my anger, I would lash out violently to counteract what I was feeling. Punching walls. Punching myself. Throwing shit. Pushing. I felt misunderstood, sad, regretful, embarrassed, and unloved. Tania and I would say the foulest shit to each other, drink to numb the pain, and fall asleep without ever truly talking about what happened. That unresolved shit would simmer and sauté until the next time the shit stew would be ready to get thrown up again as violent word bile. And more often, those words would devolve into screams and shoves and slaps and now . . .

Now she's yelling at me from the back of this stupidly lit bar with these big-ass lamps while I'm stewing in shit and sipping nasty-ass rum and Coke. DIET Coke. She's mad because she didn't make the fucking all-star team. When it came to Roller Derby, she wasn't an all-star bitch. She was taking it out on me, and I was throwing up word bile right back. I wasn't the only one she was yelling at that night—a few bouncers got some choice phrases thrown at them—but I sure got the worst of it.

And now, we're yelling outside the bar. And now, we're shoving each other and screaming at the top of our lungs, and I'm trying to wrestle her into the car because she's blind drunk and I'm not, because I knew I'd be driving. But I may as well have been drunk because I'm yelling outside of a bar at my drunk girlfriend, trying to pick her up and literally throw her in the back of her own automobile. That little foul-mouthed beauty was heavy as hell when she wanted to be. Maybe I undershot a few paragraphs ago when I said 103 pounds soaking wet. Cuz shit, that night she may as well have had bricks in her pockets. She wasn't getting herself thrown into that car for shit. This was so embarrassing.

"You can't do anything right! You're a worthless, broke-ass rapper."

"You're only good at drinking and fucking but not so much fucking! Oh, or skating! You're not good on any fucking team!"

People had already left the bar, and we were just yelling into the night. Then it devolved into a wrestling match. Then I heard sirens.

Those law-enforcement motherfuckers sure pull up fast, and all of a sudden, you're putting your hands above your head with Officer Drunk Tank shining his fucking flashlight and asking you what the problem is. At this point, I'm so fucking angry and looking around to point to my girlfriend. As I'm pointing, would you believe this woman takes off running? This lawyer. This adult. This drunkard takes off running down the street, and one of the officers takes off after her in a squad car. At this point, I'm hysterical and telling the first cop that my girlfriend and I are having relationship issues and all I want is to get her home.

"Wait, that's your girlfriend?"

"Yes, officer. What's so surprising about that?"

"Don't get smart."

You would think in one of the gayest destinations in the US, cops would understand a lesbian issue. No. Not at all. Or maybe they were just super entertained. As the other cop rolled back up with Tania in the back seat, I was busy convincing Officer Drunk Tank to calm her down and allow me to drive us both home.

I was sobbing on the curb as she was being advised to allow me to drive us home. Since it was her car, I had to get permission. I told the cops I was afraid she was gonna hit me all the way home and I'd get into an accident. During our screaming match, she'd mentioned that she didn't care if we died together on the road. That was the reddest of flags, and I didn't give a fuck if she was blackout drunk. I wasn't gonna be dying with this person tonight. I now know that was some super narcissistic abuse shit. Some if-I-can't-have-you-nobody-will, scary shit. I wasn't gonna be on no *Romeo and Juliet* shit, though. Hell nah. To tell you the truth, I was hella scared to drive us home, but Tania assured the cops that she'd keep her hands to herself. It was so interesting watching her sober up a little and do the lawyer code switch to talk to the cops after she tried to FUCKING RUN AWAY. If I'd have run like that, I might've gotten shot.

After a few more minutes of stern, confused police work, the cops let me drive away. No drunk tank for us. I drove us home and she was quiet as a fucking church mouse the whole time. She damn near fell asleep. It was the longest ride ever and the tensest I'd ever been up until that point. I was scared of my partner for the first time in my life. I was afraid of what passion could do. I was stone sober and had my guard all the way up. She was amiable towards the cops, but as soon as we got home, she revved right back up. It was like she was charging her evil battery and the motherfucker got to full right as we pulled into our garage/laundry room. I unlocked the car doors and as soon as we approached the front door of our crib, she jumped on my back like a fucking spider monkey and bit me in the face. You read that right: my fucking FACE.

In a fit of rage and strength I slammed her to the ground, yelling at the top of my lungs that this fighting was gonna get us evicted. I blamed her for everything. I believe she was shocked by the fact that she was now on the ground, so she didn't get back up right away. We were both so hurt and tired. This was our first night out together in a long time, and I was not only getting hit but getting my face eaten. Luckily her body wasn't in sync with her brain anymore so I didn't have to defend myself too much after that. I just had to kinda bob and weave.

After a few minutes in the doorway, I was able to guide her into our bedroom. Then I ducked off and hid in the little closet they called the half bedroom and locked the door behind me. I'd been sleeping in there most nights anyway. The master bedroom wasn't inviting—it was sad. I was dripping blood and terrified that I was gonna have to leave Tania sooner than I was planning to. Abandonment issues kicking right on up. The cops being called was a new low, a new level of embarrassment. And I was fucking BLEEDING. A lover had never made me bleed my own blood before. It wouldn't be the last time, unfortunately.

Our relationship was dangerous and the pseudo death threats were eating me up inside. I really couldn't let this person, or this place, swallow me whole. I curled up on my leather recliner, which was basically my bed, and whimpered myself to sleep. It was about three in the morning.

About three hours later, I heard a knock on the door of my safe zone. Tania was yelling from the other side, asking me what happened last night. She said she didn't remember ANYTHING. Tragic. How do you hold someone accountable when they don't remember shit? How do you know they're telling the truth about not remembering shit? How do you yell at them for ruining your life for the millionth time, when they were blacked out? Toxic with a side of PTSD, please.

I opened the door.

"LOOK AT MY FUCKING FACE."

"Huh, what?"

She burped, then frowned the frown of a person realizing they had a bad hangover. She squinted while wiping her eyes. She was looking very confused.

"LOOK AT ME. YOU BIT ME IN THE FACE LIKE A FUCK-ING ANIMAL."

"What? I don't remember anything about last night."

Chemicals wash away lots of pain. They numb it and allow you to temporarily forget. I've been in love with what chemicals do my whole life. Everything is made up of chemicals. Chemistry is the study of everything. And with all of my fancy schooling, I wasn't smart enough to stop feasting on the toxicity and chemicals of a tortured lover. Tania may be coming off a bit psycho on these pages, but you have to consider the source. I'm a kind person, but the mad version of Psalm One doesn't leave room for pleasantries. I was tortured, too. I was also a bit psycho.

I don't subscribe to the crazy-girlfriend narrative often. That's some gaslighting shit people use to avoid accountability. We were both foul to each other. We were both sad. I loved Tania and when things got physical, I tried to go easy, because I'm taller and bigger. When you're defending yourself, though, there's a thin line between thwarting and striking. I struck. So, I'm guilty. But that morning, standing there leaking blood and nursing a swollen, bloody face and scratched up arms, Tania looked like Lucifer. She stood there, her face puffy from crying, speaking to me, her throat scratchy and sore from hollering at me—and the bouncers and the cops. I suddenly felt a rush of despair I'd never felt before. I'll never forget how I felt standing there. I could write an album on that feeling right there.

But this wasn't a contest of who could "out toxic" each other. This was life we were playing with. YOLO (you only live once), right? I didn't have any fight left in me. I wanted to yell at her, lash out and grab her, and make her see how much she was hurting me—and how much she was hurting *us*. She swayed drunkenly in the doorway and looked at me blankly. I was sobbing and sputtering up rage and couldn't even get my volume up. These were thin walls. I knew our upstairs neighbors, who were also our landlords, heard us.

"Come in the bedroom with me."

"Babe, I don't wanna come in the bedroom with you."

"Come on. I'll clean you up and give you a sleeping pill. I don't wanna fight either. I'm sorry."

I fucking hated her. I hated what we'd become. I hated that we'd traveled all the way across the country for our relationship to completely deteriorate. I hated that when I wanted safety, I had a little-ass closet of a safe space to go to and she could just come and get me from that space when she wanted. I gave up any fight at that point. I was battered for real, and I wanted to die. I just knew I couldn't do it myself. I respect depression and suicidal ideations enough not to downplay the thought of doing it, or actually doing it. I respect the aftermath of said actions. I know I couldn't physically kill myself, but the secondhand effects of slowly doing it with drugs and abuse are something I'm pretty familiar with. A chemical and abusive escape is something I understand.

I took Tania's hand and walked slowly with her to our tiny bathroom. She took out some peroxide and some ointment and some gauze and patched my face up while I sobbed. After that she led me to what was supposed to be our bedroom. I hadn't slept there in weeks. She'd banned me from sleeping with her after a previous argument. Being allowed in there now, battered as fuck and sobbing, felt like some ghastly reward. She asked what I wanted to watch on her laptop and gave me some random sleeping pill. She then stroked my head lovingly as I cried myself to sleep. I can't EVER remember another time she'd stroked my head lovingly. But NOW she was stroking my head lovingly. This was manipulation at its finest, a nightmare.

Several hours later I woke up alone. Tania was gone and I went right to Matt's house. He looked at my face in disgust and horror, and told me I could move in as soon as I was ready. As fucked up as it was, I wasn't ready yet. But I put the plan in motion. I'd essentially forgiven Tania for this latest incident. The head stroking was our transaction of forgiveness. I knew shit was gonna get worse because we never talked about anything. We just exploded on one another for everything. Sweeping shit under the rug was no longer working. I was a wreck and she was just . . . not there.

When I wasn't working, I was getting drunk and mad. I started coming home later and staying out more. I had my Chicago homies and I could crash at the studio with my new producer friend. I didn't need to be inside the house suffering. Shit, I could be outside the house suffering.

That just created more despair when I did come home. One day soon after the bar incident, Tania and I were having a relatively light argument and our fucking landlords came downstairs to let us know they could hear us when we yelled at each other. I knew it. How embarrassing. We weren't even yelling that time and THAT was the time they decided to say something to us. Unbelievable.

I can't even remember exactly what was said after that, but we read between the lines. We knew that if we had any more bad arguments, fights, or screaming matches, they might not only call the cops on us, too, but they might evict us. I wasn't about to get evicted, even if I had a place to go. We assured them we'd be quieter and went about our awkward night.

Now the domestically violent cat was out of the bag. Shit, everybody on the block probably heard us fighting. I made a silent vow to not lose my cool again and get the hell out of the crib ASAP.

I told Matt and his roomie that if I was gonna come live on their couch it was at least gonna be MY couch. So I hit up Craigslist and bought a used black leather sofa that was in great condition and a little more expensive than the couch they already had in their place. That always made me laugh. I was a fancy hobo. Like, *bitch*, I'm gonna bring my OWN couch to sleep on, and it'll be a sofa.

After I had a delivery date in place, I waited for the right time to tell Tania I was leaving. It was only a matter of time before I got my heart broken again and we got into a whispering fight, cuz now we couldn't even fight in peace. We had to tone our rage all the way down. Tania had spent two nights away from home because her favorite artist, Manu Chao and his band, was in town. She'd allegedly slept with the band's former manager in the past and I always felt insecure about her loyalty to the group. They make some dope-ass music though, I can't even lie. Phenomenal performers.

She ignored my text messages, calls, and emails for two nights, and when she finally texted me back, she told me she'd be staying at the Phoenix Hotel in San Francisco. The Phoenix is known for attracting free-spirited folks and can boast having one of the coolest pools in town. It's also known for being a place where artists, like me, have had hedonistic dreams fulfilled. Even if Tania wasn't fucking, I knew she was fucking. This was the perfect opportunity to break up with her.

When she finally came home, I was waiting for her. She ignored me and went right to the bathroom as soon as she walked in. She immediately took a shower, and when she went into the bedroom to get dressed, I told her from behind the closed door I was breaking up with her. She said she couldn't believe I was breaking up with her with a door between us. I kind of loved that symbolism.

What confused me was how docile and accepting she was after I finally said the words. To be honest, I felt like she'd been in so many toxic relationships before me and stayed. I was in a toxic relationship before her and stayed, too. We were both used to getting dumped. But here I was, breaking up with her from behind a door and letting her know I'd be coming back in three days to collect my things. We were both tired. She had her life already, and I was finding my way in this strange land of cold Julys and early tech-bro gentrification. We would have killed each other if I'd stayed. Or maybe we'd have been evicted. Or arrested. Something bogus was gonna happen if someone didn't do some dumping. So, after she ghosted me for her favorite band and most likely cheated on me, most likely again, I took the opportunity to end the relationship.

After three days, Matt went with me to pick up a moving truck, get our new leather sofa, and grab the last of my things from my little hell shack overlooking the ocean. Tania stood in the garage, scowling at Matt. He didn't say shit to her. I just pointed him in the direction of the last of my boxes and he went right in to retrieve them. She looked gutted. I didn't feel anything at the time. I just knew I was free of this dangerous relationship. I was also free of the disposable cash that came with this dangerous relationship.

Safety nets are funny: Even when they're toxic, they still feel kinda safe. When I left Tania, she had to eventually move out, too. Even though she was making good money, she'd taken a major pay cut to take a job in California, where the cost of living was way higher. She also couldn't afford life without a roomie. Now we were *both* alone. New addresses. New roommates. There's a lot of couch surfing that goes on in these cool-ass cities. People will do anything to have the proper zip code for their investments or dreams. Fortunately, I had friends who opened their home to me when yet another relationship blew up in my face.

I tried to pick up the pieces by working all the time. When I wasn't working, I was commuting. And when I wasn't doing either, I was finally trying to make my next album. This new producer friend of mine, Pat, had so many beats. From where I observed, it looked like he'd made it in the music business. Even without a label, he could afford to live sans roommates and eat fully off the music. At least that's what I thought.

I had only been able to live fully off the music for a few years. After that, it was odd jobs, and when the education sector called, I made it a part of my life. However, I still had more raps in me. I'd only released one album since my critically acclaimed entrance to the big indie world. I was so close to big-time indie artists but I wasn't close to being one myself. I was learning so many lessons, but if I was gonna be the artist I knew I could be, I'd have to drop some new shit.

Pat was doing these underground shows around town, and after we'd recorded a few songs and established a rapport, he asked me to host a few with him. He'd even pay me. GETTING PAID TO RAP ONSTAGE? That hadn't happened in such a long time. Sure, I'd hop onstage from time to time when my rapper friends came into town, maybe cipher with them onstage. But for money I was teaching and tutoring, tutoring and teaching. Rap dollars weren't coming in, so when Pat asked me to get down with him, I was all in.

Dubstep takes elements of hip hop, so it kinda *sounded* like a hip hop show. But it was a hip hop show without rappers and where the producer was the main attraction. I was intrigued. I remember the first time I walked into one of these underground, pre-dubstep parties. Gliding through the doors, into a foggy, bass-heavy cave of people dancing. Dancing? DANCING? I never saw niggas dance at hip hop shows. I've seen your favorite rappers BEG people to dance at boom-bap hip hop shows and people would nod their heads off. They would jump or throw their hands in the air. But dance? Please. Stop it. Niggas don't dance at hip hop shows. Ninety-beats-per-minute hip hop tracks about anarchy or gripes about women or other rappers ain't gonna get the booties shakin', even if there are a thousand asses in the crowd. Those asses are at the hip hop show to mean mug, throw their hands in the air (like they just don't care), and repeat chants from the emcee. You know, that "real" shit.

But I saw blissful prancing and hip-twisting rage-makers ready to shake ass above all else at this new kind of party. Everyone was grooving and people weren't even really paying attention to the stage. Like, people weren't there to see rappers at all.

My job at these parties was to come onstage with Pat halfway through his set and pump up the crowd. I'd also rap at some point over a previously agreed-upon beat and flex my skills. But my job wasn't really to rap. It was to guide. To be someone on the microphone who was comfortable and understood the flow of the party. A selfless vocalist who was encouraged to say less, but have a true presence on the stage. Basically, it was like being the ultimate emcee at a show that wasn't your show at all. I was actually very into it. I could work on my presence and tease new music to a whole-new audience.

Some people knew who Psalm One was when I came out to those early dubstep parties. Most people were getting introduced to me. But this was very different music than the shit people were used to getting from me. This was electronic and dancey as hell. It moved me. It encapsulated what I was going through because I was so sensitive and in my feelings at the time. And these parties had soundscape and movement. It didn't fit to write hard-edged hip hop–rapper stuff all the time. The electronic backdrop allowed for different lyrics. The stuff I was writing was more personal and melancholy. But I wasn't getting through to my label. At this point I was blowing the office up every other day, trying to get some clarity on expectations.

Because I was getting little to no response and alone as fuck, I just had to eat the silence and trust the music I was making would turn into something wonderful. Pat and I were definitely making some jams. It was weird and quirky and sexy and really interesting stuff to listen to. I remember asking a few of the rappers on RSE what they thought. Here are a few of the responses I got:

" . . . "

"Why are these all electronic beats? Are you going to a rave?"

"This is fucking awesome, and you're certainly rapping good shit, but they're never gonna put this out. I don't know what else to tell you."

"This is not hip hop."

Remember, this is pre-dubstep, or pre-EDM, or post-electronic. EDM wasn't even a term that was used yet. The only people who were really into this type of music were still in the ultra-underground, and only European dubstep was getting love in the States. I was on the cusp, the precipice of that whole EDM invasion, and I had so many new tracks that were right on brand. And yet my label couldn't understand. Frankly, I think they didn't *want* to understand. I know the powers that be actively ignored me.

It always bothered me that, years later, Rhymesayers embraced the EDM sound. The bubble had already popped, though. Pat and I were making that kind of music years prior and were all but laughed at. But RSE jumped on the wave when it wasn't even exciting anymore. The tide had come and saturated the genre. And just like plenty of other things, I was too early. Or maybe RSE was just too late. I was learning a hard lesson: This label that was looked at as so progressive was anything but when it came to me.

This happens a lot in all industries. The lone woman goes out on a limb with an idea, and no one has the balls to back the idea until a dude comes in and suggests the same idea, but later. RSE is lame as hell for ignoring the music I made in San Francisco with Pat. I can't say with any certainty that it would have been a smash if they released it, but it *would* have been a precursor to the wave of EDM-centered rap that was coming. Most rappers weren't attempting what we were doing yet. RSE could have tried something different, believed in me, and seen a big return. I was already building a name in this underground scene. We had the city riding with us at these shows, which were growing in attendance.

I sent in a full project of Pat-produced tunes, and after months of ignoring me, RSE finally just said no. No feedback. No notes. Just an expressed aversion to the type of beats RSE eventually couldn't ignore, because they were everywhere. Years later, rappers made millions doing EDM shit. But when I was doing it, RSE acted like a bunch of cowards.

That was a devastating blow to Pat's ego. He'd always loved what RSE did, and I know the possibility of working with an artist on a legendary label was something he wanted. I'd even gotten my homie Del the Funky Homosapien on one of our tracks, plus a few other Bay Area legends. We were really happy with the music we were making, and for the first time in a long time I was excited about a project. But having to go and tell Pat the label didn't like his beats was extremely hard. The disappointment put a very real strain on our friendship, which was never quite the same after the project got rejected.

CHAPTER 10

BEAMING UP LOW

Psalm One on the roof of Pat's house working on music that never got released, San Francisco, early 2009. Why two mics? LOL.

When she came out, Nicki Minaj was something the music industry hadn't seen in a very long time. If we're talking about mainstream-rap superstars, we were several years past the Lil' Kim era and still several years before the onslaught of great women rappers we enjoy today. Around 2009 there were slim pickings for rap queens.

Beam Me Up Scotty was Nicki's breakthrough mixtape, and when she started to blow up in the streets, I got VERY antsy. It was difficult to see her ascension and not wonder why a record label couldn't back me the way people were starting to back Nicki. She'd gotten cosigns from Gucci Mane, Diddy, and damn near every rapper with clout, and she was about to sign her deal with Cash Money/Young Money Records, Lil Wayne's label. She was a megastar. She had backing. She had support. She had everything I wanted, but I was at a completely different level, several tiers below. And I certainly wasn't comfortable in my body like she was. When you're not secure in yourself and your trajectory, it's so easy to compare. I was comparing my ass off.

Her song "Itty Bitty Piggy" is the one I would blast all the time. Her performances were captivating. She was timed so properly. Even though Nicki Minaj was a superstar and I certainly was not, she gave me insight. She gave me inspiration to fight for the kind of support she had. Even if that would eventually make me a gigantic bitch in some people's eyes, especially the label head.

"You're hardly Nicki Minaj."

"Well, with all due respect, you're not Birdman, and this ain't Cash Money Records. I'm simply asking for a little more support. I'm sending in songs and you're telling me no after months of silence. And then it's just a no. Nothing about how we can improve or make the necessary changes. Everyone else gets at least tangible feedback."

"We're busy with Atmosphere. Why would we stop doing that to help you now? Just send in more music when you have it."

Niggas constantly shooed me away like an annoying insect. A gnat. I wasn't asking for a million-dollar booty-short budget. I wasn't asking for caviar lunches or big features. I wasn't demanding release dates or bursting through the doors like some of my peers were doing. I wasn't yelling at label staff or making interns nervous. I just wanted some acknowledgment. I just wanted some constructive criticism. RSE went from being responsive to ghosting me like a bad Tinder date.

I'd taken a short hiatus, like plenty of artists, but I wasn't prepared to accept a whole CAREER hiatus. Being ignored from another time zone sucked major ass. Hip hop was moving at light speed, and I was at a standstill. That shit hurt. And I was starting to become extremely nervous about everything under the sun.

In the midst of this professional anguish, Matt told me he was moving to fucking Hong Kong for his dream job. That was really bittersweet news to hear. I was just getting comfortable in these new surroundings and finding my footing lyrically, and I loved living with those guys. Matt had gotten the job and relocation offer all at the same time—a blessed avalanche—and he had to be gone very soon. But Matt deserved all of it. My other roomie was getting serious with his girlfriend and was planning to move in with her. All in all, what it meant was I had to figure out my next move within about five weeks.

Even though I was terrified about what would happen next, those guys had provided me with a safe space when I really needed it. I was super happy their lives were becoming more stable and they were fulfilling some personal, grownup goals. Adulting is hard, and dream jobs and serious relationships have to be pursued. Unfortunately, my dream job was ignoring the fuck out of me, and my serious relationship had exploded, a violent blast of intoxication and distrust.

I was teaching way more and recording less. When I went to Pat's house, it was a lot of escaping. I don't know what else he was doing, but together we were dabbling in drinking absinthe, sometimes taking shrooms, and smoking tons of weed. Sometimes he'd throw on some Alex Grey or Sun Ra or some really deep-dive hippie shit, and we'd ramble about existential shit for hours. We were both hurting about music, and other things, but we weren't really talking about the elephant in the room. We were hanging out more than working and that was somehow ok with me. His male energy felt safe at the time, and I definitely needed any homie who was willing to homie with me.

Craigslist came through for a player, again, and I found a six-month sublet around the corner from Matt's place. Even though I'd be moving for the third—but not the last—time since moving to San Francisco, it wasn't that much of a pain in the ass. I didn't have a lot of shit, and the little shit I had didn't have to get moved very far. The sublet was also furnished, so I'd have an actual bed (movin' on up!) and tons of privacy. My only roommate was a boat mechanic who rarely came home. I hadn't had much privacy the whole time I'd been in California, except for when Tania and I weren't speaking. Now I had six months of alone time to figure my shit out.

Right before I moved out of Matt's, I'd booked my own gig in Chicago and had it double as a food drive. I'd made a few phone calls, booked my show at my favorite small venue in Chicago, the Hideout, and prepared for a homecoming. I was so immersed in teaching work, giving back had started to become second nature. I believe I was subconsciously balancing all the darkness in my life with that. I also was super homesick.

"Home" was now weird. I hired a friend to DJ for me. I was kinda broke from moving, so I didn't have much money for a new stage outfit. I remember throwing something quirky on and prepping to do the show, more worried about the after-party than the actual show itself. Drugs, man. They really do sneak up on you.

Many old and new friends showed up to the Hideout. I was headlining, which was rare, one of my friend's old bands played, and another local rapper was added to the bill. At the last minute, I got the bright idea not to headline the show and let the local rapper headline. It was an idiotic update to the set times, but I tried to justify it by saying the local rapper had a new album out and I didn't, so he should headline. He was ecstatic and so was I. Now I'd be able to drink and do drugs and hang out with my friends during the show. Headliners don't get to enjoy the show. But the penultimate performer usually has tons of fun. I was there for fun. Music hadn't been fun in a while.

The show at the Hideout was a success even though it was kind of a blur. All I remember is going to the bathroom a lot and that the venue was packed when I was on. I don't even know how good my set was. What I do know is that it started to clear out once the headliner went on. More than half the crowd left because they were, in fact, there to see me. In retrospect, I really shat on the local rapper with that last-minute call. If I had headlined like I was supposed to, he would have had a packed house to play for. It was a dick move on my part, but I didn't care. When you're fucked up, all you care about is doing the bare minimum so you can get more fucked up.

I was getting the opportunity to party with some old friends. All I cared about was the familiar faces I saw—except one: Tania. The show was around the Thanksgiving holiday, and I had no idea Tania was also planning a homecoming trip. Of course. She'd come to the show blind drunk and on crutches. She'd broken her leg—a Roller Derby injury—and was hobbling around Chicago doing the same shit I was doing. She finessed her way backstage and asked me to fuck, but I didn't want to. I rarely want to fuck an ex. I mean, I'll certainly do it, but I wasn't interested in fucking Tania anymore. I was still so very hurt from our breakup, and I knew turning her down would crush her ego, which I was totally down to do. I pretended I wanted to come home with her until the last minute, then I rejected her in front of some mutual friends. Besides, even with all those familiar faces, I was really into the idea of fucking someone new. Even if they were someone I'd kinda knew, I'd be ok with that. But I didn't wanna look back. Looking back was too painful.

One of my best friends in the world, Colin, was chatting it up with a very interesting-looking, and vaguely familiar, woman by the bar, and she seemed to be totally into him. I was excited about that. When they saw me walk up, they both held out open arms to me. I was loving all the love. Colin was closing the deal.

"We were talking about having an after-party, and I was convincing her to come."

"Oh, you wanna come?" I asked.

"Only if you're both there."

"Oh, yeah?" The woman and I locked eyes like fools.

ZIIIINNNNNGGGGGG. Colin and I both beamed at each other like we'd hit the jackpot. We decided to have a few more drinks while we texted our friends to tell them we were, in fact, having an after-party. I was thrilled. In San Francisco I was feeling like nothing. However tonight, at this venue, in my hometown, I felt a tiny bit like a STAR again, even if the feeling was fleeting.

The after-party was at Colin's crib up north, near Logan Square. About twenty of our closest friends piled into his second-story walkup with a few gallons of booze plus the end of a keg to share. We also had the powdery stuff that gets everyone into trouble. Little did I know, this night would be the beginning of a downward spiral that would last more than eight years.

Tabby was her name, and I remembered her from Whitney Young. We didn't exactly frequent the same circles at the same time, but we knew of each other and had a mutual respect. I also remember at one point, senior year, we were after the same guy, Misfit. He ended up choosing me over her. She loved joking about it, that I stole her boy-friend. But I didn't steal Misfit from her—that Negro chose me.

At the after-party she was getting a little choosy herself. Even though I was invigorated by the chase, I was in the kitchen feverishly calling my old Chicago fling, Nu-Nu, who'd stood me up for the thou-sandth time. Nu-Nu had promised she'd be at my show and she wasn't. I was devastated because I really wanted to come home and hang with her. This girl was always the one I couldn't fully trust with my heart cuz she ghosted me a lot. But I loved her so much. (I still love you, Nu-Nu.) While I was calling her and not getting through, I was dodg-ing texts from Tania, who wanted to know what I was doing later.

Tabby suggested I leave both girls alone and talk to her. After a little while I pulled her into Colin's bedroom and we had a minor tag-team make-out session in. Now, Colin is one of my oldest friends and, minus the time I'd tried to make him my boyfriend in tenth grade (he turned me down and we became even better friends), we were purely platonic. So having the prospect of a threesome with him and Tabby was exciting. I was down for it. She was down for it. He was not. In retrospect, he was Neo dodging bullets at the end of *The Matrix*. Tabby and I ended up making out all night. She was casting spells.

By the next morning we were making plans to hang out again. I knew we were gonna probably do the nasty. The next evening, I was hungover but ready to go. She lived in an artist loft in Wicker Park and getting to her space was like navigating a labyrinth. I wasn't sure what kind of art she did to be staying in an artist's loft. She had a very corporate, very demanding job. That was the whole reason we didn't just go home together the night of the after-party: She had to get up super early and work a whole-ass corporate gig the next day.

I walked up the winding artsy-fartsy stairs to Tabby's loft after receiving a text from her that read, "Bonus kisses if you don't get lost." I didn't get lost, and when I got to her door, she opened it before I could knock. She yanked me inside and pressed her full lips against mine. She kissed me long and passionately, like she was trying to cast another spell or some shit. When you're fascinated by someone, you'll let all kinds of shit slide.

We ate pizza from Lou Malnati's and drank Goose Island beer, quintessential Chicago hipster shit. And I don't really care what you say. Lou Malnati's is the best deep-dish pizza in Chicago. Tavern-style pizza is a different debate for a different book. I'll show a few other deep-dish pies love every now and then (shout out to Pequod's), but Lou's is my go-to. Both Tabby and I agreed on Lou's butter crust and chunky-tomato-on-top-of-the-cheese situation. She got cool points for that.

I don't think I have a type, but through therapy I've learned that I definitely need intense attention. And I like busy people who make a lot of time for me. There's nuance to it, though. There's a thin line between intensity and creepiness. I was super into the idea of being super into Tabby. I knew I was hopping on a plane in a few days and heading back to my weird-ass, lonely life back in California. I was laying it on thick because I knew this was just a one-night thing.

Ok, maybe a two-night thing. We talked for hours, but I didn't eat any of the pizza the first night because I had butterflies in my stomach. We drank our beer and went to third base. I was trying to take it kinda slow. We didn't end up sleeping together that first night. We did some sexy stuff; we just didn't go all the way.

The next night was all pizza and pussy eating.

Lou's and mind-blowing sex, followed by existential conversations and all the nice beer and scotch the corner liquor store had to offer, had rendered me putty in Tabby's hands. We were both less nervous, so we finished the pizza and started up some undeniable shit. She challenged me to stare into space and think whimsically just for the sake of it. We shared so much of ourselves I couldn't help but feel a little bad about leaving. That was the best date I'd had in years. I also know that it wasn't really a date, as we didn't go anywhere. It was more of a come-over-and-fuck outing, but that was enough for me. My ex, Tania, wouldn't go anywhere with me unless there were a few other friends involved. Me and Tabby sat alone and spilled ourselves all over the room. I flew back to San Francisco a few days later, still buzzing from the time we'd spent together as well as whatever toxins were still swimming in my bloodstream.

So, you could imagine my surprise when, after about a week and a half of talking to Tabby on the phone long distance, she hit me with the cryptic question.

"What are you doing tomorrow?"

"I'm proctoring an exam and gonna see what Pat's up to."

"No, you're not. You're hanging out with me."

"What are you talking about?"

"I'm gonna come see you."

"Liar."

"I'm not lying. After your exam tomorrow, you're gonna meet me at the airport and we're gonna hang out all weekend."

I can't even lie. I was frightened by this. I thought it was psycho she was gonna fly three and a half hours just to come see me, especially since this was supposed to be a little after-party two-night stand. Now she was spending money to come see me? Curious.

"I fly for free."

"Oh, word? Well, that's not so crazy then. I thought you were about to buy a ticket and all that."

"Nah, my sister works for the airline. I get to fly for free."

Still psycho, but a little *less* psycho. So, the next day, after proctoring my exam, I met Tabby at the airport.

Dressed in a huge floppy black hat, like an actress in an old movie, and leather, thigh-high boots stood Tabby, looking out the baggage-claim window like she was ready for her fucking closeup. I came down the escalator not quite understanding why someone so sophisticated would fly all this way to come see a downtrodden rapper like me. I was all but too prepared to find out.

Like some of the affluent women before her, Tabby was down to pay for EVERYTHING. I was broke most of the time. After spending most of my earnings on rent, a little on bills, and the rest on food and some mood-altering substances, I wasn't exactly able to pay for much. Tabby's demanding corporate job paid a handsome salary, so she had broke-rapper money to spare.

I reached the bottom of the escalator and she twirled around to greet me, as if on cue. I couldn't help smiling from ear to ear. My ego was being stroked in a way I hadn't experienced before. I was determined to show her the best time I could in this strange land. After a ride on the BART, gazing into each other's eyes and giggling uncontrollably the whole way, we tossed her bags in my room and fucked like rabbits on the floor. After that, we took a stroll around my neighborhood.

The Mission neighborhood in San Francisco is probably tech bro'd out by now, but twelve years ago it was still a multicultural, funky dream. I loved the restaurants, the shops, the diversity, and the overall vibe of it. An Ecuadorian spot, a soul-food spot, and a hipster tattoo shop could all be on the same block, with at least ten different cultures coexisting. Tabby fit in perfectly with the backdrop. But I couldn't let her distract me from the fact that I was still getting over Tania. This was just a rebound.

This was some weird weekend fantasy. This wasn't a real relationship. Besides, I was worse for the wear after my last breakup. And I was poor. The cost of living was kicking my ass and I was very depressed. Music has always been the refuge for me, but since the music Pat and I had made had gotten rejected by the label, we were completing fewer and fewer songs. My Bay Area mentor was busy with his own life, and my Chicago friends were all but gone. I didn't really have any friends beyond that. My ACT-proctoring job didn't require me to interact with any other instructors. I wouldn't want to kick it with any of my tutoring clients' parents. That would be too weird. And at Gymboree exactly one of my coworkers was cool. But she liked going to clubs and getting her rent paid by a sugar daddy, so I didn't really mesh with her after-work activities. I was terribly lonely.

Tabby would fly in on the weekends to visit me. At first it was sporadic, then it became a weekly thing. My new roomie was never home when I was, and when I did see him, he was in transit. I'd catch him scarfing down a can of sardines and swigging a beer on his way out, or I'd hear him in the shower. I think I saw him three times my entire sublease. We essentially had a house to ourselves in the Mission. She had money. I had loneliness and pseudo poverty working for me. She would rub my head and tell me how great of an artist I was. I was perfectly ripe for manipulation.

Tabby was different from Tania. She sparked my creative brain in a way that had me working on big ideas in her absence. When we hung out on weekends, we would discuss all these ideas, and she spoke as if she was down to fund something huge. She wanted my label to notice me again. She wanted my music to grow, and she wanted to help. In my immaturity, I was immediately drawn to her class and education. We had a lot in common: We'd gone to the same high school and grown up on the same side of town. We both loved hippie shit and weren't afraid of a little mind expansion. We were both too smart for our own good.

At the time, her vices were scotch and weed. I still had a party-drug issue, but it wasn't even close to getting to the point where I was fucking up my daily life. At least I didn't think so. There were a handful of times I could remember not being my best onstage because of partying. But my regular jobs weren't in jeopardy. And that's what abuse fools you into believing. Being sober, as I type these words, lets me know being clearheaded and more secure in myself could have made my life and career very different. I was escaping because of major depression and social anxiety. And that's ok, now. A lot of folks lie to themselves. I was no different, but I thought I had everything under control. I had a job, a fledgling career, a roof over my head, and a new love interest. Things couldn't be that bad, could they?

I continued to dabble in MDMA. Most times I did it in secret. It was cheap in the Bay and I just wanted to feel better. Tabby also wanted to feel good. She hated her job and loved the escape of these weekend trips. She also loved psilocybin (psychedelics). Some days we would spend walking around Haight-Ashbury and talking about what we would have done if we had been there in the '70s. Some days we'd spend in the house, engaging in a beautiful cycle of drinking and fucking and tripping and plotting.

"You need to move back to Chicago," Tabby said one weekend while munching on a big-ass burrito.

"What? Nah, fuck no. I'm doing good work here." In reality, I was really lost and didn't know what the fuck I was doing. I still didn't have any new music to show. I was holding onto faith that me and Pat would figure a project out. My sublease was ending and I still wasn't quite prepared to leave. When I mentioned to Pat I was possibly moving back to Chicago, he quickly offered up the weed room in his condo.

Yes, I said WEED ROOM. Pat dabbled in growing marijuana and had turned one of the spare rooms in his crib into a mini–grow house. He told me he'd charge me a modest rent and I could live there as long as I needed. Damn. Living with my producer? I was convinced this was some sort of benevolent sign, an indication my work was not yet finished. I could live next to the studio and save a little rent money every month? I was in. He had me at weed room.

He stayed in the Fillmore District, which was an even better commute to any of my thousand jobs. He smoked and grew weed, and he played music all day. I was inspired, and upon first moving in, we'd wake up and get right to it. Bass thumping, breakfast cooking, and blunts burning. Sometimes it'd be Brazilian drumming. Sometimes it would be the latest pre-EDM producer from across the pond. Sometimes it would be Mac Dre.

I was so happy to be living in a musician's household, I didn't realize the psychological games being played. I also didn't know Pat was dealing with his own addictions. We both did drugs in secret, so it was hard to tell if anyone was struggling. If I'd learned anything in San Francisco, it was how to keep up appearances. There was a lot of floundering happening in social circles, but I couldn't, and wouldn't, recognize it. Everybody seemed to have it more together than me, and I was actually surprising myself by how I was able to keep it together. I will say that if it wasn't for Matt and a few others, I probably would have had to move back to Chicago within the first year of being in Cali. But there was work to be done, and my career wasn't nearly as over as I thought it was. I just had no clue where my next musical blessing was coming from.

Tabby and I were talking multiple times a day, and by the time I moved in with Pat, she was super comfortable in my world. She'd met Pat once at a show before I lived with him, but now it was hella weird. (You can tell I've spent a lot of time in the Bay because I say *hella*.) They clashed a lot. To me it looked like they both wanted to be right all the time and I was caught in the middle, trying to keep things from becoming too awkward. I also know now that's a byproduct of abandonment issues. I was always trying to make things better, even if it wasn't my place, because I wanted folks to want to be around me.

I failed at that, because the second time Tabby came to visit me at Pat's, he banned her from the studio. They'd gotten into an argument the previous visit, and when she returned, he'd placed a note on the door that read NO GIRLFRIENDS ALLOWED. We both saw it for the first time when we returned from the airport.

I was extremely annoyed by this, and when I confronted him about it, he muttered something about girlfriends ruining the vibe and Yoko and not wanting all that extra energy around. To me, it seemed as though he was a little jealous of how happy she was making me. And that she had ideas about my music. I hadn't had anybody show me that kind of attention in a long time. Banning her from the studio made Tabby mad as hell, so the tension in the condo was terrible when she was around. It wasn't the biggest place to begin with, and I was essentially rooming with a bunch of weed plants. It was close quarters, and with my producer and girlfriend at odds, it started to feel downright claustrophobic.

After the banning, Pat became even more cold with me, and when we made music, we never finished it. I would always be ready to put final touches on things, but he would always want to make some changes, or he'd "lose" the files altogether. I didn't know anything about these little manipulative tactics. I was a vulnerable, lost musician who was needy for acceptance. I wanted everyone to get along, but the shit just wasn't happening. Home was becoming a tense place again, and now the music was getting involved. I was revisiting being miserable.

A constant light in my darkness was teaching and tutoring. I was offered an opportunity to do a workshop with America SCORES and the American Society of Composers and Publishers (ASCAP), combining tutoring with music creation and team building. They would pay me a modest fee to run a three-day workshop, something like $750, but to me it was so much money. It was the first time in a while I'd be getting paid to do my own music, and the first time doing work like this with kids. I was used to teaching soccer, or poetry, or reading comprehension, or precalculus (my fave). Getting paid to make music with kids was new territory. I jumped at the chance, determined to give it my all. I knew that a job well done here could open up another lane in my career. I didn't know how, but I just knew it could.

This blessing was a welcome distraction to life leading up to my departure from San Francisco. I was in a month-to-month situation with Pat, so essentially, I could leave at any time. There was no lease keeping me there. When it's time to leave somewhere, I believe the universe finds ways to let you know it's time to go.

Working on this special music workshop with these new students proved to be a lot of work, but it paid off. I was supposed to come up with a family-friendly song with some third graders and record it within three days. The writing of the song itself wasn't that big of a deal. I write fast. The challenge was figuring out how to involve more than twenty students in one song. And then, how the hell was I gonna record it? My laptop was super janky and I couldn't afford a MacBook with all the bells and whistles. The latter challenge proved to be my first lesson in engineering.

A teacher's aide came to my rescue with her own MacBook, and a volunteer brought in a microphone. We were able to record the song we came up with in the final session. Of course, the kids wanted to rap about soccer, so that's what we did. In the two-hour block we came up with a chorus for all the kids to say, and we broke up tiny verses for the more confident kids to rap by themselves. I never knew how much I loved all types of writing until I started working with kids on rap songs. The whole process of coming up with a concept to rap about, writing and editing the raps, and then recording the raps with children is no easy feat. After we had about seven minutes of recordings, I was given a week to arrange that into a song that could be delivered to the powers that be. Essentially that was my first demo as a children's rapper.

I played with the recordings in GarageBand, which is Apple's version of Pro Tools for dummies. It's very easy to understand, and if you play with it for a few hours, you can get music done. I'd been sitting in studios most of my adult life, and I'm a scientist, for Chrissakes, so I understood sound waves. The interface on GarageBand was hard at first but not impossible, so I was able to splice together a low-quality version of a song that brought high-quality joy to some kids that looked just like me.

It took me the better part of ten hours to get a four-minute song, but soon after that I started to figure out what would become my niche in the education sphere. The song I sent in was a huge hit with the kids, the instructors, my supervisors at work, and our partners at ASCAP. Once a few more people in charge figured out I was Psalm One, I was offered another opportunity to do the program in another city, should I find myself traveling again. I had no idea it was a national workshop and they worked with all kinds of musicians, all the time. Bingo.

My first thought was doing a workshop in Chicago, but I didn't know when I'd be back home again. The universe was working, though. As soon as I thought I'd be living in musical Xanadu with Pat, things turned into an awkward quicksand where my dreams were slowly deteriorating. We would drink absinthe and get nothing done, or he'd do this weird thing where I'd be super tired on indica weed, and as I'd be drifting in and out of sleep, he'd play around with beats. Music that hits my soul will wake me out of my sleep, so when something he played woke me up out of this dream-like state, he'd record the beat right away.

One time he did this I got so excited I recorded a full song right then and there. It was that lucid thing again. The beat was something he'd made from leftover Psalm vocals, so my voice was truly the instrument. The beat jolted me out of my half-sleep, I feverishly wrote to it, excitedly recorded it, and spent the rest of the night buzzing from the brilliance of it all. I thought it was the best song we'd ever made together and one of my instant personal faves. I was so happy we were back to making beautiful music again—until he "lost" all the files between the time I fell asleep and woke up again. No beat. No vocals. No demo. No version of it whatsoever. This was absolutely the last straw. Tabby had thoughts about it.

"He's stealing your soul and playing with your emotions," she said quietly in my bedroom, where another batch of weed was growing.

"What? You're always saying some trippy shit."

"Nah, babe. It's one thing to just record. He was having a fucking ceremony with your creativity while you slept! Damn near a ritual or some shit and then he loses it? He's playing with your soul now, and I don't like it."

Damn. Once she put it like that, I vowed to stop making music with him. He was hoarding my best work to date and conveniently "losing" it, and he was getting more and more lifted on drugs most of the time. I couldn't judge him. I had no place to judge him. But I did.

In another instance that always stuck with me, Pat, in a moment of intoxicated forgetfulness, let it slip that he got paid way more for one of the shows I did with him. At the time of the show, he said he'd gotten paid way less, and that my cut was bigger. So, I thought he was being generous. It was a show at Club Six in San Francisco, where I rapped and emceed for him for more than two hours—and he paid me $100. He told me he couldn't pay me more but he split the profits evenly with me. I didn't expect him to give me half his earnings, but he insisted and I thought he was the coolest guy for doing that. I found out later in his ramblings that he got paid $1,000 for the show. So, he was lying to me for no reason at all. It wasn't even the money so much as it was the lie. He didn't have to gas me up like he was doing me this big favor, when really, he was underpaying the fuck out of me.

I couldn't shake the thought of deceit, and Tabby started a real campaign for me to make my homecoming permanent. Between the success of this new workshop and it being offered in Chicago, Tabby, my as-yet-unclaimed girlfriend, plus my entire family living there, and the prospect of making music with Pat all but null, home was looking more inviting by the day. I had to make a plan. The signs were plentiful, but what if I returned to Chicago and felt like a failure? Wasn't returning home without blowing up some failure shit? I didn't know if I had the balls to find out.

One weekday soon after Pat told me about the $1,000, I received a random email from Chicago producer MP. He sent me a lovely cost-free beat and told me he'd be honored if I rapped over it. He also told me that whenever I was in Chicago and needed a studio, he'd be my engineer. He told me he just wanted to work with me; he was missing my voice in the game.

C'mon, universe. So now, I was being offered an opportunity to continue my workshops in Chicago, I was being offered a working studio with a producer who was reputable, and I also found out my proctoring job was a nationwide gig. The world I had been building for myself in San Francisco could be transferred back home. But moving was gonna be so expensive. It took all my little-ass savings to move to San Francisco in the first place. I knew it would take at least that much to be able to move home.

Tabby came in with an idea to make some quick cash—some under-the-table tutoring—and she was all too willing to help front a few of the costs for my departure. I promised myself I wouldn't make the same mistakes I'd made with Tania. I told Tabby I wouldn't be moving in with her if I moved back to Chicago. She only half-believed me. Hell, *I* only half-believed myself. The last thing I wanted to do was move back home, not be famous, and live with my mommy. The horror! Why was moving back in with your parent so scary? I wanted no parts of it.

No matter what my next move was going to be, I knew I couldn't live with Pat any longer. The trust between us was gone, and there was always some passive-aggressive shit going on. Our friendship was superficial—weed and dubstep beats. We weren't even making any music. There was so much tension I didn't know where to start to even try to repair what we had. And when I looked into moving into another apartment, I realized I just couldn't afford San Francisco anymore. Rent was too damn high.

If I wanted to accumulate anything, pay down any debt, or ever have nice things, I felt I would have to either move very far away from San Francisco or move back home. Moving back to Chicago also meant being closer to the label that was ignoring me. Being closer to the beast meant I could tackle it. I had to do something. Chicago was looking better and better by the day. I hated the tension where I was living. I never hated Pat, and I know he never hated me. Tabby helped to drive a wedge between us and I let her. Years later, Pat and I would reconcile, and he revealed that he had been dealing with so much personal shit when we lived together. Stuff I never could have inferred, or helped with. Hindsight is a helluva drug. But in 2009, I had to get the fuck outta there and make some big changes, especially if I was gonna create even a ripple in the Nicki Minaj wave that was making women rappers relevant again.

CHAPTER 11

I, TOO, WANNA BE SUCCESSFUL

From the only Psalm One photoshoot before leaving San Francisco.
Photo credit: Maja Saphir.

I t was spring 2009. I was packing up the life I'd built in San Francisco and saying my goodbyes. I walked out of my job at Gymboree in a last-minute decision. My boss was yelling at me about the way I was blowing up balloons and something in me snapped. I'd never walked out on a job before in my life. But, balloons? *Nobody on earth will ever yell at me over some damned multicolored balloons.* It was a promise I made to myself then and there.

I gave Pat my move-out notice. I also started staying away from the crib. He and Tabby hated each other at this point, so when she visited, she would cop a hotel room. We didn't speak for years after I moved out but when we finally did, both he and I had gone through enough trauma to pinpoint how much we weren't expressing ourselves properly as roommates. Pat, if you're reading this, I still have a lot of love for you. I understand now why we clashed so hard. You're extremely fucking talented and you're sensitive about your shit. Samesies. I pray you're doing well and that your family is healthy. I hope to make music with you again someday. And even if we don't, maybe lunch at a conservatory. I always liked our walks through nature.

During my final days living in San Francisco, I had a couple of tutoring sessions left. I'd visited with the powers that be at the ACT test–prep office in the Hunter's Point neighborhood, and they told me I could do my job in Chicago. I also set up a workshop for kids with ASCAP back home. My tax return was nice, because of all those damned jobs, so I was able to come back home with a little bit of money. Things were falling into place. And Drake's breakthrough mixtape was the soundtrack to my arrival back home.

Let's talk about Drake.

Aubrey Drake Graham, the Canadian rapper who was once on a teenybopper television show, was having an incredible year. His nonregional yet somehow still kinda southern-for-a-Canadian accent, combined with his commitment to melody, plus his *Degrassi* background made him a new kind of heartthrob. Drake came right on the heels of Nicki's ascension, and the one-two punch of their mixtapes—*Beam Me Up Scotty* and *So Far Gone*, respectively—made the Lil Wayne–backed duo an unstoppable force. At the same time, Wayne was reaching iconic status and could do no wrong. He lived on the charts.

Young Money, as a collective, was a way for Drake to break out. But super indie-rap nerds will remember Drake before he became a household name. He's actually quite the student of hip hop and collaborated with some of your indie-rap faves. A listen to his earlier work will also give you clues about his influences, like Phonte of Little Brother, and knowledge of the genre.

But it was the floating on the tracks between singing and rapping that did it for me. He was toeing that melody line like the most skilled ballerina. I don't care if he doesn't write all his lyrics, his HOOKS are the stuff of legend. I believe Drake writes a lot of his music, but every hitmaker has help. Some of our favorite songs have hella writers on them, so I give Drake a pass on that. He's R & B and pop and rap all rolled into one Wheelchair Jimmy.

With "Best I Ever Had" blaring out of damn near every car window I passed, I walked the streets of Wicker Park, getting reacquainted with home. Coming back to the Chi wasn't nearly as hard as leaving. My time in San Francisco was over. My work there was through. I'd learned some valuable lessons. I had a knack for music in the educational sphere, I'd gained a new hustle, and I'd realized I had to work even harder if I was gonna revitalize my rap career. Making music in San Francisco didn't exactly work out for me, but I did have a toe in the world of pre-EDM dubstep. My performances at those parties back in the Bay had strengthened my onstage skills, and for that I was grateful. For everything I'd lost in California—my relationship with Tania, a producer, contact with my label, several brain cells—I'd gained knowledge and resourcefulness.

I figured out I didn't only wanna be a boom-bap rapper. That style of hip hop is classic, but it wasn't my preferred cup of tea as an artist. I wanted to branch out more. I also realized that, even with my vices, I always needed to keep a fucking job and I couldn't just sit around daydreaming about rap all day. I found out I was a good teacher. I found out I was good with students. I found out I was lonely. And I found out I missed being in love.

Chicago was so fucking different from what it was when I'd left. It had only been about two years since I'd been gone, but it felt like thirty. If I thought shit was weird after my first years touring and coming home, this was ten times weirder. None of the new hot rappers in the city were recognizable. The heavy gentrification of Wicker Park and Humboldt Park was just beginning, and new stores were popping up where sketchiness and funk used to be—the same sketchiness and funk that had given a lot of neighborhoods their spice.

My mother was ecstatic I was home. She's a big-time worrier. But

I still didn't wanna live with her while I figured out my next move. I'm not sure how she felt about my rap career at that point, but I am sure she wanted me to have stability. She couldn't really see what my stability was like when I was living across the country. She knew I wasn't rapping as much and had no music out. She knew I had multiple jobs. I think she was probably preparing for me to get a "real" job permanently. To this day she always mentions the chemistry career I'd left to be an artist. (Not just yet, Mom.) She's not *unsupportive* by any stretch, but she don't want her baby out here starving. I get it. But I wasn't letting go just yet. I just had to find my bearings.

I hadn't released a shred of music since my RSE album in 2006 and I was getting very, very antsy. I had been recording stuff in San Francisco, but none of it was seeing the light of day. And I was kind of afraid to release any music on my own. Once a big machine releases your music, it's hard to think about releasing anything without its backing. It feels like moving backwards. But I had to do something. Myspace was over, Facebook was beginning its reign, and Twitter was the new girl on the block. Social media is a funny bitch, and I soon became stuck between it and a website called WorldStarHipHop, which, during its heyday, was where you could break through as an artist with videos. It was also a lowbrow place where folks went viral for fighting or arguing over stupid rap beefs. But it gave a lot of artists a ton of visibility.

I mailed home some weed and shrooms, so in the first few weeks of being home, Tabby and I spent time in her loft giggling and plotting. Weed and shrooms definitely help me think more expansive thoughts about my art, but I know now they ain't necessary. Then, I felt it helped more than it did. Tabby and I essentially had had a long-distance relationship the several months we'd been talking, but now we could see each other every day if we wanted. It was a bit of a shock, but my life has been a series of shocks. Fuck it, right?

Tabby was weird. Like, weird as hell, and I was ignoring all the red flags in order to be around her. I didn't know until I came home

that she was ACTUALLY MARRIED—and had been for a few
years. She claimed it wasn't a big deal, and I reluctantly met her hus-
band the night I arrived back in Chicago. This man actually picked
me up from the fucking airport and—get this—this motherfucker
KNEW I WAS PSALM ONE. HE WAS A FAN. What in the actual
fuck? I was literally living with and fucking his wife and he was picking me up from the airport. This was too hot for TV.

Tabby's loft at the Flat Iron Building in Wicker Park was just
that—a loft. Artists lived there, but it wasn't a regular apartment
building. There was one bathroom on the floor for everyone and no
showers unless you built one in your loft. She didn't have one. There
was also no kitchen, so unless you wanted takeout all the time, you
had to make do with raw foods, sundries, and shit that you could
stick in a dorm-sized refrigerator. It was like an indoor camping trip,
and it was so trippy and different. My dumb ass fell right in.

I felt creative in this quirky-ass space, and the creativity was
encouraged. MP, the producer who'd hit me up while I was still in
California, made good on his promise to send me beats and give me
studio time. He never hoarded our tracks and was super cool about
anything I wanted to do. I collected my masters when songs were finished and we began a friendship. Another friend of mine gave me an
epic pep talk about using social media to release my own music. At
the time, this was a new concept. The old ways were quickly falling
away. I needed to learn some new shit. I needed to adapt.

I was scared about putting out music without Rhymesayers, but
they were ignoring the shit out of me. I wasn't about to be a shelved
statistic. I had to let Psalm One fans know I was still around and still
making music. The rap game was moving faster and faster, and I really
didn't wanna get left behind. I made a few phone calls and reconnected
with my old crew chief, Pugslee Atomz, as well as some artists who
were doing self-releases. I started figuring out a plan to make my rein-
troduction to music, but on my terms. I was scared as shit. But Tabby
was very instrumental in helping me strategize during this time.

While I was working on new stuff, I started scheduling my comeback to education. Proctoring in Chicago wasn't as lucrative as in San Francisco, and the commute was even more brutal. Chicago is so much bigger than San Francisco. And the competition in the job meant I didn't get a schedule I could work with, so I didn't work with ACT prep much. And they didn't even offer private tutoring to students in Chicago. So, my most lucrative endeavor in San Francisco did not actually carry over back home, which was a bummer.

After being back for a few months, though, I was able to secure a paying rap gig as well as my ASCAP workshop, so I had a little bit of work lined up. The paying gig, as unusual as it was, gave me a connection that, to this day, has proven to be invaluable to my career.

Rhymefest, the legendary Chicago rapper, was running for alderman and asked me to play at one of his campaign shows. This was to happen in the fall of 2010. The audience was filled with local power players, and one of them, Mike Simons of the Intonation Music Workshop, was impressed with my performance. I shit you not: Mike asked me right after I got off stage if I'd ever worked with kids and if I'd be interested in starting a hip hop after-school program with him.

God really works in crazy ways. I was gonna go from working at an after-school program to creating and running one myself. We both agreed it would take some time but we were both committed to making it happen. I'm getting a little bit ahead of myself now, so let's rewind a bit.

Tabby had previously suggested I enter a contest run by the Chicago Public Library. It was called Not What You Think, and they were giving the local artist with the best ode to Chicago an outdoor show in a popular downtown venue. She thought it'd be the perfect opportunity to reintroduce myself to the city, and if I won, I'd get a free show at Pritzker Park.

The contest sounded simple enough: Write a song about your relationship to Chicago and shoot an accompanying video. Tabby had a shitty camcorder and a memory card, so we knew we'd be able to shoot the video. But I needed a beat. Randomly, a fan of my work named Ethan sent a beat to my email with the hope that I'd want to use it for something. It was a wall of sound: big drums like a marching band and something I hadn't rapped over before. It reminded me of the "bucket boys" on the South Side, who used makeshift drums to entertain, hustle, and put some food in their bellies. Coming home and commuting to the South Side to do my rare proctoring put me face-to-face with bucket boys all the time.

"Purple line, green line, blue line, red/speed through the city where I rest my head . . . "

The lyrics were clicking, the beat was fitting, and after recording it I felt like I had a contest winner on my hands. Besides my early battles I wasn't too big on rap contests, but the Chicago Public Library thing was different. Winning with them and collaborating on a show meant really good exposure. I'd get some marketing dollars behind my name and a chance to get a bigger show at home. It wasn't exactly easy to come home after a few years and just insert myself back into the scene, especially without label backing. Things were much different than when I'd left. I had to think outside the box.

We had the song, but the video was another obstacle entirely. At this point I still never had a music video associated with Psalm One, so technically this would be my first. I didn't have a budget, so I just took Tabby's camera and shot it myself. This was the same commitment to learning new technology that I had back in San Francisco with GarageBand. If there's no other way, do it yourself.

Having a song centered on Chicago transit and the bucket boys gave me an easy backdrop. I charged the camera and hopped from the blue line to the red line one crisp morning to shoot the footage. I would get a backdrop of the city, our famous transit system, and, of course, some bucket-drumming stuff. It took me a few hours, and when I got back to Tabby's loft, I realized I had no idea how to get the footage off the camera onto a screen. Technology was helping me but failing me.

I put out an APB for some assistance and ended up at the Apple Store, using iMovie and a SIM-card adapter to make some sense of the footage. I wasn't actually in any of the clips—I'd shot it—so it was all B-roll. I was hoping this would be enough for the contest. I knew the song was dope enough to win, but the video was iffy. After submitting the media, we waited about a week to find out who the semifinalists were.

When I finally got an email from the library, it instructed me to log on to their special website to find out the results. They were being so dramatic. I feverishly logged on and scrolled down the dozens of semifinalists and stopped on . . . PSALM ONE. Fuck yeah. I was in there. I was super nervous about being considered, but being a semifinalist gave me a real boost of confidence. And because we were both petty, Tabby and I decided to look at all the semifinalists and judge them harshly. I mean, size up the competition.

We took a few hours and looked through all the bands that were still in it. Tabby and I would yell out "trash" when we didn't like the entry and look at each other worryingly when an entry was good. To our delight, we were mostly yelling out "trash," but there was one entry that was truly concerning: a young man named Chancelor, a senior in high school.

His entry was just a video of him walking around Chicago, but the song almost brought a tear to my eye. It was a beautiful coming-of-age ditty about how all his friends were leaving town to go to college and he felt like he was losing a part of himself. He completely encapsulated what it felt to be in that weird vortex between being a kid and an adult, a little cocky and a little scared. The whole world in front of you. A whole world behind you. But no real plan, yet. Of all the entries, this was the one I was most afraid of.

After another week or so, the finalists were announced. Chancelor and I were neck and neck, with a few other entries hanging around, too. I had a feeling I might lose to a kid much younger than me, and I was prepared to take my loss like an adult, but I won.

What a fucking relief. I felt I had been taking music losses for the last couple of years, so to come home and win a contest on an entry based on my love for the city was an amazing feeling. It meant I'd get my name in the paper a few times, I'd get a lot of love from the Chicago Public Library, and I'd get a show in a cool outdoor downtown venue.

Well, it was cold as shit and rainy on the day of the show. My producer, MP, had also expressed interest in DJing for me, so I hired him. I was afraid no one was gonna come to the show because of the shitty weather, but there were way more people there than I'd expected. Even more surprising, Chancelor, the runner-up, showed up to the gig to congratulate me. To be honest, I'd never seen such good sportsmanship in rap before. Usually, rappers take losses like a baby reacts to having their pacifier removed. We cry and complain and even scream about it. Chancelor and his friend Patrick both came up to me after my set and told me they liked my stuff. Patrick was a little older and knew me from my last album. Chancelor had just found out about me through the contest but let me know that if he was gonna lose to anybody, he was happy it was me.

Fast-forward to today and Chancelor, aka Chance The Rapper, is one of the biggest rappers on the planet. We've shared the stage a couple times since that contest, and right before he began taking rap seriously, he saw me play a legendary set opening for Wu-Tang at the Congress Theater. To this day the only thing I can ever brag to him about is winning this contest. Sometimes we bump into each other and joke about it. I remember telling him to keep it up and that he was gonna go far with music. But, holy shit, I had no idea. I was right to be scared of that kid back then. He changed the game, and a few years after that contest he ushered in a whole-new era of Chicago rap. Grammys and all that. Congrats to that man. What a success story.

Psalm One and Chance The Rapper at the SXSW Festival, Austin, Texas,
circa 2014. Photo credit: Chicago Mixtape founder Eddie Seslowsky.

Winning the library contest gave me the confidence I needed to
continue working on music. Tabby and I had also started throwing
little hip hop concerts in her loft to preview new music. We both figured if I started making my presence known more and more in the
city, the label couldn't ignore me and we could start figuring out my
next album. We were also in an artist community. Putting on shows
was a no-brainer.

I'd put out two loosies, songs that didn't belong anywhere, and they
were getting some local love. I needed more exposure, though. I needed
more everything. In a few months I had compiled enough songs for an

EP. I was still very scared to release a whole project even though we were firmly in the blog era. Rappers were scoring big with unofficial albums and were able to tour off them. I didn't wanna make another mixtape, so I decided to start a series called *Woman at Work Volume 1*. A friend convinced me to stop being a pussy and put music on a website called Bandcamp. It was like iTunes but without all the hassle. You could sell your music directly to fans. You could even put music out for free.

At this time, you couldn't easily upload your music to the major streaming services. So Bandcamp seemed like a great solution. Fans could pay what they wanted, a flat fee or nothing. You could give away music and track the downloads. You could upload the music yourself and dictate the rights of usage. And you'd get paid directly, should anyone pay for your art. You'd also get the majority of your revenue, unlike iTunes. It gave artists more control. I didn't have to ask or wait. I could just upload my music and let the chips fall. So, I decided to put my first project in at least two years up for free on Bandcamp.

Tabby liked to dream big, but in retrospect, her budget wasn't competitive. But since I didn't have any budget at all, hers was better than nothing. A huge perk from Tabby was airplane tickets. She was willing to put me on a standby flight any-damn-where at the drop of a hat. My love for traveling has never waned, so I was always down to go. Right before I dropped *Volume 1*, we went to New York, networked with a few artists, saw a few friends, and shot a music video, the second of my career, also self-shot.

Tabby wanted me to show the world my sexy side. I'm a sexy motherfucker, but I don't really care about playing it up for the masses. But I was so smitten and ready to try things I'd never tried before, I said fuck it. We got a Manhattan hotel room with a great view and a bottle of Veuve Cliquot. I stripped down to my undies and shot a black-and-white video for a song called "Better Than My Last."

You can find it on YouTube. It's an odd clip but one where you can see me pretend to make a beat, take a shower, get drunk, and expose every bit of glorious thigh meat, all for hip hop fans. It wasn't exactly my visual magnum opus, but it got people talking. Fans hadn't seen me in forever, let alone IN my own music video, and here my ass was half-naked in a hotel room tryna act sexy. Oh, man. It wasn't exactly a mess, so offering Tabby a lot of creative control didn't backfire—this time. The video was getting mixed reviews, mostly good, but RSE hated it. They wouldn't promote it or mention it on social media, but that didn't deter me. I was hell-bent on making waves on my own and letting them come in with the surfboards later.

Twitter was, and is, my jam. Shakespeare said, "Brevity is the soul of wit," and there is something very cool to me about looking at a perfect little tweet. I decided this would be my platform of choice. With a few hashtags, like #realtalktuesday and #thingsrapperssay, merch contests of my own, and new music in tow, I started bombarding the timeline with all things Psalm One. I was getting some fast follows. People were rediscovering me through Twitter and I was getting new fans.

Throughout the entire time I was an actively signed rapper on Rhymesayers Entertainment, I'd sent hundreds of emails to the president of the label. A quick search of my inbox archives can scrounge up about three emails returned by him. It's actually quite sad if you look at the timeline of moments where I was super excited about something, only to have it downplayed, deleted, or outright ignored. With my first project after my debut commercial release, I wasn't prepared to go away so easily. Instead of going over anyone's head, I decided to level down to people in the building who would actually speak to me.

I pressed up five hundred copies of *Woman at Work Volume 1* on CD and sent the box to RSE. I coordinated with a store intern to put my free CD in the orders from web-store purchases. I also had them give away a few copies at their now-closed brick-and-mortar shop, Fifth Element. Even if it wasn't an official release, RSE fans were gonna know about my new shit, even if I had to give it away through their interns.

New website. New logo. New T-shirts. New promo photos. New music videos. New music. All these things I facilitated with the help of my new girlfriend. At this point we were claiming each other and definitely living together, but the difference this time was her interest and involvement in what I was doing. She was literally paying all the bills while I worked on music and dreamt up the next adventure. At the beginning, it was great. It's always great at the beginning.

With these new efforts I started learning what it took to make an artist pop. All the nuts and bolts and details that go into crafting a successful act. I had a tiny budget through Tabby's money so I could get little videos done and keep the music flowing through Bandcamp while I got the attention of the people and worked on my next official album.

As I settled into a new era in my career, I began to notice other artists leveling up way faster. Jay-Z said that if "you wanna be in the public, bring your budget." I could only do so much with what I had. I certainly wasn't the talk of the town anymore. I could barely recognize the new talk-of-the-town rappers, and they all seemed to come with a stylist. The fashions were the talk. The majority of the rappers I came up with in Chicago had either quit to live "normal" lives or faded into the background of the scene.

To my surprise a lot of rappers I came up with outside of Chicago were surpassing me. They were playing to bigger rooms and getting better opportunities. They were certainly selling more records. Sometimes, Rhymesayers would even have artists come through Chicago to play and I would have to *beg* to get on the show. In my own hometown. Where was the fucking love? Most times they wouldn't add me, but I'd still show up to show my face. That was getting tired and so was I, but I was relentless. Work smarter, not harder, right?

I was so grateful *Woman at Work* was getting love on the timeline. Thousands of people downloaded the project, and I was able to start getting a few shows here and there by myself. Becoming my own marketing and distribution person was giving me a great education in self-promotion. Social media was powerful and I'd just released one of

my best videos, "Woman at Work," the title track. It was really a man-
tra. It was a descriptor. The video had me in full chemist regalia, "cooking up" bars for my fans and not wasting a single minute. Science is a
recurring theme and this video is a slick interpretation of that. Shout
out to my PDX homie Rift for helping me shoot that. It still holds up.

I was finally back active. I was working on my shit. Which brings
me back to Rhymefest's friend Mike.

Mike offered me an after-school program at Rhymefest's fund-
raising show, and after I dropped *Volume 1,* he was ready to start
developing my curriculum. I wanted it to be similar to the three-day
workshops I'd done with ASCAP and America SCORES. Ideally,
I would go into Chicago public schools and do programs that were
extended and more frequent than just three days. Before we secured
funding for that, I would have to use my own resources while Mike
recruited my first students. That was fine with me.

It took months and several name changes but we decided on the
name Rhymeschool.

We piloted the first workshops at CICS Avalon, a charter school
on the South Side with a fledgling music program. Rhymeschool was
to be the hip hop–leg of Intonation Music Workshop, which Mike ran.
Intonation offered rock music and pop music classes; I was to be in
charge of hip hop. Using my California experience and desire to give
back, I dove head first into this opportunity. Hip hop was no longer
a niche market. Hip hop was way bigger than its underground roots.
Even people who didn't listen to hip hop knew what it was. And on the
South Side of Chicago, it was safe to say most kids at this point either
rapped themselves or knew someone who was trying to be a rapper.

My first Rhymeschool students were all very good at playing
instruments and they were already cocky. The school basically took
their star music students and gave them to me. I split them into two
groups because at the beginning I had Tabby with me as an assistant.
I would work with one group while Tabby supervised the other, and
vice versa. We would go in one week, work with them and plan what

our final project was gonna be, then maybe come back the next week. The pilot program was sporadic and had no funding at all, so it was spotty. We also didn't have the best communication with the school, and sometimes the schedules for the workshop would conflict with the school's regular programming. We even had a bit of musical drama with the first group of kids. Rivalries. It was like *School of Rock* but with kids that all looked like me. I loved it instantly. We knew we had something with Rhymeschool; it was definitely special and worth pursuing further.

We knew kids in underserved areas could benefit from this. I knew it was important for kids to see local rappers, WOMEN rappers, and rappers who cared about them. God knows they weren't seeing that too much on television. Rappers ain't really role models, but we *are* role models. What a confusing responsibility.

Again, the balance of working with kids and working on my own career proved to be a good thing. It balanced me. As much as I was aching for attention from my label, I was getting real attention from an endeavor that had me giving more than I received. It felt good. I was back on the musical map and I had new goals. It gave me a new purpose. Those first few months back home were sketchy, but as time went on, I began to settle into my work. This work also distracted me from the storm brewing domestically.

.

CHAPTER 12

THE UNRAVELING

Psalm One performing at the venue Subway, Koln, Germany, winter 2010.

There's always a bit of whimsy to the beginning mania of love. It's the heroin of emotions; someone's always chasing the high of chasing tail.

For me, the high was the first stages of falling into deep admiration for someone. Tabby was different because we'd started long distance, but the outcome, for better or worse, was exactly the same. Still, I couldn't see anything else at the time.

Coming back home with any kind of support system gave me an emotional boost. Tabby was into team building, specifically building teams for me. She encouraged me to explore my feminine side, something I hadn't really done before. We would discuss feminine

153

power at length. Would you believe I've been skating by on dashing cuteness this whole time? I've mentioned this already in this book, but I'm coming out of some pretty heavy low self-esteem. I've historically judged my attractiveness or sex appeal by the caliber of partners I've had. I've been with some hotties so I must look all right, right? Add in my battle with weight since I was a kid and it's a cocktail of body dysmorphia and negative self-image. Tabby helped me embrace my sexiness more, which ended up being a manipulative move on her part. Still, she was integral in helping me navigate my sexuality and appeal. She was integral to a lot of cool shit happening to me around this time. She was helping to facilitate my latest blessings.

I was doing music and cooking up rap workshops and selling some CDs as well. I was constantly getting more and more streams on Bandcamp, my favorite website to release music on. I was booking more shows. In late 2010, I toured Europe for the second time. We were making stops in Germany, France, Austria, and the Czech Republic. I even enlisted my old manager, Overflo, to DJ for me. We had since reconnected and were attempting to bury the hatchet. Though I suppose it was also kinda hard to turn down a European tour with all expenses paid.

Tabby couldn't go on the road with me because of work, but she helped me coordinate with a French promoter, Guillaume, who was a huge fan of my label and a particular fan of Psalm One. He said he'd been trying to book me through the label for years and had never gotten a response about it. What a shitty surprise.

It was absolutely heartbreaking to find out I had tours on the table that my label ignored. It always felt like they didn't want me to win. They just wanted to say they had a woman on the label so they could look progressive. Guillaume, after several failed attempts at trying to book me through the label channels, finally found me using good ole Facebook. When I realized a tour of Europe was possible, Tabby jumped in to help with logistics.

Psalm One Europe tour poster, 2010.

The Woman at Work: European Tour was a big flex and a great opportunity to reintroduce myself to audiences on another continent. We named it after the *Woman at Work* projects I'd been putting out on Bandcamp for free. I figured that was the latest music out and the tour being named the same thing would offer some cross-promotion. On one hand, the internet is the devil, but without it, I wouldn't have been able to do what I was doing. Not without a label budget. More money was coming in via downloads and small runs of merch, but it wasn't crazy money. Tabby was spending a lot, and when her loft lease didn't get renewed, she had some decisions to make. So did I.

I'd learned that Tabby had been in her loft for more than a year and had never had any problems with the slumlord powers that be. It wasn't an apartment by any stretch, but everyone knew artists lived in their lofts. Hell, there was a couple in the loft next to us having full-blown domestic issues every single fucking night until someone called the cops and the dude ended up moving out. Most of the people in that building used their workspace as lodging, so I know it wasn't that.

When I was growing up, Wicker Park wasn't pretentious. It was actually a bit dangerous. On Chicago's North Side and west of downtown, it was in gang territory and had some low-income housing. Starving artists could afford to live there, and it was these artists who made the neighborhood attractive in the first place. Little thrift stores and record shops and funky little diners were everywhere, and it was actually cool to hang there. Fast-forward to 2010 and it was becoming pretentious.

I believe it was this new heavy rap presence that got Tabby's lease canceled. Wicker Park was rapidly gentrifying. I wasn't the first hip hop in that building. I wasn't the first musician in the building doing shows, either. But when we started doing monthly hip hop shows and even more parties with hip hop DJs spinning, people started complaining. Specifically, white people started complaining. Tabby had been a quiet resident before I'd moved in. She did have a whole-ass tree in her loft, and some quirky, outdoorsy knick-knacks, an aesthetic she'd passed off as an installation. I came in with bass and niggas. It was only a matter of time before we were both outta there. I could never prove it was racially motivated or because we were claiming hip hop to be a fine art or anything, but we bought lots of cool niggas to the building. I'm pretty sure some *not-cool* niggas hated it.

My relationship with Tabby was my longest to date, but Tabby's next idea was the beginning of the end. The first couple of years were good—kinda. I was busy with new opportunities and getting my Chicago shoulders back to a good shimmy. I was coming to grips with doing damn near everything without label support, from marketing to promotion to booking. I was getting my presence and audience cracking online, and I was learning a lot about what was needed to release music. I was becoming friends with people in the Chicago industry, managers and party promoters mostly. But I still needed more money to make things happen in a way that could compete with the big boys. For instance, if I had a real PR budget and a booking agent, I could have toured more and had press in bigger publications, not just the bigger local ones.

And then, Tabby had to figure out her next home.

She wanted us to move back in with her mother.

What the entire fuck? Tabby wanted to move not only herself, but ME as well, back to her mother's crib. She said the money she'd save on rent would allow her to spend even *more* money on this music shit. I had avoided moving back home at all costs, and here I was agreeing to move into my girlfriend's mom's house in a few weeks.

When I was with Meg, we'd moved in with her folks until we had a place of our own. This was moving in with Tabby's mom with no end in sight. It was madness and I was right in the middle of it, ready to sacrifice and do whatever it took to chase my dreams. A friend of mine told me to keep my living costs low in order to make it. I wasn't exactly reinvesting the money I made, but my girlfriend was a real sponsor. She was my investor. And she was becoming more and more persuasive. I was giving up more than I knew.

One day, somebody will write the book on the hobosexual, a person who gets into relationships with free lodging, not people. So many artists deal with toxic relationships because they don't want to pay rent. It can be a petri dish of manipulation. But again, that's a book for another shelf.

RUNNING THE TOWN WITH A STOLEN WHIP

Black on black with the factory seats/
Why'd it happened to me? I ain't never stole shit/
Nah, that's a lie, but not in a good minute/
Wasn't even hood limits, it was right by the park/
Baby, not any park . . . WICKER Park . . .
—"Drive My Jeep"

One of the loosies I'd released before we got kicked out of the artist loft was a remix of "Run This Town" by Jay-Z, Rihanna, and Kanye West. A high-quality version of the instrumental was floating around the internet, and I'd downloaded it after leaving Tabby's loft and finding her Jeep Wrangler gone. Vanished. Stolen. I was on my way to the studio to record some new demos and just kept walking and walking up Milwaukee Avenue. I walked about three long blocks too far before I realized her Jeep had been jacked.

After reporting the vehicle stolen, I decided to tweet about the theft. I also went on Facebook and ranted for several paragraphs. My inboxes started blowing up with thoughts and prayers, but nothing concrete. A follower mentioned there was a Jeep-smuggling operation in the city. I looked on Google to see if that was true. It was. Apparently, thieves loved Jeep Wranglers from certain years because the doors and roofs were interchangeable. You could essentially strip a Jeep and sell the parts at a premium online or on the black market. What brilliant bullshit.

I put out an APB on my modestly popular Twitter page and got plenty of retweets (RTs). But after all that I didn't wanna sit in the loft twiddling my thumbs. I called my producer, MP, and asked if he would pick me up so I could blow off some steam in the studio. The best place for me after getting jacked was certainly a creative space. I wanted to talk about it, getting jacked for my girlfriend's Jeep. I was just getting used to driving it.

MP told me I should rap about the theft and we got the Kanye West– and No ID–produced instrumental for me to spaz on. It was perfect. The beat is kinda dark. It's kinda ominous. It also has that Bill Withers–type of drum pattern and Rihanna singing in her signature rasp. I borrowed her melody and flipped the song on its head. And instead of singing, "Who's gon' run this town tonight?" I rapped, "Who's gon' drive my Jeep tonight?"

The song was released via my then website and was quickly picked up by several local blogs. "Drive My Jeep" racked up thousands of plays and shares, and I got a lot of love on it. It was bittersweet as fuck to be rapping about my Jeep getting stolen, but the rage and loss I felt made for an emotional vocal performance. Niggas love conviction.

To our collective delight, after a few weeks, the Jeep was recovered. I don't know if the song helped, but I like to think it did. When we found it, the Jeep had been stripped clean like a lemon pepper wet on half-price-wing night. The rumor about Wrangler parts being a target had to be true. It needed new doors, a new roof, and all sorts of repairs, but it had been recovered. We ended up finding new parts on eBay, and when we went to pick them up, the guy who sold them to us nodded knowingly. It's like Jeep owners know the pain of getting their shit jacked and stripped clean. Or maybe he was one of the guys selling stolen Wrangler parts.

Either way, we got the Jeep back—only for it to be stolen AGAIN a few weeks later. There wasn't a Jay-Z song in the world I wanted to rap on after that. Fuck that. How fucking embarrassing. I'm not even gonna tell y'all about the second jacking because it's just *that* ridiculous. We only told a few close friends. No social-media reports this time. We ultimately decided to get another, less flossy, vehicle altogether.

BACK TO CHAPTER 12

After deciding to buy a sketchy-ass white van, Tabby was convinced moving back in with her mom was the right move to make. Different neighborhood, no rent, more parking. More privacy. She made a compelling case. Moving back in with my own mother wasn't exactly an option for me. But Tabby's mom didn't care if I smoked weed in the house. That was a point in her favor.

So, we moved in with Tabby's mom, but the new space came with some major complications. We were moving in with a legitimate hoarder. I didn't notice at first, but I quickly realized that no amount of straightening up or offering to clean the house was gonna make things better.

There's a television show about hoarding called *Hoarders*, and I still find it so triggering because I believe many people are living with varying levels of it. Hoarding is, by definition, a disorder in which the people who experience it have persistent difficulty getting rid of their stuff. The person always has a reason why they need to hold on to certain items, regardless of how frivolous the items are.

In Tabby's mom's case, she loved ceramic cows and toiletries. There was also tons of food in the kitchen, canned and packaged stuff that was years beyond its expiration date. As someone who loves to cook, I found this very frustrating, because even the act of cleaning up the kitchen to make meals was seen as disrespectful. It's like I had to go in, clean as little as possible, and leave the space as shitty as I'd found it. I wanted so badly to help out around the house—I was raised to clean up after myself and pull my weight when being hosted in someone else's home—but it was pretty much forbidden.

Tabby had never once mentioned that her mom was a hoarder, or that she spent countless hours blasting and singing along with Disney movies on the living room TV at full volume, or that she caulked up the windows on a twentieth-floor condominium because she was afraid spiders would come in and bite her cats. Oh, and the whole place smelled like cat piss. Yeah. Complications.

This new living arrangement was certainly claustrophobic, and borderline frightening. But getting a European tour while residing there gave me a nice break from the chaos. I soon learned that the more I stayed on the road or worked away from home, the more I could stay away from this new arrangement. Moving in certainly put a strain on our relationship. I hated being uncomfortable at the crib. Sure, Tabby's mom was nice and she was supportive of my music career. Sure, she turned a blind eye and nose to my weed smoking. Sure, when we blared rap music at ignorant volumes in the morning she never really objected. Sure, when Tabby and I argued, which was more and more frequent, she never got involved. And sure, we were living under her roof rent-free.

But it smelled like cat piss and there was cat poop all over the house. It was dusty from two cats constantly shedding and no ventilation because of the windows being caulked shut. There were mounds of old newspapers and magazines, a collection of old ceramic cows, and tons of useless electronics. This shit was a fire hazard. Who knows what the fuck we were breathing in daily? It was way too much for a smallish two-bedroom condo on the city's far North Side. With three adults, two cats, and a ton of clutter, it soon felt as if my shared bedroom was my only place of refuge. And that wasn't a lot of refuge.

Also, and this was *almost* as frustrating as the kitchen, Tabby was fucking dudes left and right. I found this out right when I came home from Europe.

Now, before I delve too deep into the infidelity pool, I'd like to acknowledge I've basically cheated on everyone I've ever been with. Give or take some forgiveness and some cybersex that really didn't "count," I've been unfaithful historically. I didn't cheat on Meg or Tania until the end, but so what? I was still cheating. I wasn't even thinking of cheating on Tabby. We had discussed and explored bringing men into our bedroom, but nothing ever materialized. Besides, she was always trying to fuck the wrong men. Industry men. Rapper men. Married men, mostly.

One time at South by Southwest (SXSW), the big annual multimedia festival in Austin, I awoke from a weed nap to find her making out with a kinda famous rap pal. It sucked. I flipped out. Then she quickly buried herself under the covers and went down on me to calm me down—or show her loyalty or something while he was on the other side of the room. This was not sexy. This was insanely uncomfortable. This was one of the more awkward sexual moments I've ever had. It was also a violation of my body that I ignored. It made me and the other rapper closer, after we'd sobered up and talked about it. He apologized to me, but how can you apologize for another person who will lie to get what she wants? You can't. I assured him we would still be friends, we were real homies after all, but my resentment of Tabby—and a familiar but sickening feeling of disrespect—was setting in.

I was open to the idea of having occasional sex with dudes to spice things up. I'd always had a sneaking suspicion that Tabby preferred men and was just fascinated with me specifically. And I knew I wanted to indulge in (safe) dick on the side, too. But the way she was going about it was bad. She'd always put me on the spot about it, or I'd "accidentally" find out she was doing some extracurricular shit. I'd wake up and find her making out with someone. Yeah, shit like that. Once she accidentally left her laptop open before leaving for work one morning and I saw an open email on her laptop explaining how she'd flown out to fuck some dude from her past when she told me she was going to visit a sick relative. I was all alone in our filthy digs for hours. I went nuclear.

Our bedroom was the only place in the condo that wasn't infiltrated with hoards of items and cat hair. I destroyed it. I wrote things like THIS IS DUMB and CHEATING-ASS BITCH in Sharpie all over the room, knocked down most of her shit, destroyed a few photos, packed a bag, and left. One of my best friends from college, Freddie, had recently moved from the suburbs to downtown Chicago, and we were hanging out a lot. He let me crash there for several days while I figured my shit out.

While all this was going on, miraculously, my career was improving. My rap workshops were starting to get a little bit of funding from Chicago Public Schools (CPS). I didn't have much contact with CPS, as I worked directly with Mike and the Intonation Music Workshop, the organization I was running my Rhymeschool program under, but once we were in CPS it became more of a big deal. We were getting great press for the work we were doing, which felt really good, and I was actually starting to get paid through the CPS funding, which was huge. I was also approached by two bigger companies to do a tour and an album dedicated to kids. At that point, I'd done successful ASCAP workshops in two different cities and was facilitating my own workshops through Intonation. Mike, the guy who'd initially brought me in, was very involved in getting continued help with securing schools and funding, so we didn't have to spend so much of our own money conducting the workshops. This was working.

Steady paychecks were something I hadn't had in a long time. With the additional funding, we were able to hire videographers to film some of our classes. We were also able to take some students to proper recording studios to cut our songs. It was very thrilling for the kids and it was fun for me. Watching them discover the joy of making music from scratch then upload and share it was game changing for a lot of them.

Our work with Intonation eventually got the attention of a lovely lady, Susan, who wanted to see if we could work on something even bigger. She wanted to bring national attention to these much-needed programs. She was thinking of recording a full Psalm One project of rap songs with kids. I immediately thought of doing a whole tour of schools. I could feed my soul, get an album actually supported, and get the fuck away from my shitty relationship.

My personal life was in shambles and the official RSE follow-up to my first album was stalled, but I was getting this DIY music out, and now I was being offered an opportunity to release a children's album and tour it. I was getting the support of a publishing company. We were gonna get national press, and we'd scheduled recording sessions all over the country with different schools. I would be traveling to do my workshops in the morning, recording with the kids, and possibly getting a Psalm One aftershow at a venue later in the evening. That was the plan.

Tabby, with all her faults, was great at logistics and was also very down to fund what I was doing. She was down to front a tour, rent a car, book a flight, whatever. It was conflicting. As much as I didn't trust her romantically, I could trust her to get this fucking work done. I was so focused on rap, I thought this was an ok exchange. Some artists will do anything and take anything just to be an artist. At that point in my life, I fit that mold.

I decided to call the album and subsequent tour *Child Support*. I was going through all these hoods and making songs with kids who were mostly experiencing poverty. My point was to always go to schools in underserved areas, because I'd grown up in one. I always wanted to give back to kids who grew up in places that desperately needed good programs for kids. Oftentimes, these programs were the kind most parents couldn't easily afford. This tour would have me flying into a city, visiting a school for two days to write songs with a group of kids, recording with them at a legendary studio for the third day, and then moving on to the next city. It was way different than a normal indie-rap tour, in that I'd be staying in cities for multiple days. It also had me flying to every city and renting a car instead of driving to each destination. It was a long tour and I was traveling alone. Tabby had work. It would get my mind off my troubles while bringing some joy to others. I wasn't binge drinking or doing drugs around this time, so there wasn't much escaping for me. I was depressed. And this adventure was just what I needed to keep me focused on what was important.

I was able to record with students in iconic studios through ASCAP contacts and through engineers volunteering their time and spaces for our project. We recorded at Patchwerk Studios in Atlanta, where Outkast and Gucci Mane and Ludacris and so many big southern artists had recorded, as well as some other famous studios. The kids weren't old enough to really be excited about stuff like recording where Nirvana or Stevie Wonder had recorded, but I was beside myself.

In every city, I was able to meet community leaders and activists. I was able to meet wonderful teachers, great educational staff, helpful musicians, and great kids. The tour took a few months to complete, which meant I was traveling a lot. I didn't care. I was doing a ton of work by myself in each city, but that was fine by me. It kept me very busy.

In some cities, I got invited to people's homes to share food and conversation. In some cities, I ended up playing a gig at a twenty-one-and-older club after hanging out with kids all day. In some cities, I would be bored out of my mind afterwards and would use social media to meet up with local fans. I met so many people on that tour that I still communicate with today. It wasn't your normal, run-of-the-mill, everybody-look-at-me-I'm-your-favorite-rapper, ego-stroking tour. It was a fucking giving-back tour. I didn't make any money on it, either. It wasn't about doing shows for a guarantee or door split. It was about making an album with kids with donated studio time. It was a labor of love.

Psalm One with students from Riley Elementary School, Milwaukee, Wisconsin.

Love was everywhere but home. I hadn't exactly forgiven Tabby, but I hadn't left, either. I couldn't prove it but I figured she was cheating on me every chance she got. The cheating wasn't even the problem for me by now. It was the lying. And because she felt comfortable lying to me, I wondered how that was trickling into our daily life. How was it invading our professional endeavors? These were questions I wouldn't know the answer to for a while. But the bills were getting paid. And even though there was no support from my label, the Child Support Tour was a complete success.

After winding down from the road, I was pleasantly surprised to learn my fucking face was gonna be on the cover of the *Chicago Reader*'s inaugural People Issue. This was to spotlight my work with kids all over the nation, and I couldn't believe it. Neither could my family. I had no management. No publicist. No team except myself and Tabby. As a rapper I couldn't have dreamt of getting better press at the time.

MC Psalm One Pitchfork festival presenter Mike Reed Bassist Andrea Jablonski Karaoke host Fred Wood

2 22 11

B SIDE
CHICAGO
READER
MUSIC

The
PEOPLE
issue

Psalm One for the Chicago Reader *People Issue, 2011.*

When I first came back home to Chicago from San Francisco, Chicago was a much different place. Neighborhoods were gentrified, rappers were unrecognizable, and there were a lot of new names that carried a lot more weight than mine. But this was, for me, monumental. The *Reader* called me in for the cover shoot, and I straightened my hair for the occasion. Tabby convinced me I needed to show them a new look and, again, more feminine energy. The resulting cover and feature story were amazing. The digital age was making it even harder to get your name in print. But here I was, in physical print, in color, and on the fucking cover. The day the issue dropped, I must have cleaned out a dozen newsstands.

This should have been one of the happiest days of my career, but something was off. Only my closest friends and family congratulated me. Any rap peers I had were completely silent. I even saw a tweet asking why I would even be deserving of the cover. Haters. My mom was over the moon, and the friends who've known me since I was a little girl were all very congratulatory. And even though Tabby helped me with my hair and my "feminine energy" and my work in general, she didn't seem as stoked about crossing these goals off the list.

I had erroneously been giving her more say-so in my business, and I was even putting her onstage more, thinking that would give her self-esteem a much-needed boost. She was always calling Rhymesayers and going to bat for me with the head honcho about not listening to the records I was sending. She was always willing to pay for a studio session or an invoice when I needed to create. She was helping me steer my own management and she was important. But was this new responsibility making her lose actual love for me? Did she even love me anymore? I don't know. I can't even call it. I just know it was different, in a bad way. I was blinded by new work and new press, and even though I didn't trust Tabby on the romantic side, I could still trust her to be down for the cause, couldn't I?

MP was a rock during this time, keeping me busy and always giving me a place to record. My bestie, Freddie, had convinced me the last time I ran away from home to give Tabby a chance and the benefit of the doubt. I was open to it and also open to opening our relationship. But we could never have a real conversation about it. There was always gaslighting. It was always me being told I was jealous and crazy.

Tabby allegedly wasn't interested in relationships with other men. It's just sometimes she liked dick. She really loved me and wanted to work it out. I kept operating as if I was ok with our arrangement. But it was too much for me to wrap my mind around. I started back smoking weed daily to escape my day-to-day life with her—and that dirty-ass condo.

The hoarding situation was getting worse by the week. Every time Tabby's mom went shopping, the place got more cluttered. And she went shopping every other day. Every time she cooked, she would somehow burn what she was making, and the place would smell like almost-expired pork chops for several days. But professionally my profile in the city was at a nice place, so I was getting more work and more inquiries from other rappers who wanted to work.

One day I ran into a now-famous rapper in Wicker Park and he asked me to hang out. I told him yeah. A few days later he texted me and said he was in my neighborhood. I'll never forget this because it was truly embarrassing: I was too ashamed of living with a hoarder to invite him up to my crib to chill. He was so sincere too, letting me know he fucked with me and he loved the work I was doing with kids and maybe we could just hang out. When I told him I couldn't, I saw the look of disappointment on his face. Why wouldn't I wanna hang out?

I was afraid he'd see how I was living and it would somehow get exposed. I don't know exactly what I was thinking would happen, but I was too scared to allow him access to the crib. I definitely regret not having the balls to let him up and letting the chips fall, but my reputation was important. This crib was an embarrassment. I didn't want anyone seeing me living in filth, even if it wasn't my filth.

After that happened, I started quietly dreaming of my departure. I was too ashamed to let people into the crib, and I wasn't allowed to clean said crib, minus my own little shared bedroom with Tabby. She'd since painted over my lovesick graffiti, but she was only slightly better than her mom with the messiness. Many behaviors are learned, I would later discover, and cleaning was a sore spot for her family. Something about rebelling against having to clean all the time as kids. Interesting. But fuck all that, I was making a little steady rap money. Maybe it was time for me to have my own space.

By the time *Child Support* was released, I had folded in my local work with Intonation. The national work with kids gave my local work with kids a lot of shine; things were really good within the program. I would meet with my supervisors at a place called Music Garage. A work friend mentioned to me that her ex-boyfriend secretly lived in his studio space because it was cheaper than an apartment. He'd pretend not to live there of course, but a small work studio to crash in plus a gym membership, in order to have a place to shower, was cheaper than getting a proper apartment. This had my mind racing with different possibilities. Maybe I could do something similar.

I didn't let on that I was planning on leaving the house. Tabby and I had a storage unit we shared, so I would go there and gather all the things I would need for my own space. Then I would shop for little storage items and put them back in the unit, so when it was time to move, I had everything in one place. If Tabby found my stuff at home, she would surely have had a ton of questions. This had to be a smart and delicately timed operation.

On a much brighter note, I'd managed to get some live musicians to be in my band. Through my work at Intonation, I'd met tons of musicians, and a few were fans. I met a drummer who told me he had a guitar player, a bass player, and a keyboard player. He said if I ever needed backup for my shows to call him up. A band? Like, a whole-ass band backing Psalm One? This was like Mario getting the flower or the tail that makes him fly. A band could make quite a difference in my professional standing. I was down to see what this was all about.

When you take the leap and venture into adding live musicians to your traditional hip hop show, the production value goes way up. So do the expenses. Through my drummer friend, Martin, I was given access to multiple live musicians. We had bass, guitar, drums (obviously), trumpet, saxophone, and keyboard. With me as lead vocal, Tabby as background vocal (love is blind and deaf), and MP as DJ, we quickly had a nine-piece band. I could fuck with this. They don't tell you when you're coming up that when you get a band, you get more interesting, as in mostly better, opportunities. It was a lot more work getting everyone together and on the same page, but the payoff was rad.

I named the band Sexy Decoy, a nod to the attractive distractions on the trash talk show *Maury*. A *Maury* sexy decoy would entice a guy to cheat on his significant other backstage. She would be too much to resist. The studio audience would go wild, and usually a romantic relationship was destroyed. It was like the show *Cheaters*, but without host Joey Greco. I was pulling from that playful theme to suggest me with a band would also be too hard to resist. I was right.

Our first show as a complete band was at Metro Chicago in early 2013. I hadn't played the Metro in years. I was given the headlining spot for local radio station, Vocalo's Winter Block Party, and I wanted to make a lasting impression. Nobody had ever seen me perform with a band, save being asked onstage to cameo with someone else's outfit. This time was different.

With a new band came the desire for a new look. I'd been a tomboy my whole life, and being cozy has damn near always trumped being "beautiful." But with Tabby's urging and my own willingness, I started rocking wigs and decided to wear a dress for my first band show. To add some edge, I suggested the whole band wear dresses as well. The band was mostly guys.

Surprisingly, they were very into it. My bass player, Chris, couldn't wait to try on dresses, and my guitar player, Nate, vowed to go commando for the show. Coming out on that Metro stage with a nine-piece band, all wearing dresses, instantly took me to a new level. We had that place rocking with new interpretations and arrangements of my songs. The Latin flavor of my song "Beat the Drum" was all the more accented with percussive embellishments and a fucking horn section. The live basslines were all the rage, too.

But bands are fucking hard, and expensive.

I was working with a few music students from Columbia College, a couple of music instructors from Intonation, and a few pro musicians who'd toured before. Like a drug deal, the first show was free. The musicians played pro bono to see if we meshed. When we did, I knew I'd have to break bread with them. No biggie. I just knew now we'd have to leverage the band to get bigger shows and bigger performance fees so I could finally save money and make the moves I had to make.

The biggest move was out of the condo of filth and into my own space. I pretended everything was ok with Tabby because I was tired of being gaslit, tired of fighting and negotiating for every little thing. I was tired of being ashamed of my home and tired of cleaning a never-ending mess. I was also tired of being lied to and decided with my own space I could do a little exploring of my own. That's when I decided to rent a studio space at Music Garage for around $500 a month. I could afford that. With the occasional show, sometimes for a good-ass paycheck, my workshops getting funding, and some Bandcamp money trickling in, I knew I'd be able to foot the bill. I wasn't exactly paying many other bills. Hell, Tabby was even paying my fucking phone bill. If I could afford hundreds of dollars a month on bullshit, I could certainly afford this studio.

I didn't have any music equipment, and my girlfriend was so caught up in her own world she hadn't realized what I'd done. My bandmate Martin offered up his SUV to help me move. It wasn't an apartment, yet somehow it wasn't exactly a creative space. But it was a place of refuge. I could go there, siphon a bit of Wi-Fi from other studio clients, and just BE. These days I make sure to sit the fuck down and chill the fuck out a little bit every single day. I make sure I'm quiet and receptive to the calm. But back then, when I left Tabby for the first time, sitting still was foreign. I couldn't trust the person who'd supported me the last few years and essentially took me in. Now, I was making a little bit of money and all I wanted to do was use it to get the fuck away. I was bored a lot, but I needed to get away from her and her mom. My musical life was going well, but everything else was looney tunes.

It's hard to sleep in a practice space for musicians. You're not even *supposed* to be sleeping in there, but I was curled up on a futon trying desperately to get sleep while some punk band was trying out new arrangements. Or some producer was playing a loop on repeat for hours, trying to get that groove just right. A loud mess.

Pretending you don't live in your studio is insanity. There ain't no showers, and if you take a whore bath (that term is nuts), you have to lock the bathroom door for a few quick minutes while you splash the funk off your body. My mom lived a short train ride from my studio, so I'd never get too disgusting. I would just shoot over there and take a shower when my mother was at work. I began waiting until the wee hours of the night to sneak around the studio building to find the best bathroom to occupy. I had a whole strategy. What I didn't realize was that Music Garage was hella popular. I didn't expect to bump into some of the up-and-coming rap titans in those hallowed halls.

One night it'd be Mick Jenkins. Another night, NoName. Another night, Saba. Another night, Chance. Another night, Twista. Popular niggas were recording in Music Garage left and right. And here I was, occupying the space without music equipment. I was in that space surviving and plotting my next move. I wouldn't be able to keep the secret of my new studio from Tabby for long, but while I had the place to myself, I focused on two things: a new project and getting some affection from someone new.

I took a page out of Tabby's book and started entertaining a few guys who'd shown interest. She wasn't the only person in this relationship who could go get dick whenever she wanted. And now I had a private space with a nice futon and a dorm fridge where I could keep snacks and champagne. I also had a private place where I could indulge all my vices without anyone checking in on me or strongly suggesting I was doing something wrong. I could do wrong all by my lonesome.

My friend with benefits, Jay, noticed I would only booty call him when I was mad at Tabby. He only pretended to care, because when I called, he would promptly be at my studio door with a bottle and dick to share. We would have sex and I'd send him home immediately. I would usually stay up all night writing or plotting. I was coming home less and less. My studio was also very close to my friend's downtown apartment. So I would crash over there, too. I buried myself in new beats and a nagging new idea that would not go away: a name change.

Before he was 2 Chainz, he was Titty Boy. A rapper pushing forty making a late-career name and branding adjustment was winning big? Maybe I could, too. 2 Chainz had a comeback story and I was fascinated. 2 Chainz sat pretty dormant on Ludacris's Disturbing tha Peace label, despite having ghostwritten for his boss and, while he was in the group Playaz Circle, making a classic song with Lil Wayne. The song "Duffle Bag Boy," a street anthem, peaked on the *Billboard* Top 40 in 2007, but after that, there wasn't much from him that broke into the mainstream. 2 Chainz had yet to achieve commercial success of his own. Looking at the way he rebranded himself and crafted a new sound was inspiring. I was motivated, so I began planning a rebrand of my own. Sure, the educational stuff was getting attention. We had funding for the kids. That was wonderful. Sure, I knew how to put out music without my label and book my own shows. Sure, I had started a band and we were beginning to get the opportunities rappers without bands weren't getting. But I wanted something more to happen as I saw the months and the trends going by faster and faster. I wanted a clean slate.

The slate belonged to Kizzie. Hologram Kizzie.

Hologram Kizzie is the loving wife of Hologram 2pac and a blending of the eras of Psalm One. My first rap name was Kizzie Tangents. This new name was a nod to the past and a look forward to the concept of an increasingly digital reality. I wanted Kizzie to have dark humor and be weirdly sexy but still sit firmly in the world of hip hop.

I made an EP with Compound 7, a production team run by A-Plus, of Hieroglyphics fame, and Aagee, both from the Bay Area. A-Plus, most notably, is one-fourth of the iconic rap group Souls of Mischief. Souls' song "'93 'til Infinity" is one of the best rap songs ever made. This is a fact not to be debated. The beats Compound 7 sent me complemented my time out there in San Francisco, yet were perfect for my current musical sentiments. I was musically more polished since having lived in California. When A-Plus sent me the pack of beats, I was inspired to challenge myself. I immediately started to write to the beats in order. I'm a sucker for technicality. I remember getting the files in the middle of the night and instantly picking them apart. It was electronic and dance and hip hop and R & B and funky and full of synths and personality. It was a bit of a left turn from all the music I was making, and it challenged me to explore a different attitude on the mic. It was also stuff I felt could be translated into live arrangements for Sexy Decoy.

If my label didn't wanna put it out, fine. I had another angle. My new moniker gave me the opportunity to put out music with who-ever I wanted. I'd been back in the Chi for a nice chunk of time, so I'd been rubbing elbows with the whole industry. I was doing medi-um-sized shows and had favor in the scene, but I wanted to work with other artists and be even more social. I also had this flighty dream of making my own crew, but that was short-lived.

I was starting to connect with a guy who was a longtime Psalm One fan and was coming up behind the scenes. He was looking to expand his roster for his fledgling label and was courting me pretty hard. At the time, courting me was pretty easy if you loved music and weed.

My new behind-the-scenes friend, John, was all things mari-juana and wellness and good vibes. I was digging him, and he was definitely interested in working with me. I had trepidation because I didn't wanna just change my name and jump into bed with another label. I was taking it slow. I was letting John host me and fill me with herbaceous treats.

He also flaunted his substantial bank account in a way that was slightly obnoxious, but nothing too cocky. He was still pretty classy with it and not too flamboyant in his everyday appearance. He was low-key and smart and hardworking. I'd also seen him working with another local artist, and whatever they were doing also seemed to be working.

My EP with Compound 7, *Free Hugs*, marked the beginning of my rebrand as Hologram Kizzie. The EP is filled with samples, so OBVIOUSLY it was for promotional purposes only. But whatever the case, it was a turn of the page in my career and the restart I des-perately needed. Kizzie was the more fun, explorative, and rambunctious sidepiece to the Psalm One main event. I even donned a new look: a shockingly white, extremely long wig and either work suits or jail uniforms. I wanted to streamline my presentation and stand out easily. If I know one thing, I know this: Long white wigs are a conversation starter. You'll catch people's attention with that on your head. I was building a character, but it was still all me.

John loved the concept and wanted to help however he could. At first, I told him there was really nothing we could do but collaborate on shows. I did a bunch of shows with John's artist and eventually took that artist on one of his first tours. We were forging a friendship and hanging out a lot. I brought even more credibility to John's operation and I knew that. I didn't wanna lean so much on Tabby with things moving forward, so John was looking more and more attractive on a professional level.

We decided to partner on a few projects, including smoking lots of complimentary flowers. I had the promise of John's help with a few shows, a few videos, and a few merch items. We weren't exactly calling it a record deal, but if it talks like a duck, walks like a duck, and tastes really good in a burrito, it's a duck of a record deal.

My EP with Compound 7 would be our first collaboration. A video for my song "Need Love Too" was on the table. Good videos are not cheap and good graphics in general aren't something you can always ignore. That song has a Jodeci sample, so we never put it out officially. But it's one of my most loved songs. Linking with John's label came with an upgrade in overall digital branding. He had access to great graphic designers and video directors. MP was also working with John on music stuff. It seemed like a smart move.

I released *Free Hugs* on May 28, 2013, with a new look, a new label, and a fresh new logo to place on my work. It didn't cost any money to make the music or actually upload it to the internet, so that wasn't a production cost. Although things were never ideal, things were getting done. This new label was smaller than RSE, but it handled more than what I could do on my own, or with Tabby. I'd always craved good collaborators because that's how I came up. All my friends were my first label mates. Now it seemed like my life was less of that and more about auditions and star fucking and endless transactions, especially with Tabby.

A wise man, Andrew Barber, from the influential media brand Fake Shore Drive, said there are three levels to this game: music, music business, and music industry. I've always been true to the music, and I'm pretty good at handling my own business. The industry is ugly. There are things to love about it, but I don't love it. Tribe told y'all the industry was shady. Ain't shit changed.

Hologram Kizzie show, Shakopee, Minnesota, circa May 2013. Photo credit: Adam Stanzak.

CHAPTER 13

HOLOGRAMS, POLYAMORY, AND THE RAPPERCHICKS

Say, money over hoes but them hoes be making money/
And if you ain't a hoe then you might be making nothin'/
But if you pimp a hoe then you might be making millions/
And if you procreate with hoes you might be making children . . .
—**"Abe Froman"**

After achieving some different-looking success and creating one of my favorite music videos, "Need Love Too," through this new alliance, I decided to do an album with John's label.

I had a marketing plan and a vision for Hologram Kizzie's first full length. *Hug Life* was to pick up where *Free Hugs* left off. The former would be sample-free, allowing me to get licensing opportunities and not get sued for illegal sampling. Hip hop was becoming more and more corporate every day, so sampling stuff was becoming an even riskier game. For instance, in 2011, the late Mac Miller got in trouble for using a sample that had been originally cleared on a mixtape song. When he went to release the song digitally, it became a problem. The issue was worked out, but it spotlighted the changing sample game on digital platforms. iTunes don't play. Rappers and producers have to be more careful about sampling. It can break you if you don't clear your samples.

With *Hug Life* I didn't wanna have to worry about the samples my homies used. I wanted to ensure my shit would stay on streaming services. I wanted the beats to complement *Free Hugs* sonically, and I wanted the concepts to mirror each other lyrically. I was being more ambitious with this project because that's what the name change was all about: ambitious freedom.

Psalm One was so stifling because there was this expectation of more albums from Rhymesayers. More boom bap. I definitely had a role in that. I talked up a lot of music and ideas prematurely. Some got repurposed, and some got straight-up ignored. Hologram Kizzie could do what the fuck she wanted, when she wanted. Maybe.

> And tell me how you want her/
> And that she gives you everything that you need/
> You so silly/
> Then why you right here with me?
> **—"So Silly"**

I wanted to croon more and reveal more about my sexuality through the music. I wanted to embrace EDM fully on some tracks. And by 2013, EDM was really a huge thing. I had been blocked and halted from doing electronic music after RSE rejected me and Pat's project. I was scared. I was still into some of the musical elements, so I chose beats nodding towards that. This new label was on the EDM wave and was willing to exploit that world, so creatively I felt more comfortable doing it as well. I was also working with some brand-new producers and aiming higher with my features.

My marketing plan for *Hug Life* was more involved than previous projects, save the big-label release. Since then, my projects could have been categorized under *free mixtape* or *EP*. No albums. Now the playing field was different, and it looked like I was gonna get some real support from people other than myself. I knew what I could do on my own, so anything more than just me and Tabby working the album would certainly be an upgrade.

Because of this new label's size, I thought I would be a priority, so communication would be easier. John was responsive. It didn't take two weeks for a reply. Hell, *he* replied. We hung out all the time. Kickbacks, yoga sessions, dinner dates. We did all the shit people do when they're doing business together and enjoying each other's weed—er—vibes. John was quirky as hell, but he was hardworking and very passionate about the kind of music we were making. And I could see he also got off on getting things done.

If anything was off about him, unfortunately I ignored it. There seemed to be an air of mystery about him, yet we never really tried to dissect one another. Besides, we were moving full-steam ahead with my album rollout. When I first hit the scene, it was still a big deal getting on traditional radio. Then, it morphed into the blog era. Now, blogs don't break artists as much as streaming services. SoundCloud broke a lot of rappers. Today, a viral tweet or a dance on TikTok, the hottest social-media app in 2021, can break an artist. (TikTok brought us Lil Nas X. What a treasure.) As always, this social-media era is a no-man's-land. It's the wild, wild west. Anything can break you, but social media remains king these days.

My marketing plan spanned four months, with three of them being the lead-up to the album. It included a dinner party that was to double as my listening party. I'd never seen a release party that was food related. I was obsessed with the idea of feeding people a bomb-ass meal, then asking them if they liked my album. On camera. A one-listen review. I had a crazy guest list and two tiers of participants. I had priority guests, who came for a full dinner beforehand while listening to the album, then about two hours later, I brought in the rest of the group for hors d'oeuvres and drinks while the album was on repeat. I even booked a chef, a homie from high school who was down for the cause, for the occasion. It created this weird hierarchy because the dinner guests were critics, angel investors, and close friends. The latter group was superfans and some Chicago rap-industry types. It was fun to see who from the latter group questioned why they weren't in the first group.

Creating a demand and a pyramid of access was a lesson I'll always remember from planning that listening party. Even the super important and busy guests that couldn't attend replied saying they respected what I was doing. They saw it as a unique way to preview an album. Since then, I've seen a lot of dinner- and food-themed music events. I ain't sayin' I originated that shit, but I hadn't seen anyone in the city do something like that before me. It was an awesome learning experience, and it definitely helped spread the word about the album in advance. And word of mouth will always be tops when it comes to promotion.

Another thing I upgraded during the *Hug Life* campaign was my merchandising. I recruited a very good Minneapolis homie of mine, Brian, the owner of the Sexy Quality clothing brand, to design a cute-but-edgy version of a once-popular children's cartoon character. I won't be specific cuz I ain't got no time for no stupid legal shit 'round these parts. Let's just say the image is dope and it looks great on a hoodie. My merchandising, or merch game, was ok. Before this hoodie I'd had some midlevel-quality T-shirts with a few decent designs. I quickly realized on tour the better the design, the more you'll sell. All the best-looking T-shirt designs sell the fastest on tour.

I had this image, the idea for a few different colorways, and I had hustle. John fronted me the money for production costs. Hoodies are way more expensive than T-shirts. So, we started with three different colorways: black and yellow, our best seller, which we called Wu-Tang colors; blue and gray; and red and pink. I created a campaign around the hoodies, reminding people at every turn that each purchase would "hug" us. *Hug* was really an acronym for *help us grow*, and that campaign was one people really got behind. They saw the grind and the dedication to the concept. My rebrand was official, and I was not letting up. John was bankrolling a good amount of stuff, but I was wheeling and dealing. I was making his money back.

I was the one calling and getting homie prices on college-radio placements. I was the one getting the album mixed and getting videos done with multiple directors in multiple cities. This whole time my workshops were ramping up and I was extremely busy. And the days I wasn't facilitating classroom rap activities, I was meeting with John or burying myself in recording. Or I was shooting my shot with people other than Tabby.

Through the marketing and promotion of *Hug Life*, I broke down and told my draining lover about my secret studio that was also my new apartment. I was tired of sneaking back and forth. While I'm typing this, I'm realizing the reason my relationship with her was going fairly decent at the time is because I had a space I could escape to. I was generally calmer and happier because I didn't care if Tabby was fucking around. I was fucking around too, and I didn't have time to care so much about what she was doing.

But as soon as I felt comfortable enough to reveal my new place of refuge to her, she gentrified my shit. You read that right. I said *gentrified*. You know what happens when a hood gets gentrified, right? It becomes less cool and more money comes in. That's what the fuck happened to my studio. No sooner had I let her in, she was demanding a key and moving in a few things of her own. She was hinting that being in the space would be better for both of us because she, too, was tired of her mother. She never really gave me the impression that she cared for or respected her mother. But free rent will have a motherfucker acting right.

I'd had enough of that condo. Living in squalor fucking sucks. Tabby's mom wouldn't be the last gross roommate I'd have, but she really set the tone for my aversion to living with disgusting adults. The trust was gone between Tabby and me, but I was still into making it work. Damnit, everything else was working. The album rollout was moving along swimmingly. I knew I could keep trying to make things better romantically.

I was able to score a couple of really dope cameos on *Hug Life*, but the version y'all have today is not what I intended. I won't say her name, but a legendary female rapper from the '90s did a song on the album. She called me randomly one night, months after getting my number at a festival we'd both played. She asked me to send her a beat and to make it funky and different. She said she wanted to play around with some dance-music shit and make a song. I was ecstatic. But at the last minute, she sent me a $7,000 invoice for her verse. To be honest I respected her gall, but her verse wasn't even better than mine. So, you'll NEVER hear that version. That's ok with me. I was finishing up a really special album, and one rapper wasn't gonna stop my train from pulling out of the station.

We were rolling. One of the most memorable parts of the marketing plan was a trip to Haiti a few weeks before the album's release. A trip to Haiti surrounding my album release seems random, but the timing of it couldn't have been more perfect. It also fell right in with the Help Us Grow campaign. We'd be going to Haiti to work with artists who didn't have great support. I'd be conducting workshops, doing a free show, and making music with local musicians. My promoter friend Paul was compelled to establish a collective in Haiti after attending music school there and realizing he could help. His help would come through utilizing his own networks back in Chicago, then putting money back into the Haitian economy. He recruited me to work with his collective, and the trip was scheduled to happen right before my album drop. However, before I could hop on the plane and head to this beautifully complicated island, my band had to learn some new songs. We had a fucking release party to plan.

All the little nuts and bolts were in the right place, and my Help Us Grow campaign was getting recognition. I knew I had to put all of my steam into this album, these release parties, and the merch. I was learning more about the business every day, because even with more money, John didn't know much about putting out albums. Rappers are selfish by nature, and we aren't groomed to be thoughtful about the daily operation. The music business has built empires on corrupt practices, so teaching an artist about the checks and balances is rare. There was more money to be made in making things happen, then invoicing the ignorant artist. If a certain monetary value was met, the artist was usually happy.

I was still managing myself plus doing logistics for a whole-ass band. We'd done a few shows as Sexy Decoy, and my performance fees were going up, but we had to split that money between more people. Psalm One plus a band got us bigger opportunities on bigger stages, but it was getting harder for me to justify asking my band-mates to play for underwhelming money. Shockingly, these peeps were blessings from above and were simply fans of making music with me. My core bandmates really only wanted the experience; they didn't care so much about the money. Sure, if I wanted a horn section and a synth player and the extra percussionist holding me down with bongos and triangles, I'd have to cough up bigger bucks. At the very least I'd have an awesome trio of bass, guitar, and drums. At the most I'd have nine total rocking out onstage. I had options, and *Hug Life* was getting a better treatment than anything I'd done on my own.

My hoodie game became top-notch. Having those different colorways made items more exclusive. Having that cute design was clutch. To this day, people ask me if I'll repress the design in a onesie. Hug Life hoodies were a merch item that dropped quite a few years ago, but I've been able to do the design into at least three other items. When something works, it'll sell itself.

It also helped that I knew to send influencers free shit they'd actually use or wear. We didn't call them influencers then, like we do now. Same shit, though. They use their platforms to push your prod-ucts. Instagram was becoming massive around this time and I made sure I flooded the timeline with pictures of different rappers wearing my hoodies. I sent dozens out to folk who'd promise they'd take a picture, send it to me, and allow me to post it as part of the Help Us Grow campaign. It worked. They will always be one of my top-selling merch items. In fact, while editing this book, I repressed a new COVID-normal version of the hoodie, with the cartoon character donning a mask and gloves.

Rapper, friend, and supporter johndope rocking the Hug Life mask hoodie, 2020.

On the night of my release party, the Hideout was packed with people ready to help me celebrate this new chapter. Hologram Kizzie was getting her moment in the sun. Looking out into the crowd of Hug Life hoodies and well-wishers (and probably a few haters, for good measure) was a confidence boost. Things weren't perfect, but standing on that stage at my release party with my band was all I needed. I felt an overwhelming sense of pride.

Tabby had wiggled her way into the band as well. At first, her presence was useful. After my producer started DJing for other artists, Tabby became my DJ. In 2009, a woman rapper having a woman DJ was a novelty. I hadn't seen that in a long time, and I certainly hadn't seen a woman rapper with a woman DJ in the present rap-show company I was in. Nobody was doing that at the time, but folks sure started doing it after we did it. I wasn't the first, but I certainly influenced some artists to do the same thing. And Tabby was great for optics even though she was really just triggering a MIDI controller, a small box with buttons. I would preload entire instrumentals onto this piece of gear, and she would press the buttons at the appropriate time. There wasn't much DJing skill required.

After a few gigs, a fan walked up to her and said, "I love your look but, when is Psalm gonna let you rap?" Right then a monster was born. Fans should shut up more. (I kid.) In the band, Tabby was more eye candy and less useful as a vocalist. She wasn't particularly good at rapping or singing; she did this weird hybrid of both. Every now and then we'd catch lightning in a bottle and she'd do a vocal performance that sounded interesting. Love will make you do some crazy things. Plenty of artists shouldn't have been artists, but their more famous or more talented lover gave them an opportunity. A few sips of the proverbial Kool-Aid and—WHAM—now they feel like an artist, too.

For the release party, I turned Tabby's mic down. There was a huge fight about it backstage after sound check. This was new music, a new album, and a new direction, and her wobbly croon wasn't gonna cut it this time. Even though I'd put her on multiple songs on *Hug Life*, was writing her bars, and thought she'd benefit from the experience of being onstage, I didn't care. She was a dancer and had gone further than high school with that craft. She looked incredible onstage and gave my show an interesting vibe. But that was as far as I was willing to go. This access was going to her head. It was definitely getting harder and harder to deal with her artist ego. But, Satan, not tonight.

Tonight, my band had kinks to work out. I had hoodies to sell and new label heads to impress. Our first song was a little shaky. I still remember. But we quickly fell into stride and gave a sick performance. I don't remember every release party but I remember that one. There was also a genuine air of service surrounding the night. This was the album after my *Child Support* effort, and I'd just announced my trip to Haiti. A ton of my peers were playing release parties in much bigger rooms, especially the popping local artists. But not a lot of those artists could come back from a hiatus and still have fans. I know my RSE fans were looking at me to release under that label, but I was constantly being ignored. As Hologram Kizzie, I had the freedom and the budget, albeit small, to do some cool shit. Therefore, I was doing some cool shit.

We'd pressed up *Hug Life* CDs and sold several boxes of them that night. We also sold out of the hoodies we had and quickly had orders for a new batch. I had new fans and old friends at this show. It reminded me of that first show at the Hideout, where I met Tabby. I was a hot mess. Fast-forward a few years later and she's onstage with me. Still a hot mess.

That wasn't in the plan at all, but I was doing much better during the *Hug Life* campaign than at the "San Francisco is swallowing me alive, and I need to escape to Chicago via rap performance" campaign. I remember leaving that show feeling great about everything except Tabby's backstage behavior. We'd have to deal with that later. But now, the album. Now that was off to a great start.

Next was Haiti.

When I was approached to do a tour of Haiti in 2014, I had no idea what to expect. I figured it would be somewhat like the workshops I was doing already, only with a language barrier. Speaking shitty French was certainly not the same as Haitian Creole. My homie Paul spoke it. He had an apartment down there and a lot of friends. He also had access to recording equipment and talented artists. He wanted to help Haitian acts get their music into markets in the United States. He also wanted to run workshops on production and songwriting. He knew, as a white man, he had the privilege to help, so he was using his Chicago contacts to help artists down there. It was an honor, so I had to come up with a plan. I didn't wanna waste anyone's time, plus he was allowing me the opportunity to bring two people with me.

I wanted to bring someone who would help me properly document this amazing opportunity, and of course I would bring Tabby. She would have spazzed if I hadn't given her the invite. I just wanted to have people I knew would understand the heaviness and the history of Haiti. I wanted people who would help me share my craft with Haitian artists. I wanted my homies. After much deliberation I invited Shep, an incredible Black journalist, along for the trip.

I'd already revealed my crush to Shep, and Tabby knew about it. She seemed cool with it and him. Shep eventually friend-zoned me, though. He told me he understood polyamory, but he didn't wanna deal with Tabby. That was fair. She was difficult. We remained friends through the friend-zoning, and I was stoked he agreed to come with us. He was gonna write about it, do posts on his very popular website, and make sure to help us in any way he could while on the trip. I couldn't have been more excited. It was awesome. Building with artists in Haiti wasn't some regular shit.

Fun fact: The weed in Haiti was worse than expected.

Honestly, I had no idea what to expect. Paul gave us books and a couple of DVDs but how can you prepare to visit such a complex nation? After running to the plane in Chicago and a layover in Ft. Lauderdale, Florida, we slowly deboarded in Port-au-Prince and began to disrobe. It was *hot*. English wasn't being spoken, and the Black faces outnumbered the white ones by hundreds. This was different. I'd never seen so many Black faces at an airport. It was amazing.

After waiting there for what seemed like hours, Paul decided to take action and get us to our first destination: Donald's house.

After firmly negotiating with a cabbie who seemed preoccupied with smoking a menthol, Shep, Tabby, Paul, and I entered an SUV and headed out onto the insanely packed and controlled chaos that was Port-au-Prince rush-hour traffic.

It was sheer pandemonium. Near accidents every ten seconds. I couldn't tell if that was par for the course, but I couldn't help but think if we were on I-90/I-94, the shit would've been shut down. We were moving though. We took in the sights, still clearly devastated by earthquakes. Locals were carrying random goods to random buildings with fancy American-style goods promised on them. In one interesting place, a huge, gigantic mural of Sean "Diddy" Combs stood among the echoes of a previously thriving area. It seemed like everybody was standing around trying to out-hustle one another for their next opportunity. The drive itself was intoxicating and sobering at the same damn time.

We arrived at a gated residence on the edge of town and were greeted by a handsome, very young-looking man named Terry. He was welcoming and seemingly shy, showing us around this house that was clearly inhabited, but meant for us this day. While we settled in, we again noticed how hot it was getting and the numerous chickens running around. I felt at peace in this place. After a few beers and introductory conversation, we were escorted around by our new friend Donald, a crazy, boisterous musician about town. He was abrasive for about three seconds then he was all heartwarming. I liked this guy.

The first place he took us was to his girlfriend's house for a home-cooked meal. She made us rice, beans, and conch. I ate the rice and beans. I was really trying to remain vegan out in Haiti. Yeah, I was doing that vegan shit, too.

During dinner we were also able to partake in another luxury: the internet. Oh, how I wanted to immediately start posting and calling folks on my phone, but coming back to Chicago with a phone bill the size of my student loans was not the move. For the whole trip I posted wisely. Paul had a band with Donald, so we watched videos of their gigs. It was awesome music, first of all, but it also enlightened me on how much Paul had bonded with this place. He didn't carry himself like a missionary. He didn't have a white-savior complex. Paul was a musician who fell in love with a place. No more, no less.

After leaving dinner and thanking our lovely hostess, Donald took us to his friend Tifan's house. Tifan was a Haitian pop star living on many acres of property. The main house also had electricity, internet, and people everywhere. Pop-star shit. We were welcomed by her mother and uncle, and hung out there all night, talking about what brought us to Haiti.

Tifan's mother told us she also worked with youth in underserved communities, so we formed an instant bond. Her work involved providing educational services in areas where the schools were no longer standing. She revealed her hope to one day include a music curriculum. And when she does, I would love to go back and help. I expressed this to her and we exchanged info.

After a little more Haitian rum, my body started to wither and I asked if we could go back to our living quarters. Paul assured me we could and we made our way back. He let us know we had an early day ahead of us: We were going to travel for more than one and a half hours to Jacmel to begin our first studio workshop. I was excited as hell.

After many mèsis (thank-yous) and some bottled water, we hit the hay. Me and Tabby in one room, Shep in the next, and Paul outside. He was hardcore—sleeping with the chickens.

Overnight I was eaten alive by cocky mosquitoes, heard loud screaming, had crazy dreams I was in the Arctic, and welcomed every second of it. Well, I loved everything minus the mosquitoes. My flesh was tore up. Also, around five in the morning, the roosters sang. Oh lord did they sing. I'd never heard roosters like this in my life. No way you could sleep through any of that madness. They cockle-doodle-doo'd my fucking ears off.

We left around 6:15 a.m. and headed towards Jacmel. We were to check into our suite and then go to a facility called the Audio Institute for a production workshop. The drive was, again, insanity. I soon realized rush hour wasn't no damn rush hour. That traffic was the norm. Winding, narrow roads up mountains were also par for the course. Crazy public-transport vehicles, motorcycles, and pedestrians were all fighting for space. While the ride was frightening at times, I didn't really think we were gonna die. I was getting used to it. But a couple of those close encounters made me hold onto my seat a little tighter.

When we got to Jacmel, we stopped at Paul's residence to see where he lived when he stayed in Haiti. It was a three-room shack, basically. It was extremely small. He housed a friend named Deneen and her children Giovanni, who was about nine, and Fredericka, who was about sixteen, who we called Cassou. They also had a cute mutt named Bouloo. We saw how modest it was, and I understood how it could cost $1,200 a year to maintain. Paul had met Deneen while studying in Haiti. When she fell ill, she got fired from her job. Sadly, without insurance, they couldn't be sure what was wrong with her, so they got rid of her position. Brutal. Paul wanted to help her in any way he could. He truly was giving back the best way he knew how. He wasn't all flashy about it either. That was true service. I began to respect Paul even more, and I fell in love with Deneen and her family. (Rest in power, Deneen.)

After visiting Paul's Haitian family, we went to the hotel to drop off our belongings. It's crazy how quickly the opposite ends of the economic spectrum reveal themselves. We got to the suite and everyone was looking at us crazy, like we didn't belong there. I felt the Dominican stares, the white stares, and the stares of the Haitian staff, who were not too happy with our presence either. It was weird as fuck. Maybe it was the tattoos? The American accents? I don't know. I tried to befriend an old man at the bar with my terrible French. He managed a fake smile and rolled his eyes. Motherfucker.

After checking in, we went to the Audio Institute and, because we were early, we were able to sneak in some Wi-Fi time and marvel at the beautiful location. It was basically bungalows (classrooms) overlooking a sprawling cliff with views of the ocean. After a little coffee and some light snacks, I didn't mind at all that we were starting super late.

We met Joel, the instructor for the class. Joel was a white dude from Vermont who loved his hip hop. It was nice talking to him about music while waiting for students to arrive. Around eleven we started, and there were thirty students. I knew this was gonna be a fun challenge. After ice breakers and about an hour of backstory, we talked about our favorite American artists despite the language barrier. Then we decided that I was going to write and record to six beats students made on the spot.

I challenged myself to write an eight-bar verse and an eight-bar hook for each track, and lay the vocal foundation with the students adding vocals to round out the songs. I impressed the fuck outta myself. We made six songs at the session. The staff at the Institute said I was the first artist to run a fully interactive workshop and the first to perform in the still-unfinished studio. It was quite an honor.

As an added bonus, Paul's friends Paulson, Kezia, and a gang of multimedia artists came with us so we could shoot footage for a *Hug Life* music video. We shot a few scenes in the classroom, at the studio, and on the cliff and got the students in a dope scene where they all were screaming my lyrics. I just knew this video was gonna be the best ever. I was gonna get beach shots, mountain shots, and everything. As a Midwesterner, mountains still get me every time. I'm a sucker for some damn mountains.

When we got back to the hotel, there was food waiting for us. We had a free show back in Paul's hood that night so we took a nap and just chilled before the festivities. Shep and Tabby had a little argument about his contribution to one of the songs we previously recorded, so we spent the better part of the day getting everyone back to a good place. And the view from our suite was the perfect place to do it.

Paul was sending for us and was really stressed about the show. I reassured him that we'd worked so many different crowds that it was worth it to go and fulfill the mission. The show was to be held at a music school, free for all ages, so I knew people would come see us. Thank God I was right. Tabby and I performed a medley of songs and sweated our natural Black asses off, while our local artist friends performed after. It was a dope neighborhood party, and the best part was performing for little Haitian girls. Women rappers. They ain't never ever seen no shit like that up close. They thought Tabby and I were unicorns. We took a bunch of pics, and Tabby got hit on hard by an eighteen-year-old trying to convert her to Catholicism. Good times.

After the show we headed back to the telly and watched TV with Paul. We also drank a lot of rum and smoked some of that bad Haitian weed. It was a great day. It was so productive it inspired me to work even harder. Twelve songs in two and a half days. Workshops. Shows. Travel. This trip was showing me even more that we could do anything through this art.

Psalm One recording with Audio Institute students, Jacmel, Haiti, March 2014.

On our final day, on the drive from the hotel to the airport, we got to see the island waking up on a weekday. Even in the devastation, people had shit to do. People had lives to maintain and households to run. Poverty didn't mean there wasn't any work. I will never forget seeing a woman walking a small child to school, limping the whole way, as her left leg was horribly disfigured. But she had this huge smile on her face. A smile I'll never forget. Her resilience really tugged at me. I will never forget that image.

I wept the whole way home.

A trip like the one I had in Haiti is life changing. Haiti is breathtaking, and rich, and incredibly poor. When people ask me about my time there we speak about rebellion, and earthquakes, and the American Red Cross, but we almost always end up talking about what we ate.

CHAPTER 13.5

RAPPERS BE DYIN', SO I WANNA BE HEALTHY

Dead Prez is one of the most iconic rap groups, and their songs contain messages of life and prosperity for Black folks. They released an album in 2000 that featured the song "Be Healthy," and almost twenty years later I listen to it as a reminder. It's like an audio CliffsNotes to eating right.

Rappers ain't taught to eat right. Black people, traditionally, ain't taught to eat right. I grew up on fast food and soul food, and those will kill you. Hypertension, DIEabetes, etc. I believe we eat our feelings and we eat for convenience. As a kid, I ate out of boredom.

Dead Prez are Black-power-rap royalty, but not everyone's cup of tea. When I was a young adult, I was really into their seminal anthem, "Hip Hop." If someone played that song right now, I would hop out of my seat and shout along to the lyrics. Many people have that same sentiment. The song "Be Healthy" was lost on a younger me, but now it serves as a blueprint. Health is more important to me than ever before, so after a really close friend turned vegan and was a living example of the benefits of a vegan lifestyle, I decided to try it myself.

My relationship with food has ranged from healthy to reckless, and my weight reflects that. At the ripe old age of forty, I have finally come to love my body, no matter what it looks like. Some days are easier than others to love it, but these days I have a healthier overall mindset. Peace of mind helps with peace of body.

Food dictates so much. There's no realer place to see how it treats us than on the road. My early tours were a master class on Wendy's and Subway. I'm writing this piece of the book while on tour, and I just ate a banana and a CLIF Bar. Even my snack game has changed. A road trip across this nation proves slightly difficult eating vegan, but on an island, it's easier than one may think. In Haiti, it was relatively easy to eat vegan, because people couldn't afford much meat, and limited cows meant limited dairy.

I'm not exactly sure when I had a major dietary shift, but it was right before the *Hug Life* album rollout. So I wanna take the time now to discuss this lifestyle adjustment: veganism. The following is the journal of what I ate while in Haiti. I wanted to document and remember how food was treated there. Word to Dead Prez.

On the morning of February 27, we were served porridge/grits with spinach from the spinach tree at Donald's house. TASTY. Wish I'd eaten more of it. Oh, and fresh-pressed cherry juice from the cherry tree. Read that again. Fresh. Pressed. Cherry. Juice.

On the afternoon of February 27, we were served a lunch of pasta salad, boiled potatoes, string beans, carrots, and salad. The dressing for the salad was suspected to be vegan. It was all yummy, but I only ate about a teaspoon of dressing, if that. The dressing was too creamy and delicious to be vegan. I was really trying to stay vegan.

On the evening of February 27, we were served frites (fries), plantains, a cabbage slaw, and rice and beans.

On the morning of February 28, we were served mango, pineapple, papaya, and plantain-and-butter sandwiches with coffee and tea. We quickly sent out for snacks. They were weird cheesy poofs, but cheesy poofs nonetheless. They were not vegan.

On the afternoon of February 28, we were served a mashed vegetable stew with white rice and a bean gravy. Very tasty.

On the evening of February 28, we were served a pumpkin soup. It definitely didn't taste a whole lot like pumpkin, but it was delicious.

On the morning of March 1, we left at the ass-crack of dawn and ate granola bars. We were starving. We got to the Audio Institute and asked for food, and they gave us weird cheeseburgers and fries. Coffee was excellent. After the production workshop, we returned to the suite to what we thought was a hotel meal, but Deneen had actually prepared rice, beans, beet salad, cabbage, and plantains. It was so necessary and fulfilling. I think it might've been the best meal we had in Haiti. After the neighborhood show, we ate some fried root veggies and drank rum.

On the morning of March 2, we had fries and fruit. In the afternoon we ate freshly caught fish. We were served grilled fresh conch, whole fish, and rice and beans. This was too clutch, eating fish on the beach just hours after it was caught. This wasn't vegan but it was a once-in-a-lifetime type of meal. I had to. It was exquisite. In the evening, we ate another Deneen meal of rice and a veggie stew at the hotel.

On the morning of March 3, we had omelets, fruit, bread, and coffee. Tabby also had crepes. This was hotel food. Good hotel food, not great. The crew ended up eating two plates. I didn't wanna overdo it on the eggs. In the afternoon we ate lots of snacks: fruit and cheesy poofs. And rum.

On the evening of March 3, we had a porridge-like meal with bean gravy. It was modest and meant to keep us alive. After that, Deneen made some beignets. They were a little greasy, but delicious as hell. On the road, a home-cooked anything is always certainly welcome.

On the morning of March 4, we had spaghetti flavored with traces of onion and spices, topped with ketchup. This was the most modest of the meals we had, but still tasty. I tried to eat as much as possible. We were told this was the meal most locals ate daily. I understood Haiti a little more after that breakfast. Food is fascinating, a great way to learn about people and culture.

On the afternoon of March 4, we had fried chicken, fries, salad, and an individual cheese pizza from hotel room service. All of it was weird. All of it. Weird chicken (fried with no breading) and weird cheese on the pizza. Paul brought us Doritos and Hershey bars. I loved him for that. He knew that meal was trash.

On the evening of March 4, we ate cheeseburgers from the hotel restaurant. They were, again, gross and weird. Imagine breakfast-patty-flavored hockey pucks—with flavorless cheese. I needed food so I choked a little more than half of it down.

On our last morning in Haiti, March 5 (Port-au-Prince airport), we had a lot of beer and a grilled cheese panini. At the Ft. Lauderdale airport I had more drinks and a turkey sandwich. Not vegan.

Staying healthy in Haiti was possible. I did ok at it. Staying and eating healthy are possible anywhere. In addition to all the world-view-shaping thoughts I had on this trip, I was also reshaping my thoughts around food. When you attempt a vegan lifestyle, it forces you to think about your footprint in the world. There was much work to do upon returning to the United States. I was bumping Dead Prez on the plane back and ready to treat myself better, overall.

BACK TO THE REST OF CHAPTER 13

Haiti reconnected me to myself, and I got closer to Shep and Paul, but Tabby became unbearable on the trip. She was showing me she didn't mind ruining a vibe or straining a business relationship. Coming home, I wanted her to stay at her mom's house so I could be alone at the studio, but she wasn't having it. The studio was only perfect for ME. Having her move in just a few things and sleeping with her on a dorm-chic, single-person futon was not it.

I decided that since I could afford the studio on my own and Tabby was working, we could definitely afford to move into a proper space of our own. It was getting harder to pretend the studio was a working space and not a makeshift home. Tabby was embracing the unknown more and more, but I wanted stability. I started looking on Craigslist for apartments.

That website can be a scary place. Everyone's heard of the Craigslist Killer. There are a lot of weirdos on that site. I've had good luck acquiring jobs, living situations, and random furniture with only a few clicks. The trick was having someone to accompany you when you met up with someone through Craigslist. I never dated on there, but I've even had friends tag along when I went on job interviews I got through Craigslist. You can never be too careful in this ridiculous world. Niggas is crazy out here.

Naturally, when it came time to look at new apartments, Tabby insisted on tagging along. Me, being blindly loyal and romantically idiotic, agreed to it. She mentioned she'd be willing to be a proper roomie and split the rent with me, so I was game. I just wanted things to work out. I cited our living situation with her mom as one of the major reasons we were beefing. I really fucking hated being there. Her mom, in my opinion, is in need of some grand therapy and an opportunity to clean house mentally. I can't stand a lot of mess and living in a hoard was torture. Maybe that makes me anal. So be it. I couldn't move out fast enough.

The first apartment we looked at was in Bridgeport and was sketchy as hell. It was cozy, but the actual façade of the building and the surrounding block gave me the heebie-jeebies. I always watch my back wherever I go, but I didn't wanna be spooked all the time walking in and out of my crib. Besides, Chicago's Bridgeport neighborhood is notoriously racist against Blacks. The Chicago uprisings of 2020 reminded everyone of that. Times were changing but they weren't changing fast enough for me in Bridgeport. We kept looking.

The next crib we looked at was in the Ukrainian Village. Hell, the Village wasn't much better, but they were changing a lot in that neighborhood. In the past, renters who weren't specifically Ukrainian were frowned upon. They were lightening up on that. The neighborhood still had grocery stores, bars, and miscellaneous shops dedicated to Ukrainian customers. I was digging the diversity of it. There were a lot of artists and hipsters moving into that neighborhood, and the crib we looked at was on top of a private men's club. It was a bar for members only and the landlord was cool as fuck. He was this meatball of an older Ukrainian man who smoked weed and needed tenants who understood him and his pals would be loud most days of the week. They liked to party at that club. Our potential roommate was Luc, a white guy who worked as hard as he played, loved hip hop, and liked to keep a tidy crib. To me, it was the perfect spot.

Having two people moving in meant I had to be savvy as fuck with my opening email, because who the fuck wants to move in with an artist couple?

Furthermore, who the fuck wants to move in with a lesbian artist couple? NO, THANK YOU. As you can imagine, this correspondence had to be inviting. Instead of using my real, full government name, I put C as my signature, and I mentioned my girlfriend and I were touring musicians, so it would mean we weren't even gonna be home a lot. Shows were steady again, especially with the band, so that was true. I made no mention of being Black, bisexual, or a woman. I kept everything very concise and gender-free. As a result, when Luc opened the door to me and Tabby, he was taken aback. He was even more incredulous when he realized he was showing an apartment to Psalm One. He was a fucking fan. He was very excited.

We even had a discussion before we left the apartment showing regarding the vagueness around my identity in the email correspondence. Luc was pretty transparent in saying that as a white guy he'd just assumed by the tone of it I was a white guy dating a white chick and we were both touring artists. He'd only gotten the part about us being touring artists correct.

He even admitted that if he'd known we were a Black lesbian couple he may have been more, dare we say, prejudiced in showing us the apartment. He said when he opened the door he was shocked as fuck but decided to be open to showing us the place without any preconceived notions about the type of people we were. That was an important conversation. Luc could have activated racism right then and there but he didn't. He even mentioned the reality of what a lot of white people do, especially in real estate and choosing living partners. Shit's crazy. His candor made me like the place even more. The convo was bittersweet, but it was real. I respected it.

Thanks, Luc, for not activating your latent racism and homophobia. You're the shit.

After that, there was no need for Tabby and me to look at another apartment, but we did anyway. This one was in Bronzeville. It was cool and the neighborhood was more diverse, but it did not compare to the club spot with Luc. There, we'd again have ample parking, a true Chicago luxury. It was conveniently located, it had laundry in the building, and we had use of a second bedroom. We'd use the second room for merch and an office. It was a no-brainer.

I made the decision to be the only one on the lease because I wanted the responsibility—and the ability to kick Tabby's ass out, should I have needed to. I knew we could afford it as long as Tabby was working and I was doing shows and the occasional workshop. We were legitimately busy again, and I was ecstatic to be having steady income, not to mention the little bit of weed dealing I was doing on the side. (You didn't read that, and the laws have changed. Plus, that was eons ago.) Regardless of the hustle, we were able to afford new digs. So, I signed the lease and we planned to move in immediately.

Once we moved in, Tabby became even less interested in doing a good job at her place of employment. After several weeks of lengthy emails and incident reports, in addition to a nasty coup by the employees she managed, she was terminated. She spun the story of how she was fired so much, I never knew what was actually true. All I know is she filed a complaint, but the employees she managed filed more. She was given a paltry severance package. This happened right before SXSW, the big music festival in Austin we attended regularly. Since she'd gotten fired, she didn't have to worry about taking the time off from work to fly down there and do showcases. Schedule was wild open. Fuck it. Life change.

All of a sudden, we were both full-time musicians. To be honest, Tabby was never much of a musician, but she was great at business. It was time to put up or shut up. She estimated she had about $15,000 in personal savings and she could live off that until she figured out her next move. In the meantime, she'd travel with me without the pressures of a corporate job. She was all in. I was actually happy and hopeful about our overall relationship. Since moving in with Luc, we were fighting a lot less and doing music a lot more. For the first time in a long time, our relationship was doing well.

We went to SXSW with the band and our new friend Eddie from an initiative called Chicago Mixtape. We went down there and acted a fucking fool. It was glorious. I can vaguely remember eating shrooms and tripping for half of my performances. Only one of them was a disaster. I learned a valuable lesson on that trip about psychedelics, but I also learned I had a killer band that was willing to travel, and we were capturing something really special onstage. It was encouraging.

Coming back to Chicago from SXSW, we had very good morale. We were buzzing. We were so enthralled by the experience, we weren't even ready for the extra whammy of Tabby getting audited by the gawddamn IRS. Talk about a curveball. Apparently, she'd filed some questionable tax returns, and they ended up taking the lion's share of her personal savings. *Now* was the time to become concerned about money. We hadn't been in our new apartment six months, and I was already worrying about money again. Tabby's steady income and that big chunk of time at her mom's house had allowed some wiggle room, with extra funds to play with. Now, playtime was over. It was time for me to get on my hustle even more. Tabby had no idea what she was gonna do.

Fortunately, around that time I was approached in New York by an indie legend to go on a two-person tour. It would be him and me in his vehicle with our gear and merch only. It would be a minimalist outing, engineered to streamline expenses. The plan was to hit the road, traverse the nation, and just fucking grind it out. It sounded kind of crazy.

I was putting off responding to his offer until Tabby became a broke rapper in a matter of weeks. I wasn't exactly in a position to decline touring opportunities, and I decided to find out more. When I called Lou to tell him I was thinking about hitting the road with him, he was ecstatic. He'd grown tired of touring with loud-mouth, overbearing, pussy-drunk rappers with diva complexes, or at least that's how he worded it. He also didn't understand why my original label wasn't putting me on the road more. He wanted to be the change he wanted to see in the world. It's still cool that my reputation pulled strings like that— people feeling the same way I did and figuring out ways to collaborate without all the fucking red tape or ways to operate while being ignored.

Lou had small-room contacts all over the world, and he set out to book us between three weeks to a month of steady shows with not many days off. He wanted to grind super hard and hit as many places as possible, as quickly as possible. He knew his car and his own desire to tour like that was quickly waning. He really didn't wanna be touring without a machine behind him either, but if he didn't hit the road some way, somehow, he'd lose his fans. He had been a big deal before the internet, and his fans were accustomed to seeing him onstage at least once a year. In order to see fans all over the world once a year, you have to grind your dick off. Lou had dick to spare, but he was very tired. However, he'd never toured with a woman rapper. He'd also never toured with a queer rapper. He was down for the experience of it all. As much as I wanted to find reasons not to go, I needed the work. We needed the money. I needed to sell merch and make sure this spanking-new rent was getting paid every month.

Tabby was furious with Lou because he explicitly said she couldn't go on tour with us. I found it funny, but Tabby did not. Lou just wanted two people in the vehicle. It was a space issue. She took it personally and decided she didn't like him. Just like that. She was getting meaner— deciding she didn't like people if they didn't give her the "right" attention. I think she was forgetting she wasn't Psalm One and therefore didn't warrant or invite the same attention.

Lou was on his fourth tour of the year, and it wasn't even summer. I was also in the beginning stages of planning another European tour, but I had to do this tour with Lou first. One at a time. I was trusting him with the routing and the booking, and he was trusting me to drive a little, sell tickets, and bring an amazing show. As much as Tabby hated she couldn't go, I was loving it. I wouldn't have to see her face for about a month, and I wouldn't even wonder what she was doing, because I'd be doing the thing I love.

Lou and I were hitting the Midwest and West Coast. It was DIY as fuck. We were DJing for ourselves and selling our own merch. We were also staying with friends as opposed to hotels. Between Lou and me, we both had crash pads for the majority of the tour. A successful indie tour is a puzzle that I still love putting together. Lou, not so much. I'll never forget when he picked me up from the airport for our second show. I'd flown home right quick after the first show for some weird reason, then flew back and met him for the second. I came out of the terminal from baggage claim and hopped in his small SUV. He was blasting surf music.

"Cristalle. Can I call you Cristalle? I'd prefer to call you by your government name. Is that ok?"

"Yeah, sure thing, Lou."

"Cristalle, this is gonna be my last tour. I'm done with this shit. I'm over it."

"Wait, what?"

"Yeah, man. I can't tour like this anymore. I'm burnt. This is gonna be my last run, and I couldn't think of anyone better I wanted to end this era with. Don't worry though. This is gonna be fun as fuck because it's over."

Well, that was a downer for me, having my touring mate instantly admit to me all the shit he hates about the very thing we were doing. I sat silent for a long time and didn't know what to say, but he quickly gathered me.

"This ain't gonna be a sad tour, Cristalle. I'm just an old man. Consider this me passing the torch. I feel like your career is gonna have a very different path than mine, but since we are intersecting right now, I'm gonna teach you everything I know. We're gonna have a lot of fun, and it won't be homophobic like your normal tours!"

"No homo? Well, shit. Let's rage then!"

"Affirmative."

I consider myself pretty lucky and hyper talented. And modest, of course. No, I do not have a huge fanbase. But I've been a critically acclaimed artist with the absolute best supporters since the very start. I can go to different places in the world and people know my music. My show is dope. When I make a fan, it's usually for the long haul. For that I will forever be grateful.

One amazing night on tour was in Ft. Collins, Colorado. I'd sold a ton of merch and we'd made good money on the door, which showed me another booking strategy. If you know you can sell tickets and you have fans in a city, you can afford to accept a door split. This tour was majority door splits.

A Colorado kid walked up to me and told me that he and his friends were going on tour that week, too. Then he proceeded to ask me if I had any tips. Tips?

Um. Ok. Quick lesson. Five touring tips for newbies. Maybe you might wanna know this too, reader? Pay attention.

- Don't overestimate your draw, especially if you're new to this. If you don't have tons of fans, aim for SMALL venues. My prediction is: Post COVID-19 this will be increasingly hard. Buckle up.

- Pack light. Your merch should weigh more than your clothes at the start of tour, but by the end of tour, your clothes should weigh more than your merch. This means you should be selling merch. If you're not good at sales, get good at sales. If you're not good at talking to fans, *get* good at it. Until you have a lot of fans that will buy merch automatically after your show, you need someone who's personable at the merch table. And fans prefer to buy from the artist. Meet and greet.

- Laundry day is any day you can do it. If you can help it, don't walk around smelly. It's bad for business, unless you're a dude. Some dudes can smell like dumpster sauce and still be coveted. The patriarchy has weird scents.

- Map your route like someone who knows geography. Long drives and crazy routes will eat up your budget. Gas gets fucking expensive.

- And speaking of eating, eat as many vegetables as you can. And drink tons of water. Road food can be detrimental to your overall health. And dehydration can be the difference between a yell and a whisper onstage.

I have more tips, but that's all you get right now. This ain't that kinda book.

Lou was a beast at touring and a beauty at info sharing. At the end of our tour, he forwarded all his contacts and the friends we stayed with along the way to me. Truly awesome human beings. We ate green chile pizza in New Mexico, and I almost got into a bar brawl after a groupie thought Lou and I were fucking. She didn't even come to the damn show, but when she saw him hug me, she threw a beer bottle cap at me, all because she wanted Lou to shart on her. She literally said that. And for those of you who don't know what a shart is, it's a shit plus a fart. Lou heard that and was turned off, but she wanted to start with me because he was giving me attention as his tour mate. Needless to say, the whole bar saw her throw that cap at me, and subsequently Lou kept me from pummeling her. He saw me lunge at her and held me back. She promptly left. Lucky bitch. I would have dragged her.

The whole tour had charming moments like that. Lou rescued a dog that was running along the highway by backing up along I-94 and putting the cursed creature in the car with us for dozens of miles. We took it to a shelter and hoped it would survive. We went to Chick-fil-A and screamed "gay rights!" in the parking lot to confused employees. We crashed with a sex worker in Salt Lake City, and she ate chili before a client which, to this day, I'm still perplexed about. Chili before sex work? I stan.

By the time the end of tour came around, I was already blessed to be figuring out dates for the next one. I had all of Lou's contacts, and I'd sold the majority of my merch. He gave me the knowledge on how to hop on the road, in a smart way, at any time. Even though he was through with the life, I felt the need to keep going. The tools Lou gave me were priceless. Thanks, Lou.

Tour poster from Psalm One and Lou's tour, summer 2014.

On a dimmer note, I had no idea what I was coming home to. Tabby was spastic, and her Instagram timeline revealed she was making new "friends" all over town in my absence. How fitting for her to do this while I was away.

You know what they say about the mouse while the cat's out making a living?

The entire time I knew Tabby, she didn't really introduce me to any friends. She knew a lot of people, but not a lot of people claimed to be actual friends with her. I ignored this red flag. My folks kinda became her folks by default, but there were no new friends, cue the Drake song, to speak of. I'd been making bonds through music forever, so I was flush with pals. But Tabby was recruiting.

I'll never forget scrolling my timeline on the road with Lou and wondering why she was all of the sudden hanging out with some rappers much younger than her. Rappers from an entirely different, read: cool, part of the scene weren't historically attracted to Tabby, so why now? The difference was being able to host people in the apartment I was paying for, plus bragging about her partner Psalm One being on tour. Oh.

You couldn't exactly host parties in your hoarder mom's house or in a studio you weren't supposed to be sleeping in. But you could *definitely* wait for your partner to go on tour, then flex on rappers who were less fortunate. She was predatory, but we didn't really find that out until it was too late. In the meantime, she was plotting. Lou told me I should be happy Tabby was making new friends, because she needed them. The shade of it all. I agreed, but it was strange watching her operate like this while I was away on tour.

So, coming home, exhausted from this run that lasted just shy of a month, traveling thousands of miles and repositioning myself as an indie tour disciple, I didn't have much energy to deny her next move. Tabby's next move was courting the Rapperchicks.

Chicago's the Rapperchicks, as I was introduced to them, were two young ladies who were self-proclaimed hotties who loved to thirst trap and rap a little. Thirst trapping, by definition, is putting super-hot photos on Instagram, or any of the social-media apps, solely for the purpose of getting a nigga to thirst, or lust, after you. The OG Rapperchicks, Henny (RIP) and Angel Davanport, were both young, beautiful, and full of fresh energy. From my vantage point, they just wanted to party and bullshit. It seemed like Tabby wanted to be down with some young girls to increase her social capital. Being with Psalm One gave her access to a scene she never knew before, and she took full advantage. I don't know what she told those young ladies in my absence, but when I came home, they were there, with feet on the coffee table. Comfortable as fuck.

Henny and Angel started coming around more. The former, out of respect for the dead, won't be discussed at length in this book. She died tragically a few years ago, and it was a shocking blow to the local Chi community. It shined a light on what a lot of us ignore on a regular basis—shitty partners, mental-health issues, and drug abuse. She was a tortured soul. Henny was a reflection of all of us. May she also rest in power.

At first impression, Henny was a nice girl. On the other hand, Angel seemed dangerous. A powder keg. Trouble. I'd heard a rumor here or there about her. Something about promiscuity that I didn't care about one bit. People called her a slut because that was more entertaining to consider. I mean, Angel was one of the few women in the scene at the time who'd dare to wear revealing clothing. It didn't exactly win you respect, but it did make you memorable. Luckily, she could rap extremely well. Extremely.

Angel was making some moves in the scene. I'd seen her rap a couple times, and while I was aware of her talent, I wanted nothing to do with her. She was on her path, and I was on mine. But Angel took a strong liking to Tabby, and since Angel and Henny were best friends, a package deal was born. Angel brought Henny around Tabby, and Tabby brought me around. I was reluctant. I wasn't no damn party girl. Sure, I loved a good party, and I loved a good altered state, but I've always hated the club. Part of the reason drugs became more attractive to me was because it made being social bearable. After years of therapy, I realized I have both social anxiety and abandonment issues. Drugs love those. Drugs and alcohol helped me talk to people and socialize at times when I normally wouldn't be caught dead in the function in the first place. Socializing is literally part of being in the music business, or the industry. You have to schmooze, or somebody has to schmooze on your behalf. I was being advised by Tabby to be more social, to take these young ladies under my wing, and to possibly build something tangible. That was the mission.

So the four of us began hanging out at the crib even more. We'd drink and smoke and talk about rap and take pictures. Henny and Angel took tons of awesome pictures; Tabby wanted in on that action, too. As usual, I was all about the music. It wasn't long before I was trying to see where the music was. Why weren't these beautiful and talented young ladies releasing music? Little did I know, they were just trying to find their way in the scene. Shit was getting harder and harder.

Because of their youthful, partying ways, it wasn't always the easiest for them to be taken seriously. Tons of chicks would hang around the studio and never make music. Tons of chicks were party favors. But I saw something more in these ladies. And besides: My reputation was everything to me. I wasn't about to risk it on a couple of knuckleheads. If these young ladies were gonna be seen with me or be associated with me, some kind of music HAD to get done. But I couldn't force it. We had to hang out. We had to get to know one another or the music wouldn't be authentic. They already had the name, and while it was woefully descriptive, it rolled off the tongue like a charm. Rappers. Chicks. Chicks who rap. Fuck. Rapperchicks.

Now, before I could fully commit to this new group, I had to figure out if they had a good performance. I swear to you, it only took ONE show for me to see this Rapperchicks thing could work out. I brought the ladies onstage with me and it was pure magic. People went absolutely nuts. I couldn't ignore the signs. This group could work.

CHAPTER 14

LOUD LIFE AND THE QUIET REGRET

I ain't know nothin' when I came off tour/
Got these pretty young things in my kitchen, eatin'/
New generation of a real fly piece of/
Chi, my divas, aye Mamacita . . .
— **"RPRCHX IZ DED"**

By mid-2014, there were new kings in rap. My old crew pal Open Mike Eagle had a great year with his amazing album *Dark Comedy*. His career was taking a steady climb upward, and it was amazing to witness. J. Cole had a big album. 2 Chainz snatched a crown. And ScHoolboy Q's album *Oxymoron* stayed in rotation in my home.

Politically, we saw the police killings of two unarmed Black men, Michael Brown in Ferguson, Missouri, and Eric Garner in New York, rock the nation. Ferguson's uprisings were televised. I watched it all on Twitter. I also watched the Black Lives Matter movement, begun in 2013 by three queer Black woman organizers, become a huge deal. Black folks were, and had always been, fed up.

At this moment in hip hop, women weren't scarce, but Nicki was still queen. Now we had Azealia Banks, the problematic but talented phenom; Iggy Azalea, the problematic white pop rapper; and Rita Ora making some waves. Iggy's song "Happy" was inescapable. Oh, and Detroit rapper Dej Loaf had made a great splash with her song "Try Me." The underground was budging a little for women. But we had something special with this new group.

The Rapperchicks' first show at Tiger O'Stylies in Berwyn, Illinois, was a madhouse, but in a good way.

I remember, early in my career, people losing their shit seeing ONE woman onstage rocking. But FOUR? Four women, all different ages, all different skin tones, all different rapping styles, creating synergy and sexual energy and knocking the dicks off everyone in the room? People went absolutely insane. Afterwards we went back to my crib. We plotted all night. We were high off the show, and probably other stuff too.

The idea: Tabby and Psalm One would join Rapperchicks and give their group some more experience and validity. Henny and Angel would bring some much-needed youthful energy to my career. I mean, I liked partying, but I loved music more. I was bad at schmoozing, but they thrived on it. We could prop each other up and go far if we all worked together. I wanted this partnership to grow and morph into something we could all benefit from. I was thinking mixtapes, tours, and building a new girl rap group. My mind was thick with possibility. But honestly, I think we all had different shit in mind.

Left to right: Psalm One, Henny (RIP), Angel, and Tabby (face blurred out for personal reasons) Chicago, summer 2014. Photo credit: Leon DaVinci, Mudwing Media,

It was like pulling teeth getting those young ladies in the studio, and I was the only one out of all of them booking shows. It seemed like the lion's share of logistics fell on me. It was a lot. Tabby was keen on helping, but the more spices you add to the broth, the more you have to pay attention to the flavors.

I was used to guiding my own career and helping Tabby do little things here and there. She'd put songs online and promptly take them down from lack of confidence. Our new young lady friends had done much more in the scene than Tabby, but they were still very new to the business side of the game. Angel had an early boost to her career with an impressive appearance on indie-rap icon Tech N9ne's song "Priorities," but she hadn't done much since. Henny was a girl about town and seemed to know everyone. I was damn near a vet. Tabby had a mind for business and could send invoices with the best of them, and her aesthetic was intriguing to almost everyone we met. Almost.

This motley crew of women spitters had a dope show and even doper pictures. Men were starting to take notice in ways they hadn't before. People were curious. People were interested. We were onto something. We just didn't know exactly what it was yet.

I am a firm believer that building a band takes months—if not years—of bonding in order for the bond to last. I'm not entirely sure about that either, as I've seen bands who grew up together and spent decades together still refuse to be dragged onto the stage with their bandmates before securing checks containing loads of commas. Niggas be hating each other and still manage to get the work done. Yeah, the Rapperchicks were bonding and it was fun. But I still needed to know more about their work ethic. I needed to know I could take them on the road and succeed. I needed to know how strong the young ladies were, individually. Little did I know how small the scene had gotten. Things were often changing. I wasn't aware of how many people followed the leader when it came to their social cues. I wasn't aware of all the groupthink.

I was never the most popular in school, but I was never uncool. In college, I got *more* popular through the music. It allowed me access to spaces a science degree or these adorable dimples alone never could. The music made me popular, for a little while, but trends come and go. The music still brings much respect, though. Don't get it twisted. My pen was propping up the reputation of the group. My music was our first validation.

Angel had released music but had also recently gone through a very bad public separation with her manager. This manager was verbally and professionally abusive, and upon Angel leaving him, he circulated a very damaging yet untrue email to the entire Chicago underground–hip hop scene. This happened very early in her career. That coupled with her risqué choices in wardrobe made her an easy target. Henny wasn't an easy target and had more respect in social circles. When she was on, she was on. She was great with people when in the mood. That was the key for her. However, she didn't have a good amount of music with good sound quality, which at this point in the scene didn't bring a whole lot of shine. And Tabby?

Right. Tabby wasn't technically an artist. My career was essentially her career. I believe Tabby felt she could create a different persona through this new endeavor. But it was all riding on my ability to create opportunities for the whole group.

I was receiving a lot of inquiries about these hot young ladies I was hanging out with. I wanted to tell folks we were working on an album, but I was working on the dynamic. I wasn't the actual leader of the group, so I had no actual say on what the group did. I was the one with the most professional music experience, so naturally, people thought it was my group. But nah, this wasn't my group. Low-key I thought I was tricked into the whole thing by my bored girlfriend. I was all for creating a dope-ass female rap group, though. I really thought we were all on the same page with that. I was super cool with hanging out and smoking and plotting and looking cute in photos and turning heads at parties. But at some point, we had to get to work. We *had* to.

While on my previous tour with Lou, I had been contemplating going on a date with someone new when I got home. Tabby kept encouraging me to do it. By this point, we were firmly into the idea of an open relationship. I figured she was just gonna keep cheating on me with dudes. She didn't seem to be into women as much as men. Yet Tabby being into Angel wasn't surprising. I mean, Angel was generally hot and most people found her really attractive. We all joked that every Rapperchick was into Angel at some point. Not me though. Angel seemed like a handful and I didn't wanna fuck with her like that. But I could not ignore Angel's voice. I couldn't ignore her ability to change the energy in a room by just entering or quiet a whole club with just a few seconds on the mic. Angel was the obligatory rap crush. I wasn't gonna get caught up in all of that.

Opening my relationship meant I could do what I wanted as well. I really didn't care about fucking other people, but I had done it a few times when I lived at Music Garage. I liked having emergency dick or Netflix-and-chill dick. This new local-rapper interest was dangerous, and he was certainly persistent. According to my internet and social-media receipts, he'd been quietly and digitally shooting his shot for several months. Being in this group and having all this dynamic female energy around gave me a new confidence as well. I ended up giving this new guy a chance. And in doing so I made a few key mistakes that helped reverse the trajectory of our group.

See, the thing about being an adult is that you don't have to tell your business to anyone. I was big on discretion—if I'm gonna fuck a rapper, I want that rapper to keep his or her mouth shut. Keep them thumbs off the fucking timeline. Keep what we do quiet. Up until this point, the couple of rappers I'd slept with were unknown. But who I fuck is my business. However, when you're in a group with three other people who all grew up in the same city, having a grasp on cross relations would have been helpful.

Well, after a couple of dates and a couple of sexual encounters, including a handful of awkward threesomes with Tabby, my fling with this new rapper had run its course. I'd found out midlust that he was also fucking with Henny, and I didn't like the idea of being connected to her in that way. She seemed to like him, even possibly love him, way more than I did. By the time I'd stopped fucking with him I thought we could just go back to being cool, but the damage was done.

To add insult to injury, Tabby caught feelings and started obsessing over the dude. I couldn't say we actually dated. He was courting *me* and I fucked up and explored him with my girlfriend. I thought that would help us bond even more. That was a monumental mistake on my part, including Tabby in every-fucking-thing. She couldn't remain discreet. She liked the attention, and it didn't matter if it was good attention. She had the protection of this new, cool rap group. She thought she was a fucking rock star.

Once I realized the mistake of not talking with Henny about dude, I wanted to rectify it. And while I maintain it's nobody's business who I fuck, fucking someone my bandmate was quietly falling in love with was *dead-ass wrong*. I stopped fucking with him altogether, but Tabby kept contacting him on the low. Henny and I had mutual respect. While she didn't like what had happened between me and her love interest, she saw me pull away and leave the mess alone. She honored that. But Tabby was in her *Mean Girls* element and was mocking Henny with her innuendos. And for that, Henny hated Tabby. She loved Angel, respected me, and hated Tabby. As that became clearer, it became harder to even think about having this tight-knit rap group.

I didn't realize how sharply the dynamic was shifting, but it was happening early and often. Local rumors started swirling around me and Tabby. Angel would defend us fervently. I always wondered why she was so loyal. I believe it was because Angel and Tabby had created a bond and she saw how hard I was working to get us legit opportunities.

I was booking shows for us and taking us to studios. I was putting them into sessions when others were just trying to get them in the studio to possibly fuck. I took the whole thing seriously from the jump and even though being in this badass band got me more attention from dudes, I didn't care about that shit. I was always there for the music. Always. It was, is, and always WILL BE the music. But since only one, or maybe two, of the four of us felt that way, it was an uphill battle.

An unlikely friendship between Angel and me formed while Tabby snuck around with rappers, and Henny tried to bond with us as much as she could. When Henny came around, I knew she wasn't fully there. When the four of us were together, we commanded attention and it was fun. It was new to me to be part of a girl gang; it was empowering. We weren't exactly talking about our issues but we sure were making an impression. We were also partying a lot. We were tripping balls and cackling and talking about everything but building a healthy group. In hindsight, we were all coping.

By now, my solo career was in a good spot and I was willing to take the time to cultivate the group. I had a good touring history I had built on my own, and I was releasing good music. In 2014, the *Chicago Reader* named me Best Rapper, runner-up, second only to Chance—what beautiful irony. I'd landed a feature in *Forbes* magazine for my work in Haiti. I'd released *Hug Life* under a pseudonym and it was selling. Merch was selling. My shows were well attended. Rent was paid ON TIME. It didn't matter so much being ignored by my main label. I was working with a new, much smaller entity, and shit was getting done. I managed to slowly keep things moving for my career and over time I was seeing a return. It felt like a could breathe a little. But the Rapperchicks couldn't continue on like we were. Something had to give.

In terms of groups, there was a new one exploding onto rap, and everyone around me was bumping their music. Rae Sremmurd was mysterious. They sounded like kids and their infectious song, "No Flex Zone," was inescapable. And the name? *Ear drummers* spelled backwards? A Mike Will cosign? Brilliant. The song's hook made us want to scream "they knooooowwwwww betttaaaaa!" And that's what we did.

By this point I was starting to warm up to Angel. I couldn't avoid her. She was coming over to my crib all the time. I wanted to be friends with Henny, but she wasn't trying to get too close. I understood. She was there for Angel. Angel was there for Tabby. Tabby was there for herself. Everyone was looking at me for the opportunities. I knew deep down Angel was also there for friendship. Chicago was a war zone of clout at this point. It was hard to pinpoint who your true friends were.

We were driving around the neighborhood one night looking for cheap champagne when "No Flex Zone" came on in the car. By this point, Tabby and I'd traded in the white van for a smaller, more manageable Chevy Spark. Angel dared me to pull over in the middle of the street and run around the car screaming the lyrics. It was one of the most idiotic things I could imagine doing at the time, and because of that I couldn't wait to drag my ass out of the car to do it. As stupid as it was, it was the bonding moment Angel and I needed. The leash was off.

We spent the rest of the night running up to people on the street, in grocery stores, and at bus stops screaming "no flex zone" and "they knooooowwwwww betttaaaaa" like madwomen. The goofiness of it all was something the other ladies weren't into, but Angel and I became sisters in the joke.

From that point on I started to like her a lot more, not to mention the way she flamed people who tried my patience. Angel was loyal, even to a fault. I was starting to understand why Henny was so protective of her and the relationship they had. But their relationship was starting to strain. We were seeing much less of Henny. Sure, we would party and bullshit and collectively mob out at functions where people would inquire where the music was or if we all fucked each other or when the next performance was. But the bond was severed. Angel felt Henny wasn't present and was uninterested in growing with the group. She was right. Tabby was negligent. Out of the blue, Henny texted me and let me know she respected me, but she really didn't fuck with Tabby at all. Angel was still into being a part of Tabby's life, and that union included growing with this rap group. But the split was clear.

I could fully understand why Henny didn't fuck with Tabby, but blind loyalty to my girlfriend wouldn't allow any supposed disrespect, especially considering all the leadership roles I was taking on within the group's dynamic. After all, I was Psalm fucking One. I didn't have to be in this group. But I wanted it to work. The longer we tried to make it work, however, the less we saw of Henny. She loved music. She loved rap. She had a great ear and amazing bars, and I was very much interested in working with her. But she was pulling back in a real way.

We couldn't see it then because of ego, but Henny was really struggling with this music shit, and she was watching the group she'd started with Angel morph into something she wasn't down with anymore. Not to mention the whole sleeping-with-the-same-dude situation. It was too much for her to deal with. So, she finally checked all the way out.

Henny tragically passed away in 2018 to the shock of our local scene. It is quite difficult for me to write these words about her, because even though we had a complicated relationship and she split from the group, I know Angel loved her dearly. Angel and Henny were best friends for a good amount of time. She and I had a mutual respect for one another. She was a great emcee and I saw that immediately. I liked her. But my proximity to Tabby never allowed us to get too close. Henny knew something I didn't, obviously. She knew Tabby was a detriment to the group and opted out. I understand it now and it's too fucking late. That haunts me.

Without Henny, we thought the Rapperchicks could still work. I know I made things more tangible for the group as a whole, but the group came from Henny and Angel. We had stupid fights about guys and studio sessions. Tabby treated Henny like shit, but I never wished Henny anything but happiness. I had no idea how much she was battling in her short life. I'm so glad I got to speak to her sometime in 2016, before she passed away. It had been years since we'd spoken. I'd reached out to apologize to her for everything that happened with the group and my role in it.

I also sincerely apologized to her for the sleeping-with-the-same-guy shit, and I apologized for not being a good leader when she was around. I will always feel blessed that we got a chance to squash our beef. That was a critical moment. We texted a bit and we were supposed to meet up for drinks soon after those texts, but she passed before we got the chance to do so. Life is too fucking short to hold on to asinine rap grudges. If you can squash your beefs, any kind of beef, I truly recommend it.

Rest in power, Henny F Baby. Respect. I hope you are finally resting, and at peace.

CHAPTER 15

THE CHICAGO-
TAKEOVER PLAN

A fter Henny left the group, another shift happened. There's this weird thing about local scenes, and in life, where some people will inject themselves into your drama. The aftermath of the split was dumb as hell. People were choosing sides.

Certain rappers weren't talking to me anymore, and other rappers were coming around me even more. Every time I looked online, people were tweeting and subtweeting us. While I hated every second of rap beef that didn't involve actual RAPPING, Tabby loved all the attention. If we weren't gonna get in the booth and destroy each other with incredible lyrics, I didn't wanna engage in stupid rumors. Fuck online bullying, let's meet in the studio. But it didn't matter what I wanted. I felt powerless.

The one thing I'd always managed at this time was a work opportunity. The chaos seemed to be ever present, but I was building up a tolerance to it. A lot of people in the scene were trying to figure out what was happening with our group, but I was preparing to embark on another European tour. Another chance to show how cool we were. This time I was taking even more people along for the adventure.

The idea was a Chicago takeover. At this point in hip hop, Chicago had finally gotten the national attention we deserved, and everyone was thirsty for this Midwest talent from the City of Big Shoulders. From huge stars like Kanye, Twista, Common, and Lupe to Chance, Chief Keef, Lil Durk, Jeremih, King L, Lucki, and more, Chicago was the place it was finally very cool to be from if you were a rapper. My promoter homie Guillaume, who'd booked my previous overseas outing, specifically wanted me to co-headline a tour of Europe with another act. I chose my homies The Hood Internet, ShowYouSuck, and Auggie the 9th as well as Tabby to accompany me. And while I couldn't bring my new group, Rapperchicks, as a whole, it was a huge opportunity to tour Europe, on the strength of my name, independently.

When cool stuff like this happens, it's hard not to rub it in the faces of assholes who subtweet you on the timeline. Many of the people choosing sides in this ridiculous rap beef hardly, if ever, traveled outside of the city for anything rap related. They definitely never rocked in other countries. It was nice to be able to post up show dates and ticket links in another fucking language while a random local rapper was tweeting things like, "I hAtE rAp cHix tHey AiN't ShIt u KnO wHo i'M tAlKin bOuT tOo."

Everything was shifting. Our time living at the club had come and gone. Our roomie Luc took a job in New York City and I decided to move us somewhere cheaper. I didn't wanna struggle to pay that full rent when I could just cut my losses. My friend Paul, who'd taken us to Haiti, had a free room in his Logan Square apartment and was willing to give it to me for even cheaper than the rent at the club. Having even *cheaper* rent would help a lot because by this point Tabby still didn't have any source of income.

She really didn't wanna get a job either. Oh, how the tables had turned. Now I was fronting all the money for our living situation, and she was "working on her career." But all she was really doing was working on her image as a sultry rapper chick and trying to impress guys who didn't want her. I found out recently that, during this time, she was still texting the same rappers who were dissing us publicly. At the time, I was too invested in making this European tour happen to pay attention to all that. Because during the planning process, Tabby managed to screw up something bigger than our personal relationship: She insulted our future tour mates.

Because of her success helping with the Child Support Tour and the first Rapperchicks shows, I told Tabby to quarterback this Europe tour. She would be in contact with Guillaume, who she'd already hit it off with at a chance meeting at SXSW. When I was on tour with Lou, I'd gotten the initial offer for Europe and the task of bringing awesome acts with me. We'd gotten a verbal yes from the artists we were thinking of bringing, but none of them had completed their paperwork for the visas required to tour abroad. We were getting nervous about getting those visas in on time, as they'd likely get us held up at somebody's border if not handled properly. Because of this, Tabby sent a group email and insulted the other camps, egotistically suggesting they were disrespecting us by not moving fast enough. She also told them they were acting unprofessional. They were so pissed with her email they temporarily pulled out of the tour, stalling the whole booking process and causing us to lose a few major shows. It was terrible.

It took about two weeks of me groveling and apologizing to the other acts, getting another person on the team to quarterback the planning, and making many promises that Tabby would not be involved in the logistics to get us back on track. That was the first time I ever had to take Tabby off a project because of her actions. Sure, I'd fired managers erroneously. Sure, I fired potential interns for making unauthorized purchases with my debit card, but I always did that *with* Tabby. Being taken off the Europe planning team embarrassed her, and I never heard the end of it. Just like Haiti, I knew she'd be harboring some resentment for our tour mates before even stepping foot on an airplane. I wasn't gonna let her personal beefs fuck up this tour, though. I refused to do that. I had stages to rock and croissants to eat, damnit. And that's what the fuck I was gonna do.

Pro tip: If you're an artist, businessperson, or team player and you have somebody on your team you constantly have to apologize for, get them off your team. *They will eventually ruin your shit. I had to learn this the hard way, so maybe someone reading this won't have to go through that.*

I was a wreck at this point and had been hitting the party drugs a little harder than usual. I figured I needed some fun because I was stressed THE fuck out. We moved out of the club and into Paul's spot, which was a lot smaller than our previous spot. We had a bedroom and an office before. At Paul's we got a smaller bedroom and use of a living room that was already packed with stuff from two other roommates. But space was something I'd need to figure out after Europe.

Original Chicago Takeover Tour flyer, some additional shows were added, fall 2014.

Psalm One in the middle of a Parisian crowd of more than thirty-five thou-sand. One of the highlights of my career. TWENTYFOURFESTIVAL, Paris, France, fall 2014. Taken by a tour mate.

We barely had time to move into the new apartment before we were on a flight to Charles de Gaulle Airport. We dumped and stuffed our shit in that house, and promised to clean and organize it when we got back home from the tour. We also asked if Angel could come and crash in our bedroom while we were gone, since we'd just paid rent with nobody in our crib to enjoy said paid rent. Tabby had, again against my desire not to open my home to anyone, asked Angel to live with us, and she agreed. I was still thinking this would help with the checks and balances of the group. I was also beginning to like Angel a lot more. She was getting through my tough exterior, so I can't say I didn't want her around. Her energy was always warm towards me and she was action oriented. If there was a problem, I knew I could count on her to at least try and help solve it. She didn't pour gas on the fire often. Tabby was a fucking fire starter.

Professionally, Europe was a success. I played my biggest crowd to date (thirty-five thousand in a Parisian dome, opening for Travis Scott and DMX) and got to take not only myself but other acts from Chicago to another continent. I felt like a boss, and logistically everything was running smoothly. Tabby didn't really speak to anyone but me and The Hood Internet on the tour because she'd insulted everyone else. But I had a good rapport with the whole crew, and I think deep down she hated that.

Psalm One selfie with Travis Scott, backstage at
TWENTYFOURFESTIVAL, Paris, France, fall 2014.

Xzibit, Psalm One, and B-Real of Cypress Hill at TWENTYFOURFESTIVAL, Paris, France, fall 2014.

Onstage was amazing. Offstage, Tabby took her frustrations out on me. I remember the very first night, in Marseille, France, she got mad at me and threw a glass of champagne on the floor in a rage. I was cleaning up shards of glass mere minutes before leaving the hotel to rock a crowd of around two thousand. The very first fucking night. I knew this tour was gonna be rough on our relationship.

Back home we were also experiencing issues at our apartment. Our new roomies hated seeing Angel crash at the pad. They kicked her out as soon as we were out of the country, and I couldn't object. I mean, she definitely wasn't on the lease, but damn, they had people crashing all the time. Why couldn't we? Rethinking all of this now, why couldn't Angel find her own place? That was a better question, but I was all about the groupthink at this point and just trying to keep the peace. I was blinded by the good things in my career and wanted things to just fall into place. Angel being around was like a buffer between myself and Tabby. I wanted her around by then. But truthfully, I was jamming square pegs in round holes everywhere.

Eventually, we were able to figure out another rooming situation for Angel. That was one less thing we had to worry about, but I knew coming back home from Europe would be rough. I was gonna have to deal with Tabby behind the scenes on tour and come home and deal with this new living situation. It made me just immerse myself in the experience even more. I swear I didn't wanna come back to the States. I just wanted to keep rocking this tour forever. My growing rift with Tabby also made me hang out with my tour mates even more. Nothing was like I'd pictured it, but I was gonna rock the shit out of every stage, every fucking night.

As expected, I came home to bullshit. I thought I was flexing on everybody because we were hopping straight off the international flight from Paris with a layover in Washington, DC, and heading straight for a show at Thalia Hall in Pilsen, which is a super dope venue. I realized how much I cared about Angel on this trip, but my mind wouldn't let me fully commit to the idea of missing her like a partner. I knew because Tabby had given me hell on tour, I was probably overhyping Angel's appeal.

Nevertheless, I came home with gifts for her: a bottle of cognac and a bottle of champagne. Each of those came with layers of bad and bougie. Real champagne is what the world needs more of, not that insane American sparkling-wine swill we all guzzle at baby showers. All I wanted to do after this homecoming show was drink and get high with Angel.

But the bullshit wasn't gonna escape this arrival. No way. My roomie, who we'd let borrow our car while we were gone, had collected an impressive number of parking tickets. Even though he promised to pay them, it was gonna have to be in chunks because life is expensive. Tabby had also been in contact with the rapper who was dissing us all the time and invited him to hang out with us before the show. That was odd as fuck and a very short hang session. She couldn't keep her hands off him and he actually wanted to talk. But Tabby smothered the fuck out of him, and he ended up leaving after an hour. He ghosted her, and as a result Tabby was crabby all night. Reuniting with Angel was even more bittersweet. She'd met us at home. As soon as we got to the crib, our reunion hug was interrupted by news we'd have to be moving out soon. What the fuck. Move out? Shit, we'd just moved in.

Chicago has a crazy way of deflating your balloon. Here I was on a high from this tour. After a rocky planning and subsequent slow start, we ended up playing for tens of thousands of people across a couple of European countries. We'd played with some big-ass names and even got to do a show at a school for underprivileged youth. It was an added gig at the last minute, but I was always down to visit a school or do a workshop. We'd had a roundtable with a translator, spent the night, eaten meals with the students, and ended with a show for the students, staff, and faculty. All this plus they had the right champagne on every rider, every night. And everybody came home with some euros in their pockets. You couldn't tell me shit. But as soon as I stepped onto Illinois soil, there was some poop in it. Parking tickets, a pseudo eviction notice, weird love interests getting secretly invited to hang out. It was a lot to handle straight out the gate.

I was stressed out.

CHAPTER 16

MANAGER OF THE ZOO

In the air with mini bottles and a semimodel/
Flyin' to the destination, I'm a scene stealer/
I know some nice Blacks and some mean niggas/
And if you act up they gon' deal withcha/
Wakin' up to . . . Angel thinkin' I'm in heaven/
Rappin' for these people they be thinkin' I'm a reverend/
I'm a scientific artist and a smarter lover/
Got your woman crush callin' and she want somethin'/
I'm good! What you wanna do now?/
Claim Englewood and you know we too wild/
Pain in my past so you know I'm too proud/
They don't care 'bout the noise, but the pack is too loud/
'Gram in the land, hologram in yo synapse/
Playin' my play with a side of some get back/
Fuckin' with us you ain't really gon' win that/
Fuck your words, sentences, grammar, and syntax!/
And it's so heartfelt/
My rap be the whip with the new-car smell . . .
— **"Karma" (Rapperchicks)**

was getting used to rocking shows in distress. This was supposed to be a celebration of some dope-ass Chicago artists repping the crib in Europe. We were supposed to come home to eat peaches and cream, but room 112 was messy.

We rocked the show properly, as usual. Barring illness, coming off the road usually means you're in peak rapping shape. My voice was very strong. It was also cool to share a stage with Angel again. Her energy felt really fresh during the performance, and you could tell we were all excited to perform together as a group again. Even Tabby seemed locked in. I think she also felt the extra drama being thrown at us and didn't have the capacity to deal with it. Angel, Tabby, and I were a unit, and now we were gonna have to figure out a new fucking place to live in just a couple of months. Bitch, I was NOT going back to live at a studio or somebody's momma's house. We were again in need of housing. The lease was up. But first, we were gonna celebrate being home by getting shitfaced and hanging out with a new drug plug.

Drug plugs are all over the place. They can be scary, lonely, creepy, sketchy, or even likable types, but they're usually not fans. If your drug plug likes you or your music, things can get intense. And guess what? You guessed it. Our new drug plug came to the show to introduce himself as just that. A fan. A potential friend. He put his number in my phone and a bag in my hand and told me he made house calls. How very fucking convenient. With all the stupid shit going on—figuring out the fate of the Rapperchicks, needing a new crib, making sure my car didn't get impounded, finding ways not to be pissed off at my current roommates, my crazy-ass relationship—it was easy for me to find reasons to escape.

I'm social when I like you. But I can also be very antisocial. Again, after years of therapy and understanding my triggers, I now know I have mild social anxiety. Drugs helped with that. Some people say they do drugs to be social. That's understandable. My default is antisocial. Maybe it's genetic. I'd made a New Year's resolution, something I rarely did, to be more social, and this was where it was getting me.

Some cool shit was happening, but opening yourself up to any scene meant running the risk of stepping in some utter bullshit. It was crazy, because through all the poo and the impending threat of homelessness, we were still getting offers. Some small. Some medium. But our next offer was one we couldn't refuse: It included paid rent.

The local label I'd partnered with wanted to expand their roster to include the Rapperchicks. The main guy, John, was consolidating a bunch of expenses; he wanted to put out the squad's next project as well as my next solo album. He also needed help with his label's social-media presence. And instead of advance money, he was willing to give us a room in his brand-new crib, on the edge of Boystown, the super trendy and super gay-friendly part of the North Side.

He was downsizing and rarely home as he was on the road managing his other acts. The idea was, we would manage the crib as a headquarters while he was gone. We would look over his social media and not worry about rent while we worked on our projects. He had us at brand-new crib with no rent. We didn't really need to hear more after that.

Tabby was able to negotiate the terms for us to move in, and we came up with some paperwork to show we were gonna deliver two albums and manage the label's social-media pages in exchange for eighteen months' rent. A year and a half. During that time, we were supposed to make and drop at least two new albums, one from the group and one from me. That deal lifted a great weight off our shoulders and we were able to live out the last few months of our current living situation with a fuck-all-y'all demeanor. That roomie venom carried over into our group dynamic, too, as we took to subtweeting and talking shit online to our Twitter "enemies" more than usual.

Furthermore, we were actively looking for Henny's replacement in the group. We liked that number, four. To us that was THE number of people for a rap group. We were courting a few young ladies and even invited a few new faces onstage for some shows we had, but it was always awkward. The original four had good chemistry. The three of us had better chemistry. Playing with five was weird, and we couldn't force the fourth. We had to build a rapport for the potential fourth Rapperchick we decided upon.

It would take a long time to find someone that really stuck, and that person would eventually come from outside of Chicago. The local women we auditioned came in with preconceived notions and were also fueled by random gossip. I didn't like the messiness of our reputation, but it certainly had people talking, so it was hard to hate completely. I knew deep down I was getting too old for it. But I couldn't exactly walk away just yet. We'd essentially signed a new record deal, and we were about to move into yet another new home in less than a year. This new spot would be Rapperchicks crib number three.

We needed new furniture. Angel was coming to live with us and, this is idiotic to say, but the three of us had been sleeping on one full-sized bed. When Angel crashed with us at the club she was sleeping on my old futon from the studio. Tabby and I were gifted a full bed at the club and we were using that. But my dear friend Eddie came in with a blessing and gifted us a California king–sized bed as a housewarming gift. Now, three people in THAT bed was way better. Still odd that three grown women were sleeping in the same bed, but groupthink is a motherfucker. Plus, that bed was sexy as hell. Lots of room to . . . move around. We couldn't wait to warm up this new situation.

It was spring 2015. Even as my career was taking an upwards turn, with a great show, steady opportunities, and better music being recorded, I was in a dark place. I was frustrated a lot. Tabby and I were arguing all the fucking time, and those moments were swallowing my good moods. Things at our current spot were coming to a head, and I could feel it all. I was low-key miserable. Our whole group even had a late-night screaming match with Paul before we left. Something about when we were gonna pay last month's rent. Things came full circle when I screamed at the top of my lungs that he paid my parking tickets late as hell and I almost had to go to court for that shit. Don't you love a good breakup? You get to bring up all the nasty little bits that never got closure. Yum. It would be another few years before Paul and I spoke again, but we eventually squashed our drunken beef. But now it was time to move into a new crib.

Tabby and I needed to consolidate our shit even more before even thinking of moving into this next spot. There wasn't an extra room or an extra closet for us. It was a standard bedroom. No master suite. No Frank Lloyd Wright–style nooks and crannies for us to hide shit. Plus, there was another whole adult living with us. So, we went to our storage unit and spent several days going through our collective lives. We had stuff. Clothes, Nespresso machines and capsules, all sorts of important documents, posters, tons of books, and, the cornerstone of it all, merchandise from projects past. I had vinyl and CDs and shirts from every album rollout I'd ever done. Sure, I'd sold merch but some of that stuff sold slowly, or not at all. And it had all gone into this storage unit.

Angel didn't have much. Her immediate family stayed on the South Side and most of her personal stuff was there. She had clothes and a few books and things she needed for her daily life. Shoes. Makeup. Shit like that. Unlike the loads of years past Tabby and I were carrying, Angel wasn't too heavy on us materialistically. And this was good because this new second-floor walkup was nice. It was modern, it was clean, but boy it was mothafuckin' SMALL.

Now don't get me wrong. I love a good marble countertop and a new appliance. I fuck with new windowsills and working doorbells. Hot water, flushing the toilet with no shower getting cold, and good water pressure. Coming from the last rundown apartment in Logan Square, this modern crib in Boystown was definitely a step in the right direction. We were so happy to finally have a nice-ass spot where we could lay our heads for a while and not have to think about where we were gonna move next. I'd been pining for stability, and the shit had not been happening fast enough. Shows were coming in and opportunities to hop on songs for money were there. And our new roomie was footing the bill for rent. We only had to pay for food and our own personal bills. Not having to pay rent was gonna be the financial leg up I needed to start really figuring some shit out.

But no sooner had we gotten settled in Boystown, Tabby flew off the rails over a rapper who didn't reciprocate her feelings. Being Psalm One, I saw so many things in certain up-and-coming rappers that made my stomach turn. The lack of respect for themselves, their bodies, or their community, for starters. But I still had a long way to go before I could advocate for change and awareness surrounding these issues. And I, as an undercover party girl falling right in line with the Rapperchick way, couldn't judge anybody. However, for the most part, I'd used party-boy rappers for fun and not expected too much romantically. It seemed like Tabby was always trying to snatch somebody's son's soul.

But the shit was not working. And now, she'd started courting too close to home. The local rapper we were fucking with had chosen sides when Henny left the group. He was adamant about hating us, and while he never directly said anything about me personally, he took shots at everyone around me. That didn't sit right with me, as the group leader, reluctant or otherwise. I needed to get in there and defend the thing we were creating. Even if the *thing* wasn't worth defending. At this point, I didn't know the difference.

All I knew was that we were getting rent, weed, videos, projects, and studio time with this new arrangement. It was time to work, but settling into these new digs screamed it was time to party. Tabby was getting more and more desperate to have a guy around. Angel and I, through all the chaos, had grown closer. I believed Tabby saw that and started clinging to me even harder. I was the one person foolish enough to stick with her. She was more than a fuck to me, and I saw her as an asset, so I was still down for her. But she was treating me more like a pet and less like a partner. She saw the effortless friendship flowing between me and Angel, and she got jealous. I know that now. I could kind of see it then, but I didn't really understand how bad it could get. Jealousy can kill you. Jealousy has killed many people.

Through our new record deal, we were introduced to new social circles, and they were all filled with drugs. We were already super flush with weed, which was never a problem, but now it seemed as though every party we went to was some kind of lightweight drug den. Being considered cool and having your name ring bells and not having to wait in line for the club was nice, but it's hard to get a grip on something when you never really had a grip to begin with. These were gripless times.

These gatekeeper shindigs with all the pretty people and all the drugs were where Tabby liked finding mates. She'd started courting a dude named Dutch who had a local song people liked. Something about hoes and not being able to save them. He was a very young Black artist with a penchant for pills and white girls and getting into fights at shows. He was a captivating performer when he wasn't shit-faced and funny when he was engaged, but definitely not boyfriend material. He was always under the influence. Always. Tabby, how-ever, was desperate and needed a replacement rap crush. She had been shooting her shot—and missing a lot. Personally, I thought she was embarrassing herself, but what did I know? I didn't have a ton of experience with men, but I seemed to be making out much better with my extra relationships. She was failing. She hated that a couple of guys who were actually interested in me didn't keep me waiting.

All the girls wanted to do was party. John wasn't home much. He traveled more than us at the time, which left us with the crib to our-selves. There was a liquor store a block away and our drug plug was right on the other end of a phone call. We spent a lot of time partying in that place. Our crib was in the middle of some popping nightlife and we went out a lot. Even though we weren't paying rent, bills never stopped and I was putting a lot on my credit cards. I was spending a nice amount on party favors, too. Tabby was still paying back the government after her audit. Factor in a couple of years of not having a steady gig and shit: The bills were piling up. Tabby was gonna have to look for work if she was gonna court a new love interest. I mean, she spent good money courting me. I ain't cheap. She hated the idea of working a "real" job again. But something had to give. I was the only one bringing in any income.

Ever since I'd quit working at the lab, I knew I never wanted to work in that capacity again. I didn't have an aversion to work; I had an aversion to boredom. I am allergic to the normalcy that robs people of their passion and excitement. They become hardened to risk and easy to offend. They usually do some combination of work, TV, sleep, and repeat. They get happy over someone else's fake life on reality television before they get happy over their own. That's what I hated about "regular" life: the belief that we all have to fit into some routine, just because we have to be at this specific place eight-plus hours out of the day.

My mom worked her ass off throughout my whole life. Elaine became a journalist and then an author right before my eyes. When I was a little kid, she worked at a bank. By the time I was in high school, she was getting her first degree from college. As I type this, she's on an all-expense-paid trip to Orlando to cover the new *Star Wars* theme-park ride. She's even working through retirement. I'm hoping she writes a dozen more books. Neither one of us could have predicted her trajectory. But she never let a job or a kid get in the way of her taking risks or trying to get something more out of life. She never let life get in the way of her passion. That was important for me to see at a young age, because oftentimes people living in the hood get comfortable with that backdrop. Oftentimes, they know of nothing better in their lives. This saddens me.

Maybe I got my will to take risks—as well as the will to stick things out—from my mom. Sometimes I don't know if it's ambition or if I'm being stubborn. Those get confused a lot. I had the ability to stay even when shit was terribly wrong. My mom endured a few shitty relationships, abusive ones. I saw that. But I also saw her pull herself out of them. I, for one, wasn't quite there yet.

Tabby stressed loyalty and support. Maybe, subconsciously, that was part of the reason I was still in that relationship. I hadn't been happy with her for a while, but I wanted it to work so badly. The professional shit was working, for the most part, and Angel was a beautiful distraction from how shitty Tabby and I were doing. Tabby knew that in order to keep me happy, we had to keep Angel around, even if that meant Tabby was mad all the time. She was becoming intolerable at home.

To add insult to injury, I'd started casually sleeping with a guy who'd approached me at a label event. I was standing by the free bar, and he fought his way through the crowd to come and talk to me.

"Hey, Psalm, I think I might be in love with you."

"You *think* you *might*?"

"No. I am. I am in love with you."

"Oh, okay. That's better. I know who you're friends with. I'm gonna stalk you a little and find out if we should hang out."

"Please do."

His name was Mike and he checked out fine. He was super cute and pretty funny, but he was a handful of years younger than me. He overpromised and underdelivered, and that was okay, because I definitely wasn't looking for anything serious. He also lived a short ten minutes from Boystown, and it was really easy for me to call him up and sneak to his house for a booty call.

Angel was super excited when I started seeing him. She was seeing another guy, too, and it was fun talking to her about guy stuff. Having so many lesbian relationships meant I didn't get to go too boy crazy, but I was having a lot of fun exploring my bisexuality. Because quiet as it's kept, I love men. It's just hard for me to trust 'em.

Maybe Tabby was looking to snatch another rapper's soul and take him to hell with her, but I was using this time to explore what I liked about men. I'd always had a few dudes brave enough to holler at me. I think most guys think I hate dick. It's just I have more experience in long-term relationships with women. This new exploration was cool to me and it was awesome having Angel around to discuss it with because Tabby was not being present—and that's an understatement.

When it came to me and Tabby, the polyamorous shit was only in theory. When it came to me and Angel, we were truly polyamorous in practice. You can't be in a polyam situation and pick a fight every time your mate wants to hook up with someone else. It just doesn't work like that. Tabby never got that memo. As a result, I subconsciously opened myself up to the idea of dating even more outside of that primary relationship.

The more she tried to control the rules of engagement, the more it backfired. And deep down I liked to see it. In some weird way I thought she'd calm down if I had other people to keep me company. But Tabby was never able to date the people she wanted in a real way. They were always keeping her a secret or treating her like a quick fuck. Hell, even I didn't want to reveal the severity of our relationship for fear of professional backlash.

None of that really mattered anymore. We were firmly in a situation that was unconventional, untraditional, and unfathomable to most people. But, she'd started it. In my dark mind that's how I considered it. She kept cheating on me with dudes, and I decided that was ok with me, as long as we opened up the relationship for me as well. As someone who was a serial cheater, I was into the idea of this type of arrangement.

It was hard enough to juggle one girlfriend. But now I had this other, undefined, special relationship with Angel being cultivated and nurtured. I also had emergency dick I called upon now and then. Then I had Mike, who always wondered why I wouldn't sleep over. We'd play video games or he'd put me up on some new TV show or cartoon or a new local beer he liked. We'd debate rap and fuck like rabbits. I even fell asleep on his lap one time and was comfortable as shit, but I would never stay over. Part of me didn't wanna be cuddled up with someone I knew I wasn't gonna be serious with. And part of me didn't wanna hear Tabby's mouth if I came home from a date the next morning, even though she was staying out more often.

In addition to that, Tabby had gotten a full-time job. She hadn't had one in forever, and it was getting harder for her to pay the bills, even with this new living arrangement. She had way more bills than me. Her student loans were more expensive than mine, and she was handling the whole vehicle situation, insurance and all, not to mention the alcohol and going out. And Dutch.

She ended up getting a job at Lincoln Park Zoo and quickly got promoted to managing the culinary department. As much as I hated her business acumen sometimes, she was a damn good manager. Her ability to get a job quickly without a ton of effort is a testament to how talented and plugged in she was within the corporate world. That was her world. I'd ripped her out of that world to rap and have some fun. But corporate America was where Tabby shined. She was over it, though. Understandably.

This new job made her attitude go from bad to worse. You could tell she was jealous of our free time and access to dudes who liked us back. She was always complaining about work or picking fights for no reason. She started talking down on Angel really badly in private and doing little things to show her dominance when we were all together. Angel was loyal to a fault, like me, so she just took it. She also recognized through the drama that we, as a group, were cultivating something special. She wanted to see it through. She also knew I loved her and had her back, but it was just really fucking hard fighting Tabby on every little thing. When Tabby hit Angel below the belt, I was always there to defend her, and vice versa. Tabby was lonely and the weakest rap link and the only one in the group without a sidepiece. Yeah, she was terribly upset about that.

She would come home from work and lay in the bed in the dark and do nothing. We couldn't exactly write for a group project with her being so unmotivated. I had always done the heavy lifting when it came to Psalm One, but this was not my group. This was not a solo project. Trying to get Tabby to work on music outside of this new job and this new boy-crazy depression was extremely difficult. Angel and I decided we had to get this chick laid before she drove us all completely insane.

Tabby was really into Dutch. She even went so far as to devise a plan to sabotage his then relationship, thereby pushing him further into her arms. He'd started coming over to our crib more often, and I was really trying to get used to it. I just felt he was too young and immature to hang out with us. He was more Angel's speed, but she was way too smart to fall for him. Tabby? Not so much.

He was like a child, and he played games with Tabby's time and heart. I'm not sure what kind of game she was playing, but everybody else was just trying to party. I was hemorrhaging money. My credit card usage was painfully high, and even though we were still getting shows, things were getting more expensive living in this yuppie-ass neighborhood. We got another curveball thrown at us when Tabby came with a job offer for us. The Rapperchicks. Jobs at the zoo. You read that right.

I hadn't had a real job in forever, not one where I had a real supervisor and needed to wear a uniform and all that. This was working for a corporate-ass zoo. She had jobs for me, Angel, and Dutch. This was a really culty, manipulative move. Getting everyone under the same roof, working at the same place, on the same things, for the same cause is as groupthink as it gets. But Tabby wasn't using her powers for good. She was out for control and ego. Of course, I see it now as I'm writing this, after years apart and some expensive treatment. There goes that hindsight again.

Since Tabby was in charge of food, she got to hire folks for one of three facilities: the main restaurant, the dining hall, or the ice cream shoppe. (The ice cream shoppe got the fancy spelling with an extra P and an E because it was hella bougie.) She wanted Angel and Dutch to work in the ice cream shoppe. She wanted me to drive the snack truck through the zoo. YO, driving a snack truck is a former fat kid's dream come true. If I was gonna get up in the morning and work a "real" job for the first time in God knows how long, at least it was for a cause I could get behind: snacks. Now that's something I believe in.

Angel quickly got promoted to managing the ice cream shoppe and was given the additional task of running a smoothie kiosk. While impressive, that was a big responsibility for someone who was promised the easy part-time gig of putting some ice cream in some waffle cones. This was running two small shops at once and managing a few other employees. I was actually the one with the easiest job. Since Angel didn't have a license, I was the snack-truck driver by default. That was a cool little gig. It paid shit an hour, something like eleven dollars, but I got a lot of time to myself. I got to be around snacks, and I got to drive a vehicle through the zoo. It wasn't too shabby.

The only crappy part about this gig was Tabby and I did not get along. We would argue while I was filling up the cart in the morning. It was usually about Dutch, who couldn't even bother to show up to this job most mornings. He was constantly showing Tabby how unreliable he was, even though she'd gone out on a limb to hire him. She'd vouched for him. I think I saw him in uniform maybe twice. And when he did show up, he was so bad at his job even Angel would complain.

Tabby always had an excuse for him. She was always moving the goalpost for us, but when it came to Dutch, somehow it was never his fault. The bus broke down or he didn't feel good. She couldn't accept that he was a party guy with a bad drug habit who leached off his friends and fucked plenty of girls he could crash with. Oh, and he didn't wanna work a damn job, anyway. Tabby was delusional in thinking she could domesticate him. Eventually he stopped coming to work altogether, and she just got meaner. She really knew how to suck the fun out of a summer job with plenty of snacks.

In addition to Future's *DS2* (*Dirty Sprite 2*) mixtape taking me completely by surprise that season, I was also pleasantly taken aback by an inheritance coming through. My family, a few generations down the line, struck oil down south, and I'd been filling out paperwork for years. I didn't know if anything would come of it. Since my dad had passed away, I was next in line to receive his portion, to the tune of about $4,000. Now, this wasn't a lot of money by any stretch, but to someone who hadn't had more than $3,000 in her account for a long time, it was oodles of dough. It was just enough money to justify quitting that job at the zoo. Besides, I was tired of getting spotted and being asked, "Psalm, why you workin' at the zoo?" I LOVED QUITTING THAT JOB.

I added more reasons for Tabby to be jealous. She couldn't keep an eye on me or Dutch, and against her hopes, Angel was thriving at her job. It definitely seemed like Tabby was trying to sabotage Angel at work, but Angel was too good of an employee. Angel was handling the ice cream shoppe and the smoothie kiosk like a pro, and Tabby had too much to juggle to sit and try to meddle with that all day. She really thought this job was gonna bring her closer to controlling what we did. It was backfiring. Two of us quit and the third was doing better than imagined, while Tabby herself was starting to drown with all the work. Whodathunk managing food service for an entire zoo would be that hard?

That gig was somebody's dream job, but Tabby could hardly wake up on time and get there in order to be good at it. We shared the vehicle, so in order for me to be able to use the car during the day, I had to take her to work at like 7:15 in the morning and drive like a bat outta hell. This was so Tabby could be there in time for the morning breakfast rush. It was such a mess. I hated getting up just to take her to work, but I needed the car to get things done. And both of us were staying up later and later. Since I didn't have a supervisor or a set schedule or a "real job," I went right back to my regularly scheduled rapper activities. I started working on tracks for my follow-up to *Hug Life*, and it was slowly coming together. I liked the direction of this album, even in its infancy. The recording contract we'd signed included sessions anytime we needed. And I needed the time. The studio was becoming the only place I felt comfortable.

I'd started taking even more solace in Angel. She felt the cold shoulder of Tabby get colder. She couldn't understand it, but I knew Tabby was growing less and less fond of Angel. That made me take her further under my wing. I'm not sure Tabby really understood the depth of Angel's talent. She just wanted to hang out with some pretty party girls and make rappers swoon. Yes, she was partying, but Angel really was here for the music. I was handling the music. So, we were spending more time writing and recording. Tabby would rarely come to sessions, while Angel was taking every opportunity to make music. After all, Tabby promised to help with Angel's career, hadn't she?

Instead, she was helping Dutch at every turn and hinting to us that she didn't have the money to do things like she used to. But she was working a full-time, salaried job. Something was fishy. One morning, things came to a head when Angel woke up to see our group funds depleted. We'd saved about $600 in cash and had put it in a shoebox in our room. Since we were all working, we decided to put money in this box every week and use it for promotional costs. But Tabby had taken the cash to pay for parking tickets she got while sneaking out in the middle of the night to fuck Dutch in his mom's basement.

She knew she couldn't exactly bring him home, considering all the times he'd disrespected us. The running narrative was that he was scared of me, but I was simply calling him out on his shit. He'd come over when Tabby had a full bag of drugs and an empty vagina. Or he would come around on payday. She would compromise herself just to have him around, and it got old quick. I even tried being polyamorous with her once and agreed to share him, one very wild night that I shudder to remember.

Actually, I kinda don't remember much of it at all. I wasn't violated and it was consensual, but I loaded up on cocaine to even kick it with the both of them. I was in that dark of a space; I thought this would make her happy. Those crazy abandonment issues were kicking up again. I didn't know anything about that back then. I was living in these sex, drug, and rock 'n' roll moments, and it was mostly bad. It's absolutely crazy the kinds of guys you'll fuck trying to keep your manipulative girlfriend happy. Zero out of ten, I would not recommend it. Soon after that encounter, I knew I could never be successful sharing anyone with Tabby. That night was a true low point in my life.

Angel didn't respect Dutch. Tabby didn't respect Angel. I didn't respect Dutch. Tabby didn't respect me either but she pretended. Things in our little crib were intense. And to think we were all sleeping in the same king-sized bed. Tabby made it uncomfortable as fuck for Angel, demanding she didn't use her phone in bed or come to bed too late. So, Angel started sleeping on the couch. I felt caught in the middle, and to complicate matters even more, I was officially falling for Angel. Tabby was sneaking around with Dutch as I was pulling away emotionally. And after Tabby tried to justify spending our group cash by saying, "Well, everybody uses the car, so I should be able to use the group cash on the car," Angel started pulling away, too.

Angel took the minimum hours at the zoo and started hanging out with me more. We'd go on lunches and nice walks and have long writing sessions at the crib while Tabby was at work. On the romantic side we'd even started having meaningful sex just with each other and a couple of threesomes as well. Angel and I were secretly accomplishing the polyamorous lifestyle Tabby loved to brag about. Tabby wasn't a good partner. She just knew how to get away with being reckless. I was successfully distracted by my few fleeting love interests, yet I was also falling further for the person living right under our roof. The person I didn't want to live with all along was starting to get to me.

Tabby kept lying to us because she knew fucking with Dutch wasn't cool. All he did was make her even more insecure and inconsiderate at her job. She expected me to take her to work after sucking dick all night and forgetting to set her alarm. And my dumb ass did it, no matter how drunk or high I was from the night before, just so I could have access to the vehicle for the day. I was also slanging a few bags of marijuana here and there, so I definitely needed the transportation. That house was the catalyst for a lot of relationships, good and bad. But we were about to get the rug pulled out from under us.

John, full-time CEO and part-time roommate, came home one Thursday, looked around, left abruptly, and texted us on Friday that we had to be out of the apartment in THREE DAYS. This was less than six months since we'd signed our eighteen-month agreement. He was never home to begin with, yet he'd decided out of the blue that he didn't want us as roommates anymore.

We were being evicted.

CHAPTER 17

IT BE YA OWN PEOPLE

Tabby (face blurred for personal reasons), Psalm One, and Angel Davanport shooting the cover for now out-of-print mag Unsung Femmes. *Photo credit: Rena Naltsas.*

A h, hell NAH. We had just been kicked out of our last place and had even signed a contract with John for this new place. But we weren't on the lease. I, for one, was not going down without a fight, so I promptly referred to our signed agreement and requested a house meeting. John was this zen dude, this yoga dude, this dude who pushed meditation and not jumping to conclusions. Surely, he'd understand how unreasonable he was being.

The meeting started out ok, but then something snapped. Tabby started feeling herself and demanded to know why he'd changed his mind. She started calling him all sorts of bitches. Seeing him get frustrated was like candy to her. He started saying dumb shit in higher octaves like, "Y'all broke the faucet on the sink," or, "Y'all used the good olive oil," or my personal favorite, "Somebody left a condom wrapper in the living room." These were all minor incidents that could've been solved with some simple domestic talk. I tried my best to keep the crib clean. I was constantly cleaning. But my other roomies weren't that careful.

To me, none of the stuff he was yelling about was deep enough to kick someone out over, but we weren't on the lease. He could do whatever he wanted. We were almost to a point of figuring out John's touring schedule and a plan to buy us more time when Tabby decided she was done talking and jumped up on the couch, yelling at him that he couldn't do this to us.

When Tabby jumped up, John jumped up. When John jumped, Angel and I got involved. Physically he was the biggest in the house, and Tabby was the smallest. We weren't about to have anybody lunging at our smallest member. We broke up the screaming match, and that was pretty much the last straw. He wanted us out, and now he had a reason to believe Tabby was willing to get violent about it. I think she knew we had her back, so she felt emboldened to jump at John. We couldn't believe how NOT zen his response was, but we knew this was the end of our time with him. He told us he'd give us a week to move out. And then he changed the locks the next day.

We had a feeling he was gonna do some petty shit because of some of the things he'd yelled at us when the meeting went off the rails. Something about "ghetto bitches" and "broke bitches" and me specifically being an "Englewood hoodrat" my whole life. To hear a Black man say these things to me was devastating. I thought our collaboration was empowering, but to hear him say those things let me know I could no longer fuck with him—ever. Even if he said those things out of anger, they were very specific, and coming from his mouth after all we'd been through cut me like a knife. I took that shit very personally. So now, I definitely wasn't leaving without a fight.

We stayed at home packing all day after the big argument. Tabby and Angel had to go to work, but I didn't. I figured if anyone left, he might do something like change the locks. And I was fucking right. I left for thirty minutes to go pick the ladies up from work, and when we got back to the apartment our keys didn't work. That bastard had locksmiths at the ready. But what he didn't have was the wherewithal to remember he had a *back* door too. Maybe he was high that day? We literally used the *same key* we'd always used to unlock the back door and got in. What an idiot. I know he hated to receive that text saying we were back in the house.

"Oh hey, never mind about letting us in. We got it. Toodles! Talk soon."

By now I had read up on squatters' rights and spoke with the more powerful white people in my life. John was a petty guy now. So, I didn't have to play by the rules, either. I remembered the passwords to all his label's social media. We had digital access to his label more than he did, and I also knew the contracts we'd signed had been drawn up by a fake lawyer. We had more dirt on him than he would have liked, we had albums we could take back, and I also had access to people he had a lot of respect for. Bad words from me could hinder his progress, too.

So, I requested another meeting between John, myself, and a mediator he respected deeply. The mediator tactic worked, so we ended up negotiating a decent severance package for myself and the Rapperchicks. John coughed up around $2,000 for us to be out of the apartment in seven days. Since there was a breach of contract on his end, I was able to argue that he owed us. He was putting us out without much notice. How the fuck were we supposed to work on albums for his label if we were dealing with homelessness?

This shit was messy beyond belief, but we were able to come up with a plan. The living situation would get worked out, but this music shit was strained. How could I deliver albums to a Black man that referred to me as a ghetto Black bitch with all the fervor of . . . a rapper? I thought he was different, and the conversations we normally had about hard work, self-sufficiency, and the Black dollar now felt fake as fuck. I've been in some insane and compromising situations, but one thing a motherfucker can't call me is dumb. I've been overly amicable, altered by drugs, and even blinded by love. But a bitch ain't dumb. I lost so much respect for John with that one sentence. Few people have ever hurt me like that. We got the $2,000 and got a lot more apology studio time after that. Then we started looking for a new place, posthaste.

Tabby, still ever resourceful, put out feelers and ended up striking a deal with a chef at the zoo for a new place to live. He lived in the Pilsen neighborhood and was paying taxes on a house he didn't want to live in but didn't want to sell. The house needed a *lot* of work, but it had two floors and two separate entrances. It had multiple bathrooms, an attic, a garage, and a POOL. He was gonna let us rent it for $1,200 a month, and Tabby agreed to pay half the rent, leaving Angel and me each with a very manageable $300 a month to pay. We were so desperate to find a place to live, we didn't realize Tabby had signed the lease without us. We were anxious and made a stupid move out of desperation. But we had a big-ass crib now, with room to breathe. No more cramping in one room and frustrating the hell out of each other. We had multiple rooms now. Multiple floors. And a FUCKING SWIMMING POOL. The Rapperchicks had a makeshift mansion, bitches. It was time to have super hyper, ultra real, extreme fun—or die trying.

Moving out of John's place was hurried, bitter, and confusing. I thought this situation was gonna put us ahead, but now we were scrambling again. Our new landlord told us this house needed some work and the bathrooms were weird but everything operated ok, so it was more than livable. Upon walking in and inspecting the household, Angel and I were stoked at the possibility of taking the downstairs and making it living quarters and using the upstairs for administrative, creative, and organizational purposes. Tabby took one look at the room Angel suggested we turn into a common room and quickly decided she wanted her own room. Upstairs. Away from us.

Angel took that demand personally. So did I. We were already arguing daily, and now Tabby's venom was fully aimed at Angel. They'd gotten into a few arguments, but I was there to diffuse them. It seemed there was a line Tabby wasn't willing to cross with Angel, but with me the story was different. Because of my strained relationship with Dutch, Tabby was picking fights with me every single day. I didn't want to be in the new crib with him. In fact, I specifically begged Tabby to give us three months to settle into the new place before throwing parties. Tabby's relationship with Dutch opened her up to the druggie scene even more, and all she wanted to do was please him. I didn't want all these rap niggas in my house. I was over the point in life where I wanted my house to be party central. We'd been kicked out of our last two cribs, and we still didn't have anything close to a Rapperchicks project finished. We'd started a few songs, but this was beginning to run off the rails. I needed time to refresh and rethink our plan. I was asking for a mental-health break. I was not going to get it.

Tabby didn't give a fuck about refreshing and rethinking. The first thing Tabby did was take $600 out of the $2,000 John gave us and clean the pool. The pool. Since her birthday was coming up in August, the next thing she wanted was a birthday party. She didn't really have any friends, and Dutch wasn't the kind of guy you brought home to mama, so she invited her family. She wanted to impress them so bad, but they were never really impressed by her artist lifestyle. They were impressed by my career but always asking when the Tabby music was dropping. She'd make up some excuse about why it wasn't ready yet, and they'd go back to asking what I was up to. She hated that, too.

Angel started making her sanctuary downstairs, and as much as I wanted to fix the cracks in my relationship with Tabby, I was more comfortable down there with Angel. Tabby refused to move her bedroom downstairs with the rest of us. She'd also bought herself a new entertainment center, for *her* room. I was hurt because the whole time we were together, she'd demanded I sleep with her, room with her, live with her, share everything, share whatever. But now, in this new house, with two floors, she didn't only want her own space, she wanted to be on separate levels. That really got to me, but it also gave me an opportunity to build something even stronger with Angel. And with Tabby upstairs doing God knows what, I had the freedom to explore.

It was easy. We were already friends. We'd already been arrested, and released, together. We'd seen each other fight and puke and cry and win and lose and fuck and did I say fight? We weren't big on trying to find some big thing to put on it but we had more peace hanging out with each other downstairs than the weirdly depressive and cold energy that was permeating the upstairs. I'd basically put my foot down about Dutch, and Tabby spit on it. She didn't give a fuck about my request not to open up the house to parties for a little while. She wasn't interested in building a studio or working on music or using the crib to organize everything we had going on. She wanted to flex on the scene in this big house and have somewhere to fuck the dude who was clearly using her.

I was insulted when she compared me to Dutch. She hinted I was just as lost as he was. But I was lost in California with five zillion jobs and a career that was, albeit stalled, still very much a career. This was a druggie local rapper with a big dick and no semblance of responsibility. He wasn't signed. He wasn't motivated. He liked to bed girls with money who didn't mind taking care of him. I guess we had that last thing in common. The girl Dutch was cheating on Tabby with was a rich foreign-exchange student who took him on trips and paid for his nice clothes. Tabby was actually a downgrade, but she was still willing to foot the bill.

Cycles are a bitch, and they're so hard to break. It's even harder to recognize them when you're in the eye of the storm. I was so traumatized by cycles of mental, drug, financial, and physical abuse, I didn't know how to stop them from completely taking over.

The difference between the previous spaces the Rapperchicks had lived in as a unit and this new house was privacy. Up until this point, as soon as our morbid trio became roomies, we had other roomies and thin walls. Now, in Pilsen, with all this square footage, our screams had space and opportunity. We could stomp and tussle and yell at the top of our lungs. The walls were thick and the witnesses few. Angel and I could keep the juiciest, darkest secrets to ourselves.

While things in the house never truly got settled, I began speaking to John again about where we landed after that ugly eviction from his condo. He never wanted to lose Psalm One or the Rapperchicks as artists; he just hated Tabby. He liked Angel despite her failure to dispose of all her condom wrappers, and he really loved having me around.

We had, in fact, bonded before the drama. Before any fake deals were signed, we'd spent a lot of time together talking about music and life. We'd traveled together and done quite a few shows. I was super hurt by the way everything went down. But Tabby being a big problem was familiar territory, and bad for business. Now I can't, in good faith, put everything on her. Because the same things kept happening to me, I knew I had something to do with it, too. But up until this point all the negative-guy drama kept coming up Tabby. She was definitely bad for business.

I met with John at a coffee shop in Lincoln Park one sunny afternoon after we'd moved out, and he let me know he was hurt by the
whole thing, too. He said he was very sorry he lost his cool on us.
Tabby was relentless at that meeting and he just wanted her to stop
talking, which was some toxic shit in and of itself. On the other hand,
I really wanted Tabby to shut the fuck up a lot of the time, too. So
I could see both sides. We ended up agreeing to move ahead with
releasing my next album. We'd see where it went from there. We
were looking at a fall 2015 release. I'd been diligently recording new
stuff. Angel had also started singing melodies and helping with some
hooks. We were invested in my next project. I wanted him to pay for
my next release, but I planned to bail on him ASAP. Even with an
apology, I was never cool with what he had done and said to me.

Some people should never be roommates. Many artists room
with whomever will have us because we're usually broke—or cheap.
Some of us are just desperate. The Rapperchicks were certainly desperate for a stable residence. This was a theme for me. As much as I
said I wanted stability and peace of mind, the more I ran in the opposite direction. Even through all that mess, John and I were able to
move forward and plan to work on music. He just never wanted to
speak to Tabby again, which was completely understandable.

He wasn't the only person on the business side who found Tabby
problematic. Angel and I had an influential Chicago producer pull
us aside and tell us he'd love to work with us two, but Tabby wasn't
going to be allowed into sessions. He also said if Tabby was going to
be on any of his beats, we'd have to write her lyrics. He did not mince
words: He didn't think she was a good vocalist, or very friendly, but
she looked amazing onstage.

So, John and I still had a plan. We'd work on the new Psalm One
album, which would heavily feature our group, and hit the road soon
after. *Hug Life*, the album under my other moniker, was a great experiment, but John specifically wanted a Psalm One album in the catalogue.
He wanted to continue putting money behind that name and the group

name. We just needed to keep it together long enough to put the work in. Angel and I had time, because ice cream season was over. Fall was here. Tabby was still at the zoo. She stayed away from us. After work, she would go right in her room and stay there all night. Sometimes I'd hear Dutch come around booty-call hour and leave at dawn. Sometimes not. But as Tabby stayed away from us, Angel and I got to play house.

We also made some new friends in the form of an executive producer and a musician from the "other side" of the scene. They had a great studio, some stellar work on the books, and plenty of "it" rappers hanging around. They also had the plug on another thing: cocaine. We could go over there, make music, snort a bunch of drugs, have a shit ton of fun, crash over there if we wanted to, and avoid Tabby for long stretches of time. But, we were working. We were definitely working hard. We were just playing even harder. Cocaine can be a productive and destructive drug. The next Psalm One album was coming along better than I expected—drugs and depression fuel so much music.

It's crazy to think about how productive I was when I was in the most destructive phase of my life. I was thinner than ever because drugs ruin your appetite. I've always had body-image issues with a splash of body dysmorphia. So I never thought I was getting too thin. After all, I was always the heaviest one in the group. I didn't really grasp how thin I was because I would binge, then come down, and eat fried catfish and steak burritos. I wasn't eating healthy but I was fitting into all my clothes. I was looking edgy as fuck in pictures, and I was spending a lot of time in the studio. I felt like shit all the time. I was always freshly bruised and always heading into or out of a hangover. At this point in the madness, I was doing drugs solo. Angel didn't party as hard as me yet. She'd drink and smoke and do Molly sometimes, but never cocaine. That was another beast. I was fully strapped to and riding that beast. It kept my mind occupied while my life was falling completely apart. At least I had my own room.

Tabby hated me doing coke but she was dating the biggest coke-head I'd ever met. That nigga Dutch would come downstairs and do all my blow if I was in a giving mood. I was trying my hardest to accept him being in Tabby's life, but I wasn't doing that without numbing myself. Angel and I were becoming inseparable; Tabby and I were becoming mortal enemies who occasionally slept together. She stayed upstairs, in her room. She was drawing more boundaries after years of seemingly having none, and I didn't know how to deal. So I put it in the music and drank myself silly damn near every night. I was a functional vice-haver and I was in this dangerous place where I could still complete tasks while being under the influence. We also managed to run a thriving rap-karaoke party during this time.

It was one of the most successful weekly events in the city, and it started around November 2013. It grew very unexpectedly. We did one rap-karaoke holiday party at an unofficial venue (RIP, MultiKulti), kept doing it, found a proper venue to host it (RIP, Jerry's Wicker Park), did it monthly, and it grew to a weekly party that brought in the most money for that venue. By 2015 we were downright poppin'. People would pack our party every weekend and have tons of fun—while we were holding on for dear life. When I wasn't in town to host, we found guest hosts to keep it going. Much like our group, the Rapperchicks, our rap-karaoke party was something people found joy in, and they were showing up for us. It wasn't something we could ignore. I ain't no dummy. We wanted to see these things through and make money, even if we were coming apart at the seams.

Money helps dysfunction sustain itself.

CHAPTER 18

THE DON'T-DIE-IN-PILSEN CHALLENGE

I'm a lonely piece of shit, even when I got a mate/
Got so many demons, motherfuckers congregate/
If he say monogamy, then I wanna have my fun/
But if she say she poly then I gotta have her one-on-one/
I am never satisfied/
If I can't get my soul soothed, then being happy is a lie/
But I don't wanna hear that, I just want my rear smacked and not think
about it/
Move on and not drink about it . . .
— "So Close"

The party followed us everywhere. Because of our rap-karaoke success at the venue, the staff gave us run of the place. The spot doesn't exist anymore, so it's ok that I'm saying this. But boy, we had carte blanche in that bitch. We could do whatever we wanted.

Our drug plug was there every week. I can't believe we held that party together for so long, because our team (myself, Angel, Tabby, and Freddie) was wasted through most of it. The only person who didn't indulge was our IT person, Tyler.

As much as I was seemingly keeping it together, I wasn't. Because without all those drugs floating around and her seeing me doing it more and more, Angel wouldn't have indulged herself. I introduced her to cocaine. Angel, baby. I'm sorry. Peer pressure is a bitch, and we were both just trying to feel good. I know you forgive me, because we've had this conversation a few times, but I wanted you to see these words in print. I should have never asked you to party with me like that. I'm so blessed you stuck with me through all of it. You deserved better from a partner.

The scene can be a pretty unforgiving place. I'm typing these words on the other side of traumatic events with people I saw as peers. But these events had less to do with music and more to do with drugs, sex, and the inability to truly express how we felt outside of the booth. Fuck putting it in a song if you can't express yourself properly when it matters most. Many of us, as musicians, can't even speak up for ourselves. We have social anxiety and delusions of grandeur and God complexes and impostor syndrome and personality disorders and PTSD and all kinds of shit we can temporarily drink or smoke or snort or inject or perform away. We were doing so much at once and running around constantly. We were avoiding all the real shit we needed to do to possibly go even further as a group. We were experiencing and consuming and promising, but when we got home, the fighting started right back up. Angel and I were an official item now, so Tabby had to deal with that. If she could have Dutch, I could have Angel. Fair was fair.

I still considered Tabby my primary partner, and now I had a secondary partner in Angel. As a result of not being comfortable downstairs, Tabby spent a lot of time drunk, high, and waiting on Dutch to come hang out with her between binges. It was a sad state of affairs, and she'd resorted to not cleaning up after herself. I saw pieces of her mother come out when she gave up on cleaning and personal hygiene. Now I know really bad depression and low self-esteem don't allow some people to care too much about stuff like that. Now I'm a lot more sensitive to that. But then, I was going through my own shit. I hated being upstairs in squalor. My depression makes me clean *more*, not less. It used to be hard for me to see the other side of that.

Angel and I were more compatible in our downstairs fantasy because we both love doing domestic shit. And we did polyam a better way. She didn't care when I went to see my sidepieces because she had sidepieces. She wasn't jealous of anyone's talent, because she's super talented herself. The opposite of jealousy is compersion, a poly term, and we had that for each other. Angel was seeing me at my worst and not only sticking around, but helping me clean up. And we were making the prettiest music together.

Everything Tabby wanted with Dutch was backfiring. They tried to make music together once, and he literally told her she should never sing. I didn't think she could sing, either, or rap, but I knew she had an interesting presence and a few hot bars. And you don't have to know *how* to sing to sing songs, sadly. Ask Bob Dylan. If she'd really wanted to make bops and cute songs, she could have done it. When Dutch said that, she was crushed.

Our plan was to release a Psalm album, a Rapperchicks album, an Angel album, and a fun little Tabby EP, where she'd wax poetic over dreamy melodies and heavy auto-tune. The funny shit is, back in 2015 when we originally had this idea for Tabby, we would have been ahead of the curve. Mad chicks do that in music now, and the music sells. I wish we could've just put our differences aside long enough to complete her music. We were wasting actual weeks fighting. Tabby's gaslighting and her not-so-secret hatred of Angel slowed us down so much it was maddening. Being stalled by bickering was all too real and frequent. Tabby wasted so much time picking fights. And I wasted so much time falling for it. Every time.

Her unraveling sent more than a few people wondering what the fuck she was doing. It was clear I was doing the heavy lifting and Angel was holding us down in so many ways. Angel definitely kept our group young, considering Tabby and I were no spring chickens. At this point the Rapperchicks had three core members and we'd officially added a fourth, an amazing musician from Canada by way of Denver. She rounded out our quartet and gave our production more credibility. I'd met her during the *Hug Life* sessions. Now we could make our own shit in house and we didn't need to go to a million producers for beats. The only issue was, our new member didn't live in Chicago and she was touring many months out of the year. She was a Rapperchick more in theory than in practice, but that was ok. We were able to maintain this façade of togetherness. We were also able to book more shows and meet even more musicians through this new association.

Comedian Hannibal Buress and Psalm One at the SXSW Festival, Austin, Texas, 2015.

SXSW 2015 caused a shift. A few months prior to moving to Pilsen, we played at least a half dozen showcases as the Rapper-chicks, and I hosted a killer Chicago-made showcase at the festival. We were getting a lot of exposure, and some heavy hitters were even coming out to our gigs. We were burning the fuck out of our candles, though. Being too sloppy wasn't the best idea either, considering at SXSW you never knew who you might bump into.

While out there, Tabby was bumping into a plethora of indie rappers. Rappers were her kryptonite. She'd adjusted our festival schedule to see one in particular. He didn't give a fuck about her, but he was entertaining Tabby's shenanigans to try and sleep with Angel. He also wanted to talk to me about my problems with Rhymesayers, as he was very closely associated with them. He was messy, and he knew he could maybe even get some leftover pussy from Tabby. But it was no secret who he was trying to fuck.

We hung out with him, just kicking it around the festival, and ended up at none other than my estranged label's showcase. Of course, they would have a label showcase without me knowing. I was excluded from everything. They pretty much pretended I didn't exist shortly after my first album. At one point in 2013, the head honcho informed me that one of the many albums I'd sub-mitted had been accepted into the "maybe" pile of releases. Then, he rescinded without explanation. So I stopped sending music to RSE and focused on myself. A conversation at SXSW in 2015 was more than I had received in years. Hell, I'd started working with a whole-new label and become part of a whole-ass rap group in the meantime. It's amazing the things you can accomplish when your dream label is ignoring you. But here, at this showcase, I was getting this vital opportunity to chat with the guy who had been placing me on the back burner for years.

Psalm One and Angel Davanport at SXSW, Austin, Texas, 2015.
Photo credit: Kelly Taub.

After several pep talks in the ladies restroom and a minor panic attack, I walked up to him—and the compliments came right away. He told me I looked great, which I did. I was skinnier from drugs, I had makeup on, and I had on tiny shorts which accentuated my ample thighs. This was quite different from my boom-bap uniform of rap tees and jeans. I was femme'd up and it was noticeable what I was doing with the Rapperchicks. He complimented me on that, too. He finally informed me that RSE was planning a twentieth-anniversary show at the Target Center in Minneapolis that fall and I would "have to come out and be part of it."

Of COURSE I would come out for it. I joked that they couldn't have an anniversary show at an arena celebrating the label's history without their lone female act. He assured me they couldn't. I let him know I was touring in the fall and to please keep me abreast of the schedule so if I had to leave the road to make the show, I could. He agreed.

I felt like part of Rhymesayers for the first time in a long time, standing there with him, until I heard one of their flagship rappers yelling at the top of his lungs at Tabby. He was towering over her, getting dead in her face, shouting that she wasn't intelligent and that she was wrong for doing what she did. I couldn't have been more confused, considering they'd only met one other time before. That time, he shook her hand and said, "I have to take a shit," before promptly walking away. It was a brief encounter that left both Tabby and me feeling weird and slightly confused.

I couldn't believe the rapper that was once my favorite was yelling at my girlfriend in the middle of a SXSW venue, in front of plenty of important people. Nobody said anything. None of these men tried to calm the big man rapper down. It wasn't just the drugs. My head was about to completely fucking explode.

Naturally, the conversation I needed to have with the head honcho got cut short. Tabby and the famous rapper were both clearly drunk, and this dude was out of line getting in her face like that. Intimidation and bullying were par for my course with these guys, but even this was a lot. In December 2020, I wrote a long-overdue article on the website Medium describing just how deep my RSE wounds went—some things I've even omitted from this book— but I'm getting ahead of myself.[3] At that moment, I was in complete shock. Tabby was kind of loving this bad attention, though. She gaslit, too. She provoked, too. But we always stood up for her. Even though she was the biggest shit starter in the group. Angel told dude to calm the fuck down. I was speechless. Thank God for Angel.

We were always cleaning up Tabby's messes. I didn't know how we were gonna clean up this one. She'd pissed off a huge artist on the label. They already treated me like a stepchild. They had just started interacting with me a little bit, after years of absolutely nothing. Now I stood in this venue, shocked, trying desperately to understand why they'd blown up on each other. Nobody was willing to give a straight answer that night, so we just left the venue, embarrassed as fuck. I was mortified and sick to my stomach.

The next day we figured out the big famous rapper was mad at Tabby for tweeting about him being an asshole. Tweeting. People called him an asshole on social media every day. He's even apologized to fans online for being an asshole. Cuz he was. But for some odd reason, he was yelling at Tabby in person for some shit she TWEETED, yet he wouldn't say that specifically. He knew it would've sounded goofy and lame as hell. Because it was.

A simple, "Hey, you said I was an asshole on Twitter, and that wasn't cool," would have sufficed. But he couldn't have said that and still looked like the big man. So, he screamed at her. She yelled back. Pure class on both their parts. I lost a piece of my career that night. I didn't know how, but I knew that argument between them was gonna come back to haunt the fuck out of me. I was right.

Tabby was twisted, so she was happy with all the attention. I hated her for engaging one of the more influential people in independent hip hop. I hated that she took the bait and made such a scene, knowing what I'd been through with RSE. Maybe in her weird, tweaked-out mind she thought she was taking up for me? Who knows what she was thinking? She was feeling herself. Worst of all, she was throwing herself at the rapper who was friends with this guy. Just plain sloppy. This was a huge faux pas and I knew there was nothing I could do to stop the fallout. This was a runaway train.

We argued the whole drive home from SXSW, a little over a day of driving. It was horrible. Heading back to Chicago, I knew I had to work harder at the music and less at the drama and the bullshit. I had a tour to plan and an album to finish. But the damage in Austin was done, and it was irreparable.

I had been able to clean up the mess of the Europe tour, the mess of the rappers she'd fucked and pissed off. I had been able to keep Angel from kicking her down a flight of stairs, which was something Angel was apparently good at. But coming to SXSW, throwing the pussy at a kinda famous rapper, and yelling at another really famous one who could fuck my career up was not a good move. I only had one way to counter it: keeping busy. There was only one thing to focus on now: *POLY (Psalm One Loves You)*.

This album had been years in the making, yet the events of the previous few months colored the project. If you're educated on my discography, you can hear the shift in the music. Besides the warmth of the live instruments, the silkiness of Angel's voice, and the crooning in my voice, you can hear something else. There's a new pain there. There's a knowledge that I was going through a lot of bullshit. I believe *POLY (Psalm One Loves You)* shows me at my most human, for the first time in my career.

Before I go any further, can we just talk about how genius that acronym is? It was made for me. The title fell out of the fucking sky. It was the first album I'd worked on knowing Rhymesayers wasn't gonna touch it. It was the first album I'd worked on with the Rapperchicks. It was the first album I'd worked on with a band at my fingertips. I laugh when I talk about it now. I don't know how the fuck I completed such a solid piece of work given the space I was in. I wasn't well. But damn, I was still *dope*. I know now there was a lot to be desired with the final mix, but otherwise, it's an important piece of work in my catalogue. It's also a reminder that many artists can't separate from the mess of life because the art is thriving *despite* the mess.

On September 25, 2015, I dropped *POLY* to critical acclaim. My lead single, "Impatient (Just U and Us)" featuring Angelenah (aka Angel), became a fan favorite and was also licensed by an independent movie that won a few awards and was featured on Netflix. It's a well-rounded album with moments and movements and live instrumentation and dreamy walls of sound and lyrics about pain. And pleasure. And surrender to love.

Home surrendered to the chaos. Tabby was spending a lot of money on Dutch and denying it. Angel was livid about the whole thing and tired of the way Tabby was treating us. The tension came to a boiling point right before my fall tour to support the album, and it spilled over onto the road. The shitty part was I felt I could do nothing to stop it. All I really did was work on the album, plan the tour, and get wasted. I was responsible enough to do all that but, when it came to doing anything else? Good luck, Cristalle.

Thankfully, because of her important zoo job, Tabby couldn't do all of the shows on the tour. She could only do the first half with us, then she had to return home to Chicago. Angel and I did the majority of the run together. She was only a seasonal employee at the zoo. This album and tour happened in the fall, post ice cream season. Tabby hated it.

Psalm One DIY Tour flyer, fall 2015.

Tabby also, for the first time since we'd been together, hardly promoted my album when it dropped. She was mad she wasn't featured on enough songs, however rarely she, if ever, came to the studio. I had to drag her to the final recording sessions. She'd just expected to appear on tracks without doing any work. It was disgusting, and I was tired of it.

Coming back home from that tour, I was more in love with Angel. I despised Tabby. She acted a fool on the few shows she was actually present for. She didn't speak to anyone offstage. I really didn't know how to pull myself away from the relationship. We'd started businesses together, done charity work, lived in many houses, worked on mad tours and albums, and at one point we were firing on all cylinders. She was integral to my career at a time when I was lost. Everything was so out of hand. And I wasn't sober enough to deal.

But I needed Tabby to be there for me when the fallout from her SXSW debacle came. Instead, she was absent. Ghost. Radio silent. It went a little something like this:

The tour for the album was over. I'd been contacting the RSE office to figure out when their big Target Center show was taking place. Since the head honcho told me to keep the date open for the event, I did. Twenty years in the game is a big deal. I wouldn't miss it for the world. I even tried emailing and calling up to the office but never got to speak to anyone. I never got any straight answers—until they announced the fucking bill.

I was at home, chilling, thinking maybe they'd pushed the show to 2016 since they hadn't said anything about it. And then my phone blew the fuck up. People were all excited about the announcement and wondering if there was gonna be another round of names announced. There was one glaring absence: Psalm One. They had every act ever on the bill, except me. I was their only woman presence, too. At the time, it was only ME. It was terrifically embarrassing.

I started pacing the house while my phone melted with notifications. Questions poured in asking why I wasn't on the show and if I knew my name had been omitted from the flyer. Of course, I knew. It was all over the internet. I tried to ignore it but I couldn't. Even if I logged off, people who had my phone number texted and called to see how I felt about it.

On the internet, my mentions and private messages exploded with requests for clarification. How could this hip hop label, after making a big deal about signing me during their fifteen-year celebration, literally leave me out of the twenty-year extravaganza at a fucking arena? They'd even invited people who weren't officially on the label anymore to perform. The fans wanted answers. A few of my label mates wanted answers. I wanted answers, too, because of all the things to leave me out of, this felt deliberate. It felt personal. This was not just some oversight.

Soon after the announcement, I was invited to do an interview with a local Minneapolis publication, the now-defunct *City Pages*, to talk about being left off the anniversary show. For the first time since signing with that label, I was ready to answer questions candidly about my time there. Being the biggest cheerleader for them wasn't doing anything but making me feel stupid. When the reporter asked how I felt about not being invited, I answered honestly. I tried to be as poised and articulate as possible, but this was years of pent-up frustration coming out. Years of feeling like people at the label were secretly holding me back or laughing at me or maybe just straight up intimidated. Who the fuck knows? All I knew was I was fucking over it.

I was the one running around the whole earth screaming the Rhymesayers name, letting them take credit for my work whenever I did something noteworthy or dope enough to be covered by a publication. There would be whole tours where I would walk in venues and have to field questions about the label and when I was gonna work with them again. Experiencing neglect, intimidation, and non-communication from them, I'd have to dig into my classy bag and say something nice about the whole fucked-up situation. But nah, not this time.

This time I spoke up, and the result was an explosive interview that put me squarely in the court of public opinion in a way I hadn't experienced before. The article was strategically released in the same issue of *City Pages* that was honoring the label for their contributions. The same issue that came out mere weeks before the big anniversary show. So, while they were navel-gazing, I was lifting the curtain to a darker revelation.

People were mad. People were shocked. People were brutal.

After the interview dropped, Angel advised me to stay off the internet. There were whole Facebook groups popping up discussing the article, my career, what I ate for lunch, and who I was as a person. Rhymesayers fanatics were setting themselves on fire just so I could feel the burn of them never liking me anyway. Some of these fans are true incel bullies. Woman hating. Homophobes. Racists. And they were proud of it. There were fans telling stories of this one time I didn't sign an autograph right away so it served me right to be left off the bill. People saying I'm wack. People saying I'm just mad because I'd never be as good as other artists on the label. I was so hurt; I believed them. I was a wreck. Angel was the only one in the house willing to help me through it.

I don't know what the fuck Tabby was thinking. Maybe she saw the article as career spoiling. Maybe my loss of clout from Rhymesayers meant the loss of clout for her. Maybe she knew she might have had something to do with it. Was this professional embarrassment part of the fallout of her screaming match with their big important artist months prior? Was this retaliation? We will never know, but it ain't too far-fetched to consider. Let's recap: Artist is invited to play on a huge anniversary show, artist's girlfriend gets in a screaming match with one of the most influential dudes on the label, artist is uninvited.

I could never prove this. I don't know this to be truth. But come on.

All I'm saying is: It's not too baseless of a theory. If *important* folks didn't like me, or my girl, or *whoever*, they could dismiss me.

But you could never erase a bitch like me.

I am years removed from the moment, but I was absolutely gutted at the time. When I even thought about going on social media I was smacked in the face with a tweet or post about me being bitter or not good enough or awesome. But you're never as good, or as bad, as they say. People said some fucked-up shit about me, and it only pushed me deeper into the bottle. I wouldn't be sober for this. If there was any incident to push me completely over the edge of addiction, this was it. I couldn't be sober for this. I felt like everything I'd built was crumbling.

My primary partner was absent. Tabby told me a week afterwards I shouldn't have done the article. She all but declared she wasn't gonna support me through this anniversary-show shit. I had some rapper peers show me some undercover support, but most of the rappers I know would never do what I did. There are musicians and employees of plenty of labels who felt the same way I did regarding intimidation, professional abuse, and gaslighting, but they would never say anything. You'd never know how they felt because they'd rather be disgruntled on a label than exist without that affiliation. I understand that. But I was fed up.

I didn't have the luxury of support after my first album; they'd done the bare minimum. What were they gonna do, NOT put out my next album? Nah. Even though it hurt, I did the right thing. And it got the conversation of abusive RSE practices and inclusion started. A conversation we are still having about them to this day.

At home, Tabby showed us the music didn't matter to her anymore. She wasn't a great artist. She wasn't even a good artist without help. Her contributions to my actual music were negligible. She was supposed to be my friend at the very least. Fuck the romantic shit, we were friends. And during one of the hardest times in my life, she turned her back on me. I was broken.

My explosive *City Pages* article dropped in November 2015, and the arena show was shortly thereafter. I spent the holidays in an exhausted stupor. The house had calmed down a bit, but there was an irreparable shift in energy. I hated Tabby but rent was cheap, and *POLY* was surprisingly making a lot of year-end lists. Angel and I cared. We were gonna get this Rapperchicks music out, even if it killed us.

Between Thanksgiving and Christmas, Tabby and I warmed up to being cordial. I was too tired and inebriated to fight all the time. My dumb ass even agreed to go celebrate with her family. Dutch flat-out refused to go to family functions with her, yet I was a fixture at these gatherings. Tabby had been telling her mom about us fighting, and her mom told everyone in the family. Being with Tabby's family as the bad guy was excruciating. They all gave me the cold shoulder while still asking when I was taking Tabby on tour again. I promised myself that would be the last holiday season I spent with her family. Even if somehow she and I worked through our relationship issues, I wouldn't go back over to her aunt's house for dry turkey and burnt brisket, even if I did enjoy speaking with her grandparents. The whole family shit was over. Ain't no family in hip hop.

The 2015 New Year's Eve show offers were coming in, so we decided to do a big one at a convention center with some friends who were given a slot. We were gonna be opening for bigger acts like Gucci Mane and Skrillex. As a group we felt we had something to prove. Tabby invited Dutch, and even though he was lightweight unimpressed by us, he was on our dicks after the performance. We killed that shit. Maybe it was the pent-up anger and aggression. Maybe it was because it was my first show since the article fallout. Maybe it was to remind us we were a powerful group with a great message and awesome music. Maybe it was because deep down, I knew it would be our last show as a unit. Next year, 2016, wasn't going to, and couldn't, be like this last year. It was getting harder to survive.

We came home after that show and did all the drugs. It was New Year's Eve, after all. I wanted to lock myself in a room and get bent. I didn't care to stay at the convention center where the show was taking place. I didn't want to go out to a party and actually celebrate with my friends. Nah. I wanted to numb the fuck out. I feel dumb as hell writing this, but I now know how depressed and broken I was. Plenty of artists deal with daily bouts of insecurity, anxiety, depression, addiction, and the like. Most of us don't know how to deal. We don't have insurance. We can't talk to our parents. We don't have the language or the tools. We feel like we can't talk to our friends or peers because we should be grateful for the opportunity to do music for a living. So we self-medicate. I was self-harming. Thankfully, things are changing, and we're having more conversations about how artists suffer in a nonromantic way.

The year 2016 came with my face in a pile of drugs and my heart broken in the corner. Tabby retired to bed early because she was being antisocial, and Dutch didn't wanna be curled up in a bed with this older woman with low self-esteem, no drugs, and no desire to have fun. She'd risked a lot to have him around and he was around at a minimum. He came over on Thanksgiving to get a plate and barely spoke to Tabby. He wasn't around on Christmas but popped back up around New Year's Eve. He was more interested in hanging out with Angel and me downstairs because we were actually partying. At this point Tabby was just mean. Nobody wanted to be around her. She was just paying half the rent.

January 4, 2016, is a night I'll never forget. All of the previous month had been spent in a dangerous haze. After sobering up from New Year's, by the fourth day of January, I decided I was gonna get my act together. I was gonna detox, damnit. There was stuff to look forward to, and I still thought we could get our act together as a group.

I needed to run an errand in the suburbs that night so I was taking a nap. Angel was gonna join me because it was late and she hated being in the house alone with Tabby. Dutch had stumbled into our crib in the middle of the night and was sleeping off a Xanax high. He was in a coma-like state for over half a day and the house was quiet. It seemed as though everyone was sleeping one off.

At approximately 7:30 p.m., we heard loud bangs and noises upstairs. It went from silence to fireworks, and next we heard Dutch screaming at the top of his lungs, then another loud crash. Angel and I weren't gonna just pretend nothing was happening. Dutch knew he had Tabby emotionally, so he was getting meaner and meaner. We'd heard them arguing before and we'd seen him get mad at other people, so it was only a matter of time before he turned on her. But now he was breaking shit in our house? OUR HOUSE? Angel and I ran to the top floor to see what was going on. He was having an absolute fit.

He was screaming something about Tabby ruining his relationship with his real girlfriend. Tabby was standing there docile, allowing it to happen. A much different person than she was with us. Angel tried to rationalize with him, but he was screaming and punching shit. He turned his venom on me and told me he hated me and so did Tabby. His boldness told me how much they were pillow talking. She was definitely telling him shit he shouldn't have known. So, he felt comfortable coming at me.

He cursed me. He told me I was a wack rapper and I was a jealous bitch and that's why I didn't want him there. He said I should be afraid of him and pretty soon my house would be his kingdom. He said those words. All of this was disrespectful enough, but none of them was as triggering as when he threatened to shoot me in the face. In my own home.

My body flooded with triggered reactions. Dutch had no idea, or maybe he did, that my father had been killed by his father in a domestic incident that left me without a dad. I grew up with varying memories of domestic violence. Walking on eggshells and having the thickest tension in your own home was no way to live. This nigga didn't even pay rent and he was threatening to kill me, all with Tabby standing right next to him in silent approval. This was a purely violent cycle that needed to be broken somehow. But not tonight.

I flashed furiously. Dutch's threats sent me into a tailspin and I dared him. I dared him to kill me and I told him the foulest shit I could think of. I spoke about his deadbeat parents, his drug addiction, his nonexistent economic and professional status, his inability to make women come, even with a big dick. His ex. I talked big shit about his ex. She'd liked a few of my pics on Instagram. The latter hurt him the most, and after he got violent with me, I made a move.

He was barefoot and it was the dead of winter. I ran outside and said I'd fight him out there. My plan was to get him outside, barefoot, run back inside, lock the door, and let the chips fall. Without shoes, the Chicago winter would freeze him before he got back indoors, and by then the cops would probably have scooped his drunk ass up. But before any of that could happen, before Dutch even reached the door wielding a wine bottle, Angel tackled him with the strength of a hundred linebackers.

They both flew into the air, and Dutch went crashing down below Angel. She was sober and scary strong. He was frail, drunk, and coming out of a pill coma. He wasn't scary. He was loud and wrong. Angel is *not* the one to fuck around with. He didn't even get close to me before she lunged at him. He got body-slammed. It was perfectly horrible.

Dutch was now writhing under her and Tabby had the nerve to yell at Angel. This guy was tearing up our house and demeaning the fuck out of her, not to mention threatening my life, and all she could do was yell at Angel for tackling him? Wow. Tabby also ended up under Angel's grasp when she tried to stop Angel from stopping Dutch from attacking me. I couldn't take it anymore. I pretended to record the whole thing on my phone, then grabbed both sets of car keys while they were tussling on the ground. Angel got them both to submit. They were both too frail and weak to do anything else as we quickly bolted out. If Tabby wasn't gonna defend us, our house, or herself, why the fuck should we? If I stayed, I knew somebody was gonna get beat the fuck up—or worse.

Angel hopped in the car as I was about to pull off. She said she didn't trust me to drive safely or stay sober. She was right. We drove to my homie Freddie's house—he'd since moved back to the burbs—and decompressed. I was so hurt. This relationship had deteriorated too much. Tabby wasn't willing to stand up to Dutch; she'd sacrificed us to be with him. Not to mention the highly traumatizing death threat. I knew I could never be in the same space with him again.

I also knew I had to leave Tabby. Dutch crossed all the lines. Several hours later, when I was sober enough to drive us home, Angel and I approached the front door of the house and noticed the front door was broken, and the front window of our house was shattered. This motherfucker broke our door, our front window. He destroyed the house and even went down to the basement apartment. Who knows what Tabby had to endure in our absence? He didn't do too much downstairs, but I realized he had been down there. I noticed some of my weed was gone and there was a little broken glass in my bedroom. Even through this I hesitated to call the police. As much as I despised Dutch, I didn't actually want him to go to jail. A Black man in the hands of the police is usually a death sentence. And even though he threatened to kill me, for some reason I didn't want calling the cops to be on my conscience.

When he lunged at me, I had the bright idea to lock him out and let the cops find him, but that never happened. Angel dealt with him before I could. This latest incident proved he would hurt us if given the opportunity. I didn't give a fuck about him hurting himself. He did all the drugs and got in all the stupid fights, but that never involved me. Now, I was involved. And it took everything in me not to call the unsavory characters in my life to fuck him all the way up.

After coming home the next morning to a broken door, an arctic house with winter air screaming through because we had NO FRONT FUCKING WINDOW, and Dutch and Tabby cuddled up among broken bottles, empty pill bottles, blunt guts, and dirty underwear, I made an absolute vow to leave the house and break up with her—for good. My heart was completely demolished and we were now in danger. I'll never forget the way I felt walking back into that house and seeing them in bed together after all that. I wasn't going to be a part of it anymore. I didn't care what was gonna happen with the group when I left the house. That picture of them was everything I needed to see. It's burned into my brain. Before it was too late, I was gonna leave this place and change my life. I just had to get out of Pilsen first.

CHAPTER 19

PSALM ONE LOVES YOU (ETERNALLY)

Gettin' mad at me because I tame goddesses/
What the fuck you done about it? I just been a boss about it/
All this pleasure sho' nuff get ya game up/
See all these dudes talk shit when they mad/
But they ain't open up to talk about it/
Thought I'd be the bigger person/ Ain't no dick gon' make waves/
So swingin' it my way you look impatient and untalented/
Really wanna challenge what is ritual/
And when they look into my face I notice envy show/
Wanna get down with my team, it's an investment, Joe/
And I don't need no pythons in my jungle book . . .
— "Taming the Goddess"

I can count on one hand the number of significant fights I'd gotten into as a child.

One fight that sticks to my ribs was the one I had in an Englewood playground across the street from my Granny Thelma's house when I was about nine years old. I'd hit my friend Jamal's cousin in the back with a two by four, then kicked him in the nuts for talking shit about my family. He punched me dead in my face. He had a ring on. He split my shit. I had to go to the hospital for stitches, and the doctor said if he'd hit me an inch higher, I could have been blinded for life. If you look closely under my left eye, you can still see the scar where they had to sew me up. Not being able to handle my emotions when people talked shit about me would fuck me up a lot. I hadn't fully recognized it yet, but as an adult, I was violent.

Domestic violence fucked my life up. It almost killed my rap group. For the next two weeks after the Dutch incident, Tabby stayed away from the house and smeared my name, and Angel's, to whomever would listen.

We had one more fight, the worst one of all, on January 21, 2016. I won't get into all the ugly details, but during a heated argument about promotional and PR costs for the Rapperchicks, of all things, Tabby tried to push me out of a moving car. She also kicked me in the face with the new purple Timberlands I'd gotten her for Christmas. I, in turn, busted her lip and lumped up her right eye. We ended up stopped near the park across the street from our house, screaming and wrestling in the street. Yes, we were drunk. The cops were called. It was especially heinous and we were in front of our own crib.

The neighbors saw everything. I told the police, through hysterics, it was a domestic dispute and promised them we would calm down. They laughed, sent Tabby on her way, and left. The whole thing reminded me of San Francisco. Cycles are a motherfucker. It certainly hurts to type this, but it's necessary. These stories are important. What a mess. How you gonna kick me in the face with the boots I BOUGHT YOU? Ungrateful.

Tabby left with the car and stayed with a friend of Dutch. She told everyone all our business, but with her own special twists. She was actually telling people we weren't together and I was just jealous of her and Dutch. She even took the opportunity to say some wildly homophobic shit about me and Angel, which really cut deep. She also said I deserved everything I got from Dutch. That killed me, as we were always defending her from people. I couldn't believe she actually told people we *weren't* in a relationship. Who knows the lies she spread about Angel, who she hated even more? While Tabby stayed away, I started packing my shit. I was officially preparing to leave. Like, FOR REAL this time. I didn't tell her anything. She wanted me to stay and pay rent, and I knew that, but staying meant dying, literally. I wasn't gonna die in this Pilsen den of hurt.

I would have gotten fucked up in a tragically stupid way if I'd stayed with her any longer. It was obvious the romantic relationship had to end, but after the purple-Timberland fight following the Dutch fight, there was absolutely no doubt I had to leave the crib ASAP. Something clicked inside of me. God knocked me upside the head. There would be no debriefing. There would be no sweeping under the rug, boarding up of windows, patching up our wounds, or moving forward. None of that. Angel and I also decided that we had to kick Tabby out of the Rapperchicks as well. There was no time to waste. Tabby could rot alone, or with Dutch. Either one was fine with me.

Angel and I went halfsies on a new storage unit and moved all of our big and important items there. I still had a storage unit with Tabby but I didn't care. I rented a U-Haul, and one icy winter morning we moved everything I wanted to keep into a nice warm unit. Of course, I couldn't leave the crib without doing a few petty things upstairs. I wouldn't be Cristalle aka Psalm One if I'd left without leaving Tabby something to remember me by. I won't incriminate myself any further, but I'll give you a taste of what I did before leaving.

I knew the real tidal wave of bullshit was gonna come after she realized I was gone. I knew there was gonna be retaliation. But I did do this: I took her favorite shoes, the ones I knew she loved, even some expensive ones I'd purchased myself, and threw away the left one because THAT BITCH AIN'T RIGHT. Let her buy a whole-new pair of purple Timberlands with her raggedy ass. She'd already stolen quite a few special items from my wardrobe. After one of our tussles, all of my limited RSE merch disappeared. She also stole a few of my dad's pictures. I was big, big mad. I'm surprised I didn't destroy more of her shit when I was packing my stuff. I guess I figured I was being frugal in my bullshit. I wanted to get my shit out of that house more than I wanted to destroy it.

Leaving Pilsen meant homelessness. I didn't secure a new place to actually live. I couldn't go home to my mother. There was too much baggage I had to sort through. I couldn't crash with friends forever. I didn't know what to do. So I swallowed my pride and did something I rarely did: I asked for help. I hollered at my old buddy who worked at Chicago Mixtape. The friend who'd been an angel investor for a few merch items and a couple of albums could possibly be an angel investor for me reclaiming my soul. I was at rock bottom. There was no doubt about that. I just needed to get away from the chaos for a little while to figure out my next move.

I choked back tears and asked him to help me. He gave me a few thousand dollars to get back on my feet. I paid my new storage unit fees for six months, and booked a bus ticket to my pal Nate's house. Nate told me whenever I left Tabby I could come up to his crib in Minneapolis. He knew things were getting uncontrollably fucked up. He wanted to help me, too.

People ask me about the years leading up to my 2019 album, *Flight of the Wig*, so I've decided to provide a loose timeline for perspective. We tend to forget the musicians and entertainers we hold so dear have actual lives. A hiatus from the art could mean much more than we think. Just because someone has a dream job doesn't mean they don't need a break for their own livelihood. My dream had turned into . . . I don't have to say that corny shit. My life was fucking awful.

People on the internet mocked me for speaking my truth in 2015 about being on RSE. The public scrutiny was eating me alive. I was still dealing with that. I had blocked so much pain surrounding my time on RSE out of my mind. I flooded my life with writing and recording and shows to try and save face to my fans. I had these little secret competitions with my peers to show I was still relevant. I was in an abusive relationship that had helped my career, but killed my self-esteem. All of that blew up in my face. It wasn't until the uprisings of 2020 and the demands of the Minneapolis community for Rhymesayers to be held accountable for even *more* allegations, that had nothing to do with me, that I began to sift through all the trauma and accept it for what it was. I also had to accept my role in ALL of it. Let's sift.

In 2017, after an eye-opening bout of depression where I realized I *had* depressive episodes, I dragged myself to a behavioral-health clinic, puffy eyed and exhausted. But before I could do all that, I had to settle into a new life, away from Tabby and away from Chicago. If I'd stayed there after purple-Timbo night I might have gone to jail, hell, or worse. So off to Nate's house I went. But Nate lived in Minneapolis. The belly of the beast I *thought* had calmed down a bit. The date was February 1, 2016.

I really had to put the pieces of my life back together before I could even think about music, but I had some tunes ready to go: a three-song EP from the Rapperchicks. Angel ok'd it and we decided to put it out without telling Tabby. We'd written all her lyrics anyway.

The morning after arriving in Minneapolis, I released the Rapperchicks' *Shitty Punk Album* on my Bandcamp page and let fans pay what they wanted for the project. It did surprisingly well and got a writeup in *Vice*, for what it's worth. We even got iconic southern rapper Gangsta Boo on a track called "Rules and Regulations" and that did really well. Even through the worst days of my life, I was still getting love for the music. What a mind fuck. I sold enough copies to pay bills for a few more months.

Angel was back in Chicago. Leaving her was so hard, but I knew I had to get out of the city for my own sanity. I needed to be far enough away from Tabby so I wouldn't be tempted to find her, OR Dutch, for that matter. I was still wildly triggered by him telling me he was gonna shoot me in the face. Under all this nerdy exterior, I'm a real nigga and you don't tell a real nigga that. Nah. It was better for me to go.

I didn't wanna break up with Angel. We were closer than ever. Of course, we got closer through trauma, but we'd already established a friendship before things fell apart. I told her I'd send for her, like we were in a fucking black-and-white film. I needed two weeks away from all of it. So she packed a small bag and crashed with the friends who were partying a lot. Yeah, *those* kinds of friends. She promised to be safe, and I promised to get better.

But before they could get better, things got so fucked up. Getting back on your feet after leaving an abusive relationship can take years. Sometimes decades. Some people die trying to leave these kinds of relationships. Crimes of passion make up a frighteningly large number of murders and assaults. Look it up. This shit is very real, and it may help somebody to read this. At that point in my career, in 2016, I wanted to give up. I was having suicidal thoughts again and music was way low on the priority scale. I needed healing, like yesterday. Releasing the Rapperchicks' music had given us some creative time. I really needed that time.

In Minneapolis, I was technically homeless. I was taking the Megabus back and forth from Chicago to the Twin Cities and crashing with friends every time. Here and there I'd crash with my mom or my aunt, but I didn't want them to know how bad it had gotten. I had to come clean about a lot of shit to my mom after deciding to leave Chicago, but I didn't wanna tell her *everything*. Mama's gonna read this and worry about me more. Note to my mother: I know you're reading this, Elaine. I'm ok now, Mama. It's ok now.

I've split myself open again and again. I control the narrative now. No fan or label or mistake or lover or fight could ever define me. I made a decision after leaving Chicago, after Tabby: I wasn't going to allow my crazy life to end on such an ugly note if I could help it. After being homeless for a few months, going back and forth between Nate's house in Minneapolis and family in Chicago, plus laying off the drugs, I found a lead on a room I could rent in Chicago for both me and Angel. Having a residence meant we weren't homeless anymore. There could finally be a little stability. I had stayed away long enough and laid low enough that there was no trail. Most of my friends and peers had no idea where I was. I was moving around so much, there was no way Tabby could pop up on me. I was ready to begin a life with no scene and no music on the horizon.

As soon as we released the Rapperchicks project, Tabby started whining online. It didn't matter. She was constantly going on rants and sending me long emails cursing and threatening me. I had a few things of hers and we still shared a storage unit. The only thing I remember really missing from that unit was thousands of dollars' worth of Rhymesayers vinyl. Tabby threatened that she'd burn the vinyl if I didn't do something she wanted regarding the group. I wasn't gonna do it. So, I lost that vinyl. To this day I still shake my head about that. What a loss. I wonder if she actually burned it. Raggedy.

Because Tabby was so clearly gone from the group, we decided to reach out to our other group member, ill-esha, and see if she still wanted to be part of what we were doing. Sure, she was in Denver and doing her own thing, but she saw what was happening online. Tabby had emailed her privately and told her some lies, but luckily, she was more interested in the music. The drama was something we were leaving behind when we got rid of Tabby. We could finally focus.

We went to Denver for a month to make music with ill-esha, and it was great. It was the first time we were traveling and working without the deadweight of Tabby. Going to Denver unlocked a new level of musicianship within the group, and we were able to build a new, strong bond.

By the spring of 2016, we'd also booked a few really important shows as a group. It was crazy because I swear the exact day we released the Rapperchicks album and kicked Tabby out the group we were offered a performance slot at the Taste of Chicago. The Taste is an annual food-and-music festival in Chicago, one of the biggest in the nation. As a kid I used to go there, eat my face off, and catch world-class musicians play in Chicago's Grant Park. It had always been a dream of mine to perform there, and every year Tabby would tell me we needed to play the Taste. As soon as I left her, we got the offer to play. It further confirmed how much I was blocking my blessings messing with her.

Our music instantly got better because there was no tension. To further purge, I compiled a gang of songs I'd been recording over the course of my time at Rhymesayers for release. These were songs they either shelved or ignored, but ones that really meant a lot to me at the time. *Gender / Fender / Bender (GFB)* was self-released as a triple album of deep and previously unreleased Psalm One material. The third album, *Bender,* I filled with unreleased Angel Davanport material. She still hadn't released a proper project and I wanted to help in the little ways I could. We only made two hundred copies of the entire thing and it was never released online. It's a cool little physical-only project, and it's one I'm very proud of. That triple album felt like a weight being lifted and it symbolized starting my career over. Getting rid of those songs was like having a colonic.

Psalm One and Angel Davanport, Gender / Fender / Bender *photoshoot, Chicago, summer 2016. Photo credit: Southside Cos-G.*

Coming back home to Chicago was bittersweet because we could only afford so much. Tabby and her financial contributions were gone. Shows were slowly coming in but the reality of rent and transportation was swift. I didn't wanna sell weed because I hated handcuffs. We came back to live in a really dangerous area of the South Side, off Seventy-Ninth Street and King Drive. I was grateful to have a place I could afford while I picked up the pieces of my life, but I can't lie, I was shook. I hadn't lived in the hood since high school. I had made it out of the hood, as it were. Going back was like going back to a war zone.

There were shootings on my block every day (not an exaggeration), and it was even more dangerous than I remember it being as a kid. I was finding ways to cope and escape those thoughts, which led back to some bad habits. I needed to stay clean. I had been with Tabby for eight and a half fucking years. It was gonna take a long time for me to get over it. I'm still getting over it. There was so much work to do.

The cool thing about my after-school program, Rhymeschool, was that I could schedule workshops based on my availability. Intonation worked with several touring and full-time musicians, so they were very accepting of long blackout dates. Fall was approaching and I wanted to teach. Working with kids also helped me stay sober and brought me joy. Opening up my schedule to Rhymeschool meant closing my party schedule, and that was exactly what I needed. I also needed some income.

By the end of the fall of 2016, workshops and sales from the triple album had my bank account looking a little healthier. Numbers for *GFB* were good and even though I wasn't recording any new music, I had "new" music out there. The momentum of that plus the growth of our group with ill-esha got us through the private pain of healing from what had just happened to us. I'd also been approached with a new tour offer, one I didn't have to book myself or drive or do anything but come and rap. I would even have a DJ baked into my set. It was a refreshing change, to just show up and do that. I felt like I was becoming myself again. Thank you for inviting me on the road in 2016, Kno. It was cathartic.

CunninLynguists' Doombox West Coast Tour flyer, fall 2016.

That tour was the beginning of me finding my stride again. That fall was also the beginning of daily meditation. Or as my homie Nate liked to call it, sitting your ass down. I didn't know where to begin, but sitting still was a good start. Healing was slow but I was starting to build some healthy habits. Habits that I still hold dear, even today.

Psalm One onstage, Berkeley, California, October 2016.
Photo credit: Kayla Windsor.

Upon coming home from the Doombox Tour, I found out that my roommate was pregnant, and she was gonna need our room for a nursery. She was kindly kicking us out. This was such a familiar feeling and I was happy for my roomie, but it was a bummer because we had to be out sooner than later. It was an opportunity to get out of the hood, though. But in order to do that, I needed more money than I was making.

Here's where life really kicked in: the gig economy. I was tired as fuck of not having a car. I'd lost that in the divorce, as I called Tabby's and my tumultuous breakup. The first three years had been ok, but the last five were hell. Picking up the pieces was taking long as fuck. It was time to swallow my pride and find more work. I was making a little money off rapping and a little money doing workshops. Angel was always a blessing but she was still finding her way financially. I needed a car and I needed money—fast.

Uber has so much bad shit attached to its name, but around Thanksgiving 2016, they had a program where you could rent a car and drive for them. If you did seventy-five trips a week, they would reimburse you for the car *and* you could keep your earnings, minus gas of course. I had been on so many tours and spent so much time driving random niggas around that I jumped at the chance. I could drive all day for money. And it wasn't even my car, it was a rental. This was a no-brainer and if I could deal with possibly getting spotted as Psalm One, something that was sure to happen, I could stack some bread and continue rebuilding my existence.

After moving into yet another new apartment with an artist friend, a cool-ass white chick I'd met through a local rapper, I started driving a rented Hyundai Sonata for Uber. We found that new apartment in haste, though, which is never great. It was in a prime location, back in Logan Square, but there was one little caveat: We were living *again* with people who loved to party. There was gonna be, dare I say, *too* much temptation, and even though I was slowly getting back on my feet, I never went to rehab or anything. I was always somehow able to stop as long as I needed to. But addiction doesn't just go away. You have to be proactive at *staying* clean. I wasn't quite there yet. Angel and I were both dealing with PTSD. And coping.

Our relationship remained strong, but we had real bouts with addiction. The holidays were coming up, and it was the first time I started noticing signs of anxiety and depression surrounding that time of year. Even though things were better than they had been in months, they were still kinda shitty. I had a lot of baggage. School and workshops were done until spring. When I wasn't driving Uber, I was back to getting shitfaced. And my new roommates had all the shit I didn't need.

By the time New Year's Eve 2016 came around, Angel hit her own personal rock bottom. There was just too much temptation in that household. We were partying almost every night, and I was even back to using drugs secretly. I had a lot more disposable income from ridesharing—I was good at it!—and I could afford to indulge. But after a few weeks of heavy drinking and cocaine use, Angel got the scare of a lifetime and saw the devil in the shower.

No, I'm serious. We'd come home from blowing lines with a friend and she kept complaining of chest pains. She was convinced she might be overdosing and she wasn't, but you couldn't tell *her* that. We ended up at the emergency room twice. They released her twice. When we got home, I suggested she take a long shower. While in the shower, she hallucinated. She was so sincere.

"Cris, I see the devil in the shower."

"What?"

"I see the devil in the shower. I think he's here to kill me."

"Ok, well, since you see the devil in the shower, tell that motherfucker to kill you or go the fuck away. I'm tired of him being here."

"Me too."

There was a lot of crying and releasing that night. While I still dabbled infrequently with hard drugs, Angel stopped drugs cold turkey that night. She made a vow she'd never touch cocaine again. I would make that vow several months later, but Angel was done that night in that bathroom. And she's been sober for over three years. She's the champ.

After the scares of drugs and the realization we were both still really fragile, we looked to what was next and how we could resist the temptations of home. An old friend invited us to come to Los Angeles to work on building Angel's career. In the middle of winter, nothing is more attractive than spending a few months in California. I was afraid of being broke again, as LA is so fucking expensive, but I knew taking this risk might be just the thing we needed to keep us focused on what was important.

I gave Uber their car back, paid my rent for the next two months, and hopped a buddy-pass flight to La La Land. There, we were faced with Angel's withdrawal symptoms. Turns out her body *really* wanted to party, and there were no hard drugs allowed where we were staying in LA. Well, no *hard* drugs, but niggas drank A LOT. Angel discovered she could stave off the withdrawal symptoms with alcohol. I was worried about her but at least she wasn't doing drugs. I wasn't either.

Angel was also writing some of the best songs she'd ever written. She was healing, slowly, and was able to sing about some of the real shit in her life. These were songs young women could really relate to. It was promising. Our time back in California was not without complications, but it was a stepping stone to bigger opportunities.

Even though my time at RSE was over, I still had friends in the game. An old Minneapolis rap pal invited Angel to feature on one of his songs. That song led to hopping on a show when he toured the West Coast during our time out there. He recognized the growth we were both displaying and told us to come to Minneapolis to make music. I missed making music. As it turns out, he told lots of people to come to Minneapolis to make music with him that ultimately wouldn't materialize. But we took him seriously. He said it was time to leave Chicago more permanently, face my fears, and plant some real roots in the Twin Cities.

I decided to take his advice. It was impossible to think about getting sober in the house we were living in, and our time in LA was coming to an end. While we made some cool music, the alignment wasn't there to do much more. There were too many proverbial cooks in that kitchen. We wanted less complicated creativity. We were both so tired of making music that never got released. Music was still very much a desired career path, and this time felt like the beginning of a second chance. I didn't wanna blow it, and Angel hadn't even really gotten started. So, after deciding to move YET AGAIN, we went back to Chicago from LA to pack up our shit. Minneapolis was the destination.

Before fully making the move, I escorted my mom to Paris and Amsterdam for her sixtieth birthday. My godmother funded the majority of the trip. I wasn't balling like that, but I'd saved up what little money I had to make sure we had money for transportation and food once we got to Europe. In LA, I had unexpectedly been commissioned to do a few songs with an EDM producer, Manic Focus. Through those songs I was able to save a few dollars and have a cushion. It still boggles my mind that I was able to make and sell music during this time. But music has always been there, even when I thought it wasn't.

Through all the madness at home, I was able to leave the country and bond with my mom. She knew I had been having a hard time since leaving Chicago, but she saw me working through it. We had a wonderful time. I told her when we got back to the States, I was gonna be in Minneapolis again, but this time she was gonna see even bigger changes in my life. Thank God I was able to keep my word.

And thank God for my godmother, Belinda. She gave my mom and me an opportunity to experience one of my mom's dreams together. It was important for me to see my mother happy during a time when I was at my lowest. I have always wanted her to be proud of me. As an only child of a single mom, I've spent my life trying to be impressive, for better or worse. I didn't want her to worry, but I was very sad. That trip with my mom was so chill and so loving and so beautiful. There were times where I actually felt at peace. That hadn't happened in such a long time. I was ready to make yet another change. One of the biggest in my life.

CHAPTER 20
WOMAN-RAPPER PROTECTIVE SERVICES

Silence is violence, I beg you don't try it/
And you ain't discrediting my shit/
They even sent women of color to try to shut us up/
You worse than that white bitch/
Look at you lickin' them boots/
And you ain't came up, sucks to be YOU/
I told the truth and yo' boss is a fluke/
And I'll flame yo' ass for them subtweets, too . . .
— **"McNothing" (Big \$ilky)**

Coming back to the Twin Cities was gonna be much different this time. No more crashing with Nate. He and his partner were about to have a baby. Joy! Even though we could no longer crash with him, he told his neighbor across the street the Rapperchicks were moving to Minneapolis and needed a place to live. His neighbor was a fan of our music and she'd met us before. She had an empty room and was willing to open her home to us. Living permanently in Minneapolis was gonna be a reality.

Cue the absolute culture shock. By March 2017, we were mostly living in the Powderhorn neighborhood of south Minneapolis, and Trump had been elected President of the United States. Mothafuckin' Donald J. fucking Trump. I couldn't believe it. What a dumpster fire.

Minneapolis, while somewhat diverse, is overwhelmingly fucking white. And this Minnesota-nice phenomenon, where people are nice to you, even if they hate your fucking guts, can get you killed. I laid as low as possible. I actually didn't want anyone knowing I was living in the Twin Cities yet. I had to find my bearings. Our new roommate, Jenny, had been so kind to take us in.

While I was happy to be surrounded by folks who understood my plight and didn't care about label politics, I was still coming back to a place of real trauma as a professional musician. I didn't realize how sensitive I was until I bumped into an RSE label head at a bar. I had a full-blown anxiety attack. Living here was not going to be a cakewalk. Sure, I was fixing my Chicago problems, but I had Minneapolis baggage to unpack. Even more changes needed to be made. Again, even more work to be done.

Angel found a job right away, and I was qualified for a gang of science-related jobs, but I needed a car for all of them. I started figuring out a way to Uber again, but before that happened, I landed a job BEING A FUCKING WEDDING DJ. I was still not mentally able to record my own new shit, but I still loved music. That doesn't just go away. Working in LA with Angel taught me I could work on music that wasn't mine and be happy, just so long as I wasn't being led astray. Being a wedding DJ was pretty good money. My roomie let me borrow her car for a few weeks so I could train. I would be learning some new skills and working on my blends. DJ Psalm One? Fuck it.

After living with Jenny for a few months, we learned that she got accepted into Harvard for grad school, and we found a sublease on the other side of town. A rap pal yelled at me to get my own home studio set up and start recording my own fucking demos. It had never really occurred to me to do that, considering I was never in a crib long enough to set something up. I had always been a studio rat. People throughout my career had always scheduled studio time for me. But my homie reminded me that so many women get jerked around at the studio, no pun intended. He told me to save $1,000 and get to building. This was some of the best advice I'd ever gotten in my life.

But $1,000 was so much money to me at that time. I didn't wanna tell my friend that we were beyond broke after moving residences constantly, battling addiction, and spending the winter in LA. But fuck excuses. If I could do everything I'd done up to that point, I could find a way to save a grand.

Independent-artist tip: That weed and alcohol add up. The partying adds up. You can save money and invest in your career if you sacrifice. Maybe you don't buy that new outfit or that bag of drugs. Maybe you stop going to the bar for a few months. If you're spending money on fashion, parties, and entertainment, you can spend money on your art. Just my two cents.

The wedding-DJ gig kept me very busy, and after passing the Minnesota driving test, I was able to get my license and rideshare again. I was gonna be able to lease a new car through Uber as well. What a blessing. I planned to work both jobs, pay down my credit cards, get a new place, and eventually save enough money to buy some recording equipment. Things were looking up. I just worked. And worked. And worked.

Since coming from LA and realizing I wasn't fitting into many of my clothes, I decided it was also time to tap back into my athletic ways. When you get off drugs you get chunkier, especially if you're still drinking alcohol. Life hack: You can "gym hop" by getting free weekly trials at all the fitness places in town when you're a new resident. Free gym memberships got me back on the road to health in a lot of ways.

The following timeline has to do with therapy. In the summer of 2017, Angel and I moved into a temporary sublet with some very nice young ladies who didn't party every fucking night, weren't trying to be musicians, and kept regular jobs. Our previous roommate was leaving for Harvard and she was an inspiration to watch. We were finally surrounded by positive shit. No underlying competition or pressure to be anything but healthy.

Here's how it all went down.

A SHORT TIMELINE OF HEALING PRACTICES / BUILDING MYSELF UP TO MAKING NEW MUSIC AGAIN

Month/ Year	Medita- tion?	Exercise/ Yoga?	Substance- Abuse Level	Behav- ioral- Health Therapy?	Were you making new music?
Jan 2016	Started	Limited Yoga	Medium	No	No
Aug 2017	Almost Daily	Both	Medium	No	No
Sep 2017	Daily	Both	Medium	No	No
Circa March 2018	Semidaily	Both	Low	Yes	Yes
March 2021	Daily	Yoga	**None**	Yes	**Yes**
June 2021	Daily	Both	None	Lots	**Lots**

You will notice that quitting drugs and alcohol and starting exercise, meditation, and therapy had everything to do with my ability to make music again. And God, of course. I'm a firm believer that damn near every musician deals with mental-health issues, especially ones who've tried and failed. I've succeeded at a lot of shit, but I've had some failures that could have defined my whole life. Not to mention the detours I went on being an addict and in abusive relationships. I have been the abuser AND the abused. Hell, *music* can be an abusive relationship, if you're not careful. After moving out of the sublet and into the Minneapolis home I still live in today (over three years in the same crib—stability!), things slowed down even more on the drama front. Peace was closer than ever before and I craved it. But in this new house, I had to humble myself quite a bit.

A happy Psalm One, Minneapolis, circa October 2018.
Photo credit: Serene Supreme.

Major, positive life changes can come in the form of employment, diet, exercise, spirituality, meditation . . . plenty of shit. I don't have all the answers, but I do have the experiences. Music has been a constant in my life since I was a little girl, and from the time I became a professional musician, I lost parts of myself. Music has always been my heart, but a lot of heartbreak can fuck you all the way up. I started therapy because I was tired of using my friends as a crutch. I was tired of always venting to them or arguing with Angel about shit that I hadn't figured out in my own head.

In the fall of 2017, I started behavioral therapy. I spent the first several sessions sobbing my eyes out about Tabby and Rhymesayers and feeling like I was a failure. How hard it was driving Uber and Lyft around every weekend, knowing there were shows I couldn't attend. Shows I couldn't perform at. How hard it was seeing rap peers, many of whom really don't write or rap as good as me or Angel, succeed. Maybe it was because they were able to play the game, lock a budget, and keep their mouths shut. Maybe it was just their pure talent. But if they were upset at their labels or their bandmates, they would never say anything. I had respect, but no clout. I had to accept my fate as a nonmusician before I could become one again. My therapist has helped me out a lot with that. I'm blessed. I know therapy is expensive, but I was able to get some through health insurance. I was able to get health insurance because I was working a few jobs. Minnesota's health-insurance system is way better than Illinois's. Get it together, Illinois. To anyone reading this, there are resources out there if you're diligent. Find someone qualified to talk to you. It may help you get back on track. It might even save your life.

Around the same time I started therapy, Angel and I moved into the house we've been in ever since. Before the pandemic, my roomies were never home as they were touring musicians. I had a lot of time to myself. I had to swallow a lot of pride, moving into this home. I had to accept they were doing the shit I really wanted to do. In order to not become resentful and bitter, I had to make peace. I had to access humility. Everything in my life was getting better, albeit slowly. But slow was better than nothing, and as I was building my mind and body, the universe was clearing a path back to music.

After months and months of only ridesharing and solitude at home, I was asked to go on tour in 2018 with Insane Clown Posse for almost two months. It would be the longest tour I'd gone on in years. Even though I'd only be rapping a little bit, my main job was to DJ for an opening act. Wedding-DJ season was over, but rap-tour season was beginning. The road schedule was intense. I learned so much on that tour about longevity and what I actually want in life. I was able to get my face back out there and remind old and potential fans that Psalm One was not dead.

I was working out and meditating throughout the entire grueling tour. I didn't do drugs or binge drink once during the whole thing. Progress. I had finally started becoming the change I wanted to see. Being a rapper's DJ as a rapper was also humbling. I was starting to like it.

Towards the end of that tour, my Uncle Marlon passed away, and my family back in Chicago was dealing with it. Losing him was brutal. The timing was eerie. I actually went to see him in the hospital on the last afternoon of the tour. He was at Northwestern Hospital during our Chicago stop, and I made sure to go visit him. If I hadn't taken some time for my *real* family that day, and instead laid up resting in my hotel room, as I was prone to do, I would never have seen him alive again. That's a lesson I will never forget.

He told me that day to never bite my tongue and to save as much money as possible. Powerful lessons from a man awaiting the afterlife. I held his hand, kissed him, and told him I loved him and would always cherish him. The way he looked that day, I was entirely sure I'd never see him again. Unfortunately, I was right. He passed on shortly after I visited him, when I was already back in Minneapolis. Rest in power, Uncle Marlon. I know you're in a better place. I know your spirit is still here with your loved ones. I miss you.

Real life keeps coming, we all keep getting older, and these bills never stop accumulating. I ain't famous at all. Pretending to be some huge successful rapper isn't an option. I was never really into pretending, anyway. I needed to work out all of the things in my head. I was beginning to win because I was quieting my mind in the stillness of meditation. I was praying more intentionally. I was able to move into a nice-ass crib, send the leased car back to Uber, and buy one outright because I had another source of income that had nothing to do with music. I was not abusing any hard drugs. I actually stopped years ago. I'm getting older. Drugs ain't fun anymore. I increased my credit score and now my shit is excellent. On the surface, things were a million percent better. However, my mind still needed, and needs, a lot of help.

Trauma doesn't just up and go away. I still get mad at things I thought I'd healed from. I still cringe at the way I've treated some of my partners. I still cringe at the way I became bitter as an artist. But that's ok now. I wasn't considering how long I was depressed. When I finally considered I was dealing with some mental-health issues, I looked into getting better health insurance so I could afford therapy. God was surely looking out for me, because I was able to find a therapist here, in Minneapolis, fairly easily. When things align like that, you don't take it for granted. I've been seeing a therapist ever since, and it's made me more grounded and accepting than I've ever been.

I was able to work through a lot of the bitterness surrounding the simultaneous break up from my dream label and my longtime girlfriend. I was able to wrap my mind around this new dynamic relationship with Angel, one where I sincerely help her with her career and she helps with mine. And we have lives independent of each other. That's clutch. We are truly polyamorous, and even though we have times where we don't see eye to eye, we never resort to violence or even loud yelling. When I find myself getting upset, I remove myself and recenter. I breathe. I pray. I *communicate*. That's a huge win.

I'm also able to see the fruits of my labor here, in Minneapolis. After the ICP tour, I was empowered. I started looking to finish an album of my own and in May 2019, I released *Flight of the Wig*, my first full-length solo album with brand-new tunes since *Psalm One Loves You* in 2015. *Flight* has been my best-selling album to date. It also landed on some best-of-the-year hip hop lists. That album is my baby for real. The first project I'd created since college that was only for ME. All-new music and a new way of approaching life. I couldn't have made that album without going through hell. That's probably why it has resonated with so many of my fans. They could hear a healthy Psalm after seeing so much public backlash.

> *Racists hate me, but I'm way faster/*
> *Get a straight assassin on a gay basher/*
> *Drop ya label, they slave masters/*
> *In a field of underpaid gate crashers/*
> *I rap for women with new agendas/*
> *Got rules to bend, friend, are you offended?/*
> *If you are, bitch I meant—to!/*
> *Fuck you and whoever sent—you!/*
> *AHH!*
> —**"Nasty Jazz Hands"**

The landscape has changed a lot in the Twin Cities since I began making music again. In 2020, my story regarding the label I had so many issues with miraculously came back around. During the COVID-19 pandemic and the George Floyd uprisings, a lot of local acts started getting called out for abusive practices. Fans and artists alike were actually tired of performative local celebrities getting away with all types of abusive shit while claiming to stand for the community. Minneapolis was having its own #MeToo moment in the midst of all the chaos. We were, and still are, in the eye of a new civil rights movement. It was insane how many people alleged they had been violated by artists here in town, including some folks from the Rhymesayers camp. These are not my stories to tell here, but they are plentiful and heartbreaking. These new allegations reminded people of the things I'd said years ago, and it opened the floodgates for a lot of personal and professional trauma to come back to the surface.

But God wasn't finished with me. This time, I was strong enough to speak out in a way that was powerful. This time, I was sober and unafraid of what would happen to my career by speaking out. By 2020, I had taken full creative control of my own shit. My career is mine, and nobody runs my shit but me. In 2015, so many fans and peers just wanted to believe I was mad and bitter. While they were correct, they were incorrect about RSE. In 2020 I was proven right, but I hate being right about abuse in hip hop. Now that so much has been exposed, we *have* to rebuild.

More people believe my story of intimidation, gaslighting, neglect, and plain-old misogyny than ever before. They see the propping up of rape culture. The folks who are mad at me for speaking up for survivors aren't the kind of people I need in my life. They're telling on themselves. They're abuse apologists. I don't need them.

Minneapolis, and the music industry in general, will experience brighter days when people speak up and don't have to be afraid of talented and powerful folks playing with artists' and intimate partners' lives, especially women and queer artists. We are very susceptible to harm. But things are changing, and the wonderful Minneapolis fan and survivor community, myself included, had something to do with that. Imagine that.

Times have changed so much. I have changed so much. Hip hop is in a much different place than it was in '93. Yet I'm still here with my hands in the air.

When I started this book, I wanted to discuss my life in hip hop as a woman and my love of the culture. But it has morphed into an exploration of my career through music AND love. Music is my number-one love, and I've always been in a relationship with somebody.

The company we keep can truly shape our lives, and artists are some of the most sensitive creatures on earth. We tend to escape through many things: art, drugs, alcohol, delusion, sex, etc.

Certain lovers throughout the course of my career lifted me up, and some of those motherfuckers didn't care if I died. Talking about my art includes talking about my relationships. It also includes talking about my failures and how I dealt with them. My best, most honest music has come from not holding back on certain details of my life.

This book has been no different.

I'm a big advocate for mental-health services for musicians. I'm also an advocate of including health insurance with record deals. That's an almost-utopian fantasy, but it's certainly a good idea. There have been some strides made dealing with musicians and mental-health services. When I fell in love with hip hop, I never knew I'd be living it. Being a rapper for this long has taught me lessons about myself I thought I'd never learn.

When I signed my first deal, my dreams were small. I lived those dreams and fell in love with the lifestyle at the same time. The music kept me alive, but the lifestyle almost killed me. Artists frequently fall off the map and disappear, often prompting that age-old question: Whatever happened to so-and-so? Whatever happened to Psalm One?

In 2005, I signed my first record deal, and since 2015 I've been crawling out of a hole of depression and abuse. That's what happened to me. *Everything* happened to me, fool. And I'm right here. I'm alive and well.

I never fell off; I just never blew up. I've been living an insane life and building a legacy, usually with an unforgettable woman by my side. I've traveled all over. I have no regrets about my lost loves, because I'm sitting here navigating through the madness. I have peace. I have a home studio. I have a work studio. I have music that's selling as we speak. I just ate a bagel sandwich that was delicious. And I just wrote my first book.

And my latest group and project with Angel, *Big $ilky, Vol. 3*, was released in June 2021. We decided, in 2020, out of respect for Henny, that we would no longer record under the name Rapperchicks. It's Big $ilky now. ill-esha understood that. She's dope for that. We made our money back on the project within seven days. We have a lot of support from incredible fans. Bandcamp also honored me with a lifetime achievement award in 2020; I actually teared up when I saw the notification. It's like a Grammy to me. And to think: I only put music out on that website because a label was ignoring me. Imagine if I hadn't believed in myself enough to work independently of the cool independent label? Imagine if I'd believed what they said about me. These may be little wins to some, but these are big wins that keep me in the game. They keep me in the conversation. This is all me. I've taken my career, my love, and my life back. And then some.

Psalm One on the set of "McNothing," Chicago, May 2021.
Photo credit: Nicci Briann.

My music journey sometimes feels like a mind fuck, but this mind is stronger than ever. Life is good. God is great. Watch what I do in the next five years.

Pandemic illuminates darkness, uprisings just hit me the hardest/
And all you virtue-signaling fucks will not get to sample the harvest/
See, I don't align with no coward/
Cuz I used to be one/
Thankful that's over, I fear no human . . .
—"Jesse Got Away" (Big $ilky)

Getting back to the woman who isn't traumatized by the game and gets excited about making music took me years, but hip hop always found a way to pull me back in. It took succeeding, failing, moving, taking risks, sitting still, getting wasted, getting sober, getting therapy, accepting my mistakes, and getting real about what my life is to be here with y'all today. More than any person, lover, or drug, music has been *it*. More specifically, hip hop has been it. I'm a rap nerd through and through. I'll be loving this rap shit 'til the day I die, and I'll be doing some form of rap shit 'til I physically can't do it anymore. I'm in this thing forever. Google me. But please, don't call me a femcee. Call me a rapper. Call me a chemist. Call me Cristalle, OG $ilky, a child of God, or Psalm One. My bars are the truth.

And my word is bond.

EPILOGUE

could lie and say that so many people inspired this book. Many people didn't. God, first and foremost, has kept me protected and ordered my steps, from rap stages to these pages. My mother has been a long-time journalist and self-published her first book. She was the main inspiration for this. I also wanna thank my partner, Angel, for telling me to get to it. I've been wanting to write a book since I was a kid.

Finishing this project has been traumatic at times. Remembering some of the more awful bits of my life hasn't been fun at all. But I had to keep reminding myself that it was something I went through. Something that someone might need to read, to be inspired. My faith was restored because I've been through things I never thought I'd get through. At times I thought I was finished. At times I thought I wasn't worthy of good things. We are not our mistakes.

If you or anyone you know is struggling with addiction, self-hatred, or professional or domestic violence, do not stay quiet. We all know the cops don't have the best track record with bringing abusers to justice or dealing with mental-health issues, but we can find strength in the community. There are people out there qualified to deal with all of the things I've mentioned above and more.

Nationally, you can contact the National Domestic Violence Hotline through their secure website. They can be reached online at thehotline.org, or you can call SAMHSA at 1-800-662-HELP if you're dealing with mental- and/or substance-abuse disorders. It's confidential.

In Minneapolis, the Domestic Abuse Project is currently taking calls at 612-874-7063 ext. 232, helping with healing and therapeutic programming.

In Chicago, Deborah's Place is a resource for unaccompanied women experiencing homelessness. They can be reached at 773-722-5080. And if you have the means, donate to them.

Finally, I'd like to thank Jill Petty for her amazing guidance and skill navigating me through the completion of this book. Thank you for understanding the need for mental-health breaks! I'd also like to thank the amazing people at Haymarket Books for taking a chance on an *almost-almost* famous artist such as myself. I'm forever grateful.

Oh, and thank you to my crews PDX, Nacrobats, and Bionik 6ix. We made history.

THE PSALM ONE DISCOGRAPHY

Psalm One, *Whippersnapper*, Banarnar Records, 2001

Psalm One, *Bio:Chemistry*, Banarnar Records, 2002

Psalm One, *Personal Surplus*, self-released,* 2002

Nacrobats, *Always*, Birthwrite Records, 2003

Psalm One, *Bio:Chemistry 2: Esters and Essays*, Birthwrite Records, 2004

Psalm One, *Get in the Van Volume 1*, Birthwrite Records, 2005

Psalm One, *The Death of Frequent Flyer*, Rhymesayers Entertainment, 2006

Psalm One, *Get in the Van Volume 2*, Rhymesayers Entertainment, 2006

Psalm One, *Woman at Work Volume 1*, self-released, 2009

Psalm One, *Woman at Work Volume 2*, self-released, 2010

Psalm One, *Woman at Work Volume 3*, self-released, 2011

Psalm One, *Child Support*, ASCAP/America SCORES, 2012

Hologram Kizzie (aka Psalm One), *Free Hugs*, Bonafyde Media, 2013

Hologram Kizzie (aka Psalm One) *Hug Life*, Bonafyde Media, 2014

Various Artists, *Chicago Takeover Mixta/EP*, The Hood Internet, 2014

Psalm One, *POLY (Psalm One Loves You)*, Charm Lab Enterprises,** 2015

Rapperchicks, *Shitty Punk Album*, self-released, 2016

Psalm One, *Gender Fender Bender*, self-released, 2016

Psalm One, *Don't Get Lazy Now!*, Charm Lab Enterprises, 2019

Psalm One, *Flight of the Wig*, Charm Lab Enterprises, 2019

Psalm One & Optiks, "Cult of Ye" (single), Charm Lab Enterprises, 2020

Psalm One & Optiks, *Before They Stop Us*, Charm Lab Enterprises, 2020

Big $ilky (Psalm One & Angel Davanport), *Big $ilky Vol. 1*, Charm Lab Enterprises, 2020

Psalm One & Optiks, "What I Get for Being Brilliant" (single), self-released, 2020

Big $ilky (Psalm One & Angel Davanport), *Big $ilky Vol. 2*, Charm Lab Enterprises, 2020

Psalm One, "Gas Lighters" (single), self-released, 2020

Psalm One & Afrokeys "Anxious, Nervous, and Imperfect" (single), Charm Lab Enterprises, 2021

Big $ilky (Psalm One & Angel Davanport), *Big $ilky Vol. 3*, Charm Lab Enterprises, 2021

* *Self-released*: was sold directly, or on tour, without being released on all major digital service providers (DSPs). Can be found on Psalm One's Bandcamp.

** *Charm Lab Enterprises*: has been released on major DSPs with the backing of Psalm One's label of the same name.

NOTES

1. "Bitin' and Freakin'" featuring Psalm One, track 6 on Casual, *Smash Rockwell*, Hiero Imperium, 2005.
2. "Ginsu Knives" featuring Del the Funky Homosapien, track 1 on *Woman at Work Volume 3*, self-released, 2010.
3. Psalm One, "Ain't No Human Resources in Hip Hop," *Medium*, December 1, 2020, https://psalmonelovesyou.medium.com/aint-no-human-resources-in-hip-hop-32ecb66ae3f9.

ABOUT THE AUTHOR

Serene Supreme

Cristalle "Psalm One" Bowen has spent the better part of twenty years as a dedicated and prolific hip hop mainstay. With dozens of national and international tours and twenty-five-plus bodies of musical work under her belt, she has continuously grown her supportive and dedicated fanbase. While never boasting "famous," Bowen has historically been an inspiration to independent hip hop fans and artists alike. Described by Bandcamp's Phillip Mlynar as "an MC, [who] shifts easily between acerbic cypher-honed barbs, incisive commentary on socio-political issues, and moments of raw emotional honesty," Bowen is in a class by herself. Splitting her time between releasing music, artist development, artist education, and sitting on the board of the SHIFT Cooperative, a disaster relief organization based in Minneapolis, Bowen shows no signs of slowing down. *Her Word is Bond* is Bowen's first book, a new and promising stage in an already celebrated career.

ABOUT HAYMARKET BOOKS

Haymarket Books is a radical, independent, nonprofit book publisher based in Chicago. Our mission is to publish books that contribute to struggles for social and economic justice. We strive to make our books a vibrant and organic part of social movements and the education and development of a critical, engaged, international left.

We take inspiration and courage from our namesakes, the Haymarket martyrs, who gave their lives fighting for a better world. Their 1886 struggle for the eight-hour day—which gave us May Day, the international workers' holiday—reminds workers around the world that ordinary people can organize and struggle for their own liberation. These struggles continue today across the globe—struggles against oppression, exploitation, poverty, and war.

Since our founding in 2001, Haymarket Books has published more than five hundred titles. Radically independent, we seek to drive a wedge into the risk-averse world of corporate book publishing. Our authors include Noam Chomsky, Arundhati Roy, Rebecca Solnit, Angela Y. Davis, Howard Zinn, Amy Goodman, Wallace Shawn, Mike Davis, Winona LaDuke, Ilan Pappé, Richard Wolff, Dave Zirin, Keeanga-Yamahtta Taylor, Nick Turse, Dahr Jamail, David Barsamian, Elizabeth Laird, Amira Hass, Mark Steel, Avi Lewis, Naomi Klein, and Neil Davidson. We are also the trade publishers of the acclaimed Historical Materialism Book Series and of Dispatch Books.

ALSO AVAILABLE FROM HAYMARKET BOOKS

Abolition. Feminism. Now.
by Angela Y. Davis, Gina Dent, Erica R. Meiners,
and Beth E. Richie

All the Blood Involved in Love
by Maya Marshall

The Anti-Racist Writing Workshop
How To Decolonize the Creative Classroom
by Felicia Rose Chavez

Black Queer Hoe
by Britteney Black Rose Kapri, foreword by Danez Smith

Boots Riley: Tell Homeland Security-We Are the Bomb
by Boots Riley, introduction by Adam Mansbach

Build Yourself a Boat
by Camonghne Felix

Doppelgangbanger
by Cortney Lamar Charleston

I Remember Death By Its Proximity to What I Love
by Mahogany L. Browne

Mama Phife Represents: A Memoir
by Cheryl Boyce-Taylor